W9-BTG-601

BABYLON'S ARK

LAWRENCE ANTHONY WITH GRAHAM SPENCE

BABYLON'S ARK

THE INCREDIBLE WARTIME RESCUE
OF THE BAGHDAD ZOO

THOMAS DUNNE BOOKS
ST. MARTIN'S PRESS ⅗ NEW YORK

THOMAS DUNNE BOOKS.

An imprint of St. Martin's Press.

BABYLON'S ARK. Copyright © 2007 by Lawrence Anthony and Graham Spence. All rights reserved. Printed in the United States of America. No part of this book may be used or reproduced in any manner whatsoever without written permission except in the case of brief quotations embodied in critical articles or reviews. For information, address St. Martin's Press, 175 Fifth Avenue, New York, N.Y. 10010.

www.thomasdunnebooks.com
www.stmartins.com

Design by Abby Kagas
Photograph on pp. ii–iii © ISTOCKPHOTO.com/DW photo

Grateful acknowledgment is made to Gracia Bennish and Brendan Whittington-Jones for permission to include their photographs of Baghdad and the Baghdad Zoo.

Library of Congress Cataloging-in-Publication Data

Anthony, Lawrence.
    Babylon's ark : the incredible wartime rescue of the Baghdad Zoo / Lawrence
    Anthony with Graham Spence.—1st ed.
        p. cm.
    ISBN-13: 978-0-312-35832-7
    ISBN-10: 0-312-35832-6
    1. Baghdad Zoo.   2. Zoo animals—Conservation—Iraq—Baghdad.   3. Wildlife
rescue—Iraq—Baghdad.   4. Iraq War, 2003– I. Spence, Graham.   II. Title.

QL76.5.I722B342 2007
590.73'56747—dc22   2006050573

First Edition: March 2007

10   9   8   7   6   5   4   3   2   1

THIS BOOK IS DEDICATED TO THE WOMEN IN MY LIFE:

My wife, Françoise,

My mother, Regina,

and Bijou and Tess.

*And to my soul mate, Nana, the matriarch of a
very special herd of wild elephant.*

ONE

ON THE EASTERN SIDE of the border hundreds of civilian vehicles were jammed up bumper-to-bumper, gridlocked on the desert sands as crowds queued to get out of war-torn Iraq.

On the Kuwaiti side, there was just one car among all the military hardware waiting to get in.

Mine.

Or more correctly, it was mine for as long as I paid the fees. If the rental company had known I was taking one of their spanking new vehicles into the war zones of Baghdad, they would have had a conniption.

The border sentry held up the stamped permit granting me permission to enter Iraq. He squinted at it incredulously. It was legitimate.

But . . . still. The astonishment on his face was almost comical. This was too weird for him to grasp.

He poked his head inside my wound-down driver's window,

his face a foot or so from mine, and then looked at us as though we were escapees from an asylum. My two Arab companions from the Kuwait City zoo focused their eyes straight ahead, studiously avoiding his scrutiny.

"You guys sure you want to go to Baghdad? Don't you know there's a war on?"

I nodded. "We're going to try to rescue the zoo there."

He still looked flabbergasted, so I jabbed my thumb over my shoulder. "There's half a ton of supplies in the back."

The soldier eyeballed me, disbelief on his face, and glanced at the permit again. "There're animals in Baghdad?"

"We hope so. The zoo there was once the finest in Arabia."

"Man, people are shooting each other there. For real. Forget about animals. You've got to worry about your own sorry asses."

He gestured in front of us to the other side of the border. "Look at all these cars. Everybody else is trying to get out. And you want to go in?"

"We've got to get these supplies in. Urgently."

"Okaaay." The soldier pondered for a moment, then smiled. "This is crazy. You're the first civilians in—apart from some newsies, but they don't count."

I forced a grin. Maybe this was all insane. Maybe he was right, I should be somewhere else. My elation that my mission was at last under way was starting to deflate a little.

But it was too late for that. The soldier walked to the barrier gate and shoved it open. "Just stick to the main road, obey military instructions, and follow real close to the convoys, okay? We're getting several hits a day from the ragtops on the road."

This was valid advice, I thought. Advice, however, that my two Kuwaiti assistants, on loan from the Kuwait City zoo, had no intention of heeding. As soon as we came to an intersection on the highway they made signs for me to stop. They then climbed out, opened the trunk, and rummaged for a box of tools. With a few turns of a screwdriver, they whipped off the Kuwaiti license plates.

Alarmed, I asked what they were doing. But as my Arabic was

2

limited to "Salaam Aleikum" and the Kuwaitis' English was equally scant, communication was a challenge.

"American . . ." The Kuwaiti named Abdullah Latif made a shooting motion and pointed at himself.

I grasped what he meant. They were concerned the soldiers might target them as Arabs and equally concerned that if they were seen in a foreign convoy, Iraqi fighters would consider them collaborators.

All very well, but what about me? My instructions had been specifically to stick to the main Baghdad Highway and stay with the numerous military convoys speeding to the Iraqi capital. Indeed, in the hour or so it had taken us to drive from Kuwait City, cross the border, and enter Iraq, I had seen more military vehicles than you would find in the entire South African army. That's where I wanted to be, safety in numbers. I knew too well that a Westerner on the back roads was a prime target for remnants of Saddam's army or the scores of feral fedayeen gangs who were fanatically loyal to the deposed dictator. And I, six feet and four inches tall, with a pale complexion and blue eyes, looked about as un-Semitic as you could get.

I pointed at myself and also made a shooting motion. "Iraqis shoot me."

The Kuwaitis shook their heads and one spoke animatedly in Arabic. I gathered they were telling me they would refuse point-blank to travel on the main road, but I would be safe with them as they were Arabs and they could talk their way out of any situation.

I looked at the road ahead, a narrow ribbon of potholed tarmac, mirage shimmering in the hot air. It suddenly looked very desolate. There would be no American or British soldiers for hundreds of miles. I felt as conspicuous as a match in a fireworks factory.

But my guides from the Kuwait Zoo were not going to change their minds, so what the heck . . . there was not much I could do about it. I couldn't very well order them back onto the highway. So I might as well enjoy the ride into bandit territory and hope like hell the clouds of billowing desert dust would disguise the fact that I was a Westerner in no-man's-land.

The barren landscape we were speeding through radiated hostility, and I somewhat ruefully reflected that making a ten-hour journey through the back roads and alleys of a war zone might not have been the most intelligent thing I had ever done.

But it was too late to turn back now, so I slouched low in the front passenger seat. Well, about as low as I could. The Toyota was not exactly built for someone as big as me to hunker down in. All the while I pictured Iraqi fedayeen, militia fighters specifically trained to hail Saddam Hussein as a cult figure, hiding in the dunes and relishing the opportunity to hijack a car. An unarmed white man would be the juiciest prize for them imaginable. I had no illusions that being a neutral South African would cut much ice with renegade gunmen. I was a visible Westerner, and as far as Saddam's Ba'athist fanatics were concerned, any foreigner would do.

I forced the grim visuals out of my mind. At least I had two Arabs with me, even though they were Kuwaitis.

However, that illusion was soon dispelled when my companions confirmed, through vigorous sign language and an interesting repertoire of facial expressions, that another reason they had taken off the Kuwaiti registration plates earlier was because there was no love lost between them and the Iraqis. Thanks to Saddam's vicious propaganda, most Iraqis believed Kuwait was the reason for the American invasion in the first place. Not only was I a Westerner far off the beaten track, but the welcome mat wasn't exactly out for my Arab companions, either.

As we drove deeper into the country, passing through remote villages unchanged since biblical times, I started to unwind a little. In fact, I even began to enjoy the view. It was like diving into another world where people were rooted in time immemorial: they had survived Saddam; they would survive the foreigners; they would survive the fedayeen. In among the squat-roofed mud buildings, women drew water from communal wells as they had in the days of the prophet Muhammad, while overburdened donkeys with drowsy eyes watched children running barefoot in the swirling dust. Time truly stood still.

4

We traveled fast to make sure armed gangs weren't following us. But even so, whenever the car had to slow down for loitering donkeys or camels, villagers did stunned double takes when they realized a white man was inside. Being in the only brand-new vehicle among the banged-up relics on the road also drew a lot of unwelcome attention to us.

I felt dread creep into my belly. Surely the fedayeen would soon know about me. Indeed, the rolling desert sands fringing the road could be hiding hundreds of Saddam loyalists. At one stage I saw at the roadside a man dressed in Bedouin robes that contrasted starkly with his wraparound sunglasses. He appeared unarmed, but there could be anything under those flowing garments. As we went past, he stared coldly before swiftly turning and disappearing down the back of a dune.

Whom was he going to tell?

Behind him, the skies were black with the greasy smoke from burning oil wells blazing red and orange in the distance. It must have the most expensive pollution in the world.

At another village we passed a group of men gathered under a cluster of wizened palm trees. Hookah pipes were bubbling on top of a box, and the group's transformation from soporific lethargy to instant alertness when they noticed me was unnerving. I felt exposed, alien.

Whenever we entered larger towns we had to slow considerably to ease through the narrow, congested streets and I crouched on the floor, the gap between the dashboard and front seat squeezing me as tightly as a python. These were the most dangerous moments in the journeys. Gunmen were more likely to be lurking on these urban perimeters, and the mere glimpse of a Westerner could trigger a hailstorm of lead. Squashed, sweaty, and uncomfortable, with only a thin metallic skin protecting me, I knew how a sardine felt. Even the Kuwaitis were silent.

Abdullah, a self-assured, well-built young man of about thirty-five who was keen to get to Baghdad to find lost family, was pensive and alert. His partner, who didn't speak a word of English, was quite the opposite; slightly built and unassuming, he sat in the back of the car in silence. They were originally both as keen as mustard to come with me to Baghdad; the war was over, after all, and it was a chance for a bit of an adventure and a few days off from their jobs.

Now that we were actually here, misgivings were beginning to surface. The atmosphere in Iraq hung like a pall and had tempered their ardor somewhat. As it had mine.

But the most harrowing few minutes of all were when we had to stop and refuel. We had brought spare gasoline with us, and running almost on empty, we pulled over beside a flat stretch of desert where no dunes could be sheltering gunmen. With a speed that would have rivaled a Formula 1 pit stop, we sloshed gasoline from twenty-five-liter jerricans into the tank, not overly caring how much spilled onto the steaming tarmac. Then I heard the Kuwaitis say something to each other, alarm in their voices. I looked behind; a crowd was gathering about one hundred yards away and starting to move toward us. They may have been curious onlookers or maybe inquisitive kids just hanging out. We didn't bother to find out. Quick as race-car drivers, we were back in the car and speeding off again.

As we got closer to Baghdad, the landscape was no longer biblical. The area was littered with burnt-out tanks, shell holes, bombed bridges, and hastily abandoned air-defense systems discarded like junk. There were Iraqi missiles, twenty-five feet long and as thick as oak trees, some still on the backs of their launch vehicles, others dumped casually on the roadside as lethal litter. Scuds, I thought; they were certainly big enough.

Also among the detritus of battle were scores of toppled statues and bullet-pitted portraits of Saddam Hussein—the calling cards of America's frontline warriors.

We skirted Nasiriya, Al Najaf, Karbala, and Babylon, now renamed Al Hillah, all bearing fresh scars of the American whirlwind advance.

Then to our absolute dismay we found we were hopelessly lost. The Iraqi army had removed all street signs to confuse the American advance, and we had no idea where we were or which way to go. We were forced to double back through areas we had been glad to see the back of, asking for directions in villages and navigating by the sun in the countryside until we found a large road. This had to be the main Kuwait–Baghdad road.

We looked at one another hopefully. It was. Abdullah slapped me on the back. The relief in the car was palpable.

Eventually we reached the outer periphery of Baghdad. There we asked for directions to the zoo and a friendly Iraqi pointed ahead. "Al Zawra Park," he said. "Just keep going straight."

I felt my stomach muscles tighten. We were entering the belly of the beast.

IN BAGHDAD, the awesome evidence of American firepower was omnipresent. Even though they had bombed strategic targets with surgical accuracy and few homes or apartments had been affected, the city was still a shambles.

In the upmarket Al Mansur district, buildings such as the Department of Information and the internal security headquarters were hollowed-out shells, their shattered cores little more than piles of rubble. Chunks of concrete dangled from tangled steel reinforcing as though they were giant wind chimes. Burnt-out Iraqi tanks and trucks were like mangled monuments of science-fiction movies, stark testimony to the Americans' shatteringly superior technology. Millions of spent cartridges lay sprinkled across the streets, a carpet of confetti glinting so harshly in the desert sun that your eyes hurt.

Every now and again random clatters of automatic-rifle shots sent civilians scurrying down the streets. This is for real, I thought, as I realized with horror what was happening. They are still fighting. I couldn't see where the shots were coming from, so we kept moving, heading toward Al Zawra Park in the center of town, home of the Baghdad Zoo.

To our surprise, there was a fair amount of traffic on the road.

With all the traffic lights down, it was hard going as we swerved in and out, trying to get away from the shooting. Cars jumped intersections with reckless bravado. If one careered into another and could not be driven off, it was abandoned. The most important piece of motoring technology amid the anarchy was the horn. You sped through traffic intersections by honking as loudly as possible and praying that everyone else got out of the way.

But as we crossed Al Jamhooriah Bridge, spanning the river Tigris, everything seemed to go suddenly quiet. After the raucous gauntlet of gunshots and traffic chaos, the only noise now was the hum of the hired Toyota—ominously out of place in the eerie stillness. We were the solitary car on the road, although gutted Iraqi trucks littered both sides of the double-lane highway as far as we could see. Some were still smoldering.

From one side of the muddy river to the other, traffic had simply disappeared. We soon discovered why. Looming menacingly before us at the top of Yafa Street was a massive roadblock: Bradley tanks and machine guns spiked above sandbags and tightly coiled razor wire. Khaki-colored helmets peered above the barricades, commanding the street with absolute authority.

The desert sun was pitiless, blasting down like a furnace. Above the brooding bulk of the tanks, sand-colored camouflage nets twitched nervously in the heat, the only shade available for soldiers clad in full combat dress and ceramic bulletproof plates.

I felt uneasy about driving any closer, so the two Kuwaitis and I decided to stop right there. We were about one hundred yards from the barricade when I slowly got out and approached the machine-gun nest gingerly, my hands stretched wide to show I was unarmed and a friend.

Everything was tense. It was as if something brittle was about to shatter. I couldn't understand it . . . surely Baghdad was a liberated city? I had seen the footage on TV of Saddam's statues falling like giant metal dominoes. I had heard the reports that his fedayeen were on the run. That the Iraqis were rejoicing in the streets . . .

There was no rejoicing in this street. In fact, all I was aware of was a creepy sensation slithering up my skin like a snake.

I kept walking, slowly, with arms stretched.

The soldiers who had been watching my car as it came down the street were now monitoring my every move through high-powered binoculars. I tried to look as harmless as possible as I approached.

"Back off! Back off!" they suddenly yelled, waving me away. Machine guns now poked out from the bagged fortress, their barrels focused on my chest.

I stopped, stunned, feeling as though I had been punched. I had expected the Americans to be friendly. After all, I was here with their blessing.

"I've come to help at the zoo," I shouted back, waving my authorization papers.

"Fuck off! Just fuck off!"

Jeez, I thought, these guys are serious. They must've heard my shout, and I certainly don't look like one of Saddam Hussein's fedayeen.

I yelled out again that I was on a rescue mission for the zoo. This time there was no reply, just a sinister silence.

What the hell was going on here?

It was obvious I was somewhere I shouldn't be. But I never would have guessed I was at the entrance to the most heavily armed, highest-alert security zone in the city, somewhere nobody without top-level clearance was allowed in. In fact, I was just a block or two away from Saddam's palaces, the designated headquarters-to-be of interim administrator Gen. Jay Garner. Security was so paranoid that Abrams tanks firing 105mm shells casually vaporized any unauthorized vehicle driving or parked in the area.

This was strict "shoot to kill" territory, and soldiers at the checkpoints surrounding it were primed to do just that. Unescorted civilians were given one warning only.

I was on my second.

The Americans were understandably on hair triggers. There was a good reason for all of this security. For despite TV images of quick victory, much of Baghdad certainly had not fallen and firefights with die-hard Ba'athists loyal to Saddam Hussein were raging all over the city.

I also was unaware that a few days previously a suicide bomber had blown himself up at a roadblock near Al Narjaf, killing four marines, while at Karbala soldiers had riddled a car that refused to stop, killing seven people, including a woman and her child.

The two Kuwaitis frantically signaled to me. Al Zawra Park formed a dominant rectangle in the heart of the city; there was probably another entrance to the Baghdad Zoo. Wheels spinning, we made a quick U-turn and sped away.

About a mile or so farther on we came to another roadblock. There the heavily armed Americans, also dressed in full body armor and desert camouflage stained dark with sweat, were quizzing some Western journalists.

This time I refused to back down and got permission to approach. A soldier asked what I was doing, and I showed my authorization papers, explaining that I had to get to the Baghdad Zoo on a rescue mission.

For good measure I added that I had urgent supplies—including drugs—for the surviving animals. If there were any, of course. I still had no idea what condition the zoo would be in.

The soldier just looked at me; here they were fighting a war and, if he was hearing right, some madman had pitched up in the middle of it with animal narcotics. He asked me to repeat what I had just said. Perhaps it appealed to his sense of the ridiculous.

I again flourished my papers: "Here're my credentials from the Coalition Administration."

The American scrutinized the papers, shook his head in amazement, and smiled.

"A South African," he said. "You're sure a long way from home."

He radioed through for instructions and indicated that I should bring my hired car up to the side of the roadblock and wait.

I parked in the lee of an Abrams tank and greeted the crew, who stared at me with openmouthed curiosity. The tank was a huge, vicious monster of a machine, dirty and battle worn. Unlike the tensely wired soldiers at the first roadblock, this young crew—who looked and smelled as though they hadn't seen soap for months—was friendly, and a couple of them jumped down to shake hands.

"So you're here for the zoo," said one. "It's right behind us, just across this wall. Had the shit shot out of it."

"You mean to say you came here on purpose?" asked another.

I nodded.

"You're nuts, man. Me, I would turn around and go straight back to my girlfriend. This place is a shit hole. It's not worth fighting for."

This wasn't what I wanted to hear.

Then, as a rattle of AK-47 fire split the air, I realized why the roadblock soldier had told me to drive up to the tanks. Their brooding presence was the only shield in that hostile street.

"When did you guys get here?" I asked.

"First in," was the proud reply. The soldier looked down the street, raising his gun and taking imaginary potshots. "We came straight in. Killed anything that came near us and plenty more."

It dawned on me I was actually chatting to the same tank crews whom I, and millions of others, had watched on TV storming the city just a few days before.

No wonder the soldiers smelled as though they had just emerged from some fetid pit. They had been in continuous combat for the past three weeks, holed up in the sweaty, claustrophobic confines of their tank. The bitterly pungent odor of cordite mingled with the rank sweat of battle and acrid adrenaline was all-pervasive. I didn't breathe too deeply.

My little car looked absurdly incongruous parked among all the military hardware, like a rabbit among wolves. I realized what an absolute gate-crasher I was in this world, a million miles from my normal life. This was about as far removed from my natural element as I could get—where bullets were flying through the street and people you couldn't see wanted you dead. It was some bizarre situation and I was the supreme interloper.

Eventually the soldier on the radio got through to the right person: 1st Lt. Brian Szydlik. But it took another thirty minutes, with me marking time and feeling wretchedly exposed on the side of the road, for him to arrive. Once he did, he leaped out of his armored troop carrier, checked my permit, and nodded.

Szydlik (pronounced "shadalack"), a blond, square-jawed, compact man with bull shoulders, exuded a powerful presence that was almost tangible. He was someone you wanted on your side in a fight, and with him there you felt you would win it.

"All seems okay," he said with a curt nod. Then he smiled and I blinked, astonished at the transformation of his granite visage into sudden affability. "That zoo sure needs help all right. Follow me."

We drove under the crossed-scimitars archway, one of Baghdad's most famous landmarks, across the military parade grounds, and into Al Zawra Park, a huge, sprawling open area similar in size to Central Park in New York, where remnants of a fierce shoot-out that had raged just days before were starkly evident. Twisted metal that was once sophisticated Iraqi weaponry lay blackened everywhere. Road surfaces and paving had been powdered to grit by charging Bradley and Abrams tanks, while culverts and walls were speckled with thousands of chipped holes from a maelstrom of lead. Trees and buildings looked as though they had been through a chain-saw massacre. Irrigation pipes, vital to prevent the desiccated ground from reverting to a dust bowl, had been squashed flat.

However, I soon learned that despite the apocalyptic scenario, the biggest damage to the Baghdad Zoo had not been done in battle, fierce as it had been. It was the looters. They had killed or kidnapped anything edible and ransacked everything else. Even the lamp poles had been unbolted, tipped over, and their copper wiring wrenched out like multicolored spaghetti. As we drove past, we could see groups of looters still at it, scavenging like colonies of manic ants.

Eventually we stopped outside a large dust brown wall, crumbling in some sections from mortar bombs and pitted with countless bullet scars. Behind it wispy smoke still rose from fires that had obviously been burning for some time.

"Well," said Szydlik with an elaborately grandiose sweep of his arm. "That's your zoo." He then eyed me quizzically. "How the hell did you get caught up in this nightmare?"

It was a good question. . . .

PERHAPS THE DEFINING MOMENT was a fortnight or so previously on my game reserve, Thula Thula, thousands of miles away in Zululand South Africa, when a soft-lilting voice whispered in my ear, "Wake up, darling. Your babies are here."

Françoise, my girlfriend of fifteen years, was very French and very beautiful. I had always wondered what exactly it was she saw in me but had decided some things were better left unknown.

However, I knew exactly what she meant when she said "your babies." For the past few nights the elephants had been coming up to our game reserve lodge—something they had never done previously.

We soon discovered why. The matriarch, Nana, and her second in command, Frankie (named after Françoise), had recently given birth, and they wanted to show us their babies. Nana and Frankie's pride in their offspring easily matched human maternal love.

For the past five years I had been concentrating on restoring Thula Thula, our beautiful Zululand game reserve home, to its natural glory, removing alien plants, improving infrastructure, and allowing the wildlife to flourish undisturbed in their native environment. I had also been involved with several of our neighboring Zulu communities, assisting them to create their own game reserve and by so doing help rebuild their traditional cultural relationships with nature, which had to a large extent been eroded by apartheid.

My personal love is the African elephant. Five years ago I had offered sanctuary to a traumatized herd who were due to be shot by their previous owners for being "troublesome," and I had been working closely with them to ensure they settled down at Thula Thula. They had been wandering deep in the bush for a while, and even though it was 3:00 A.M., I was excited to know they were here at the house again.

I pulled on a battered pair of khaki shorts and unlatched our bedroom's stable door that opened onto the lush lawn, sheltered by a giant African marula tree. Sure enough, I could make out the herd's gray hulks in the murk.

I felt a warm glow spark in my core. The sheer joy of being alive was as bracing as plunging into a crystal mountain stream. Who else in the world was lucky enough to be woken up by a honey-silk Gallic voice on a game ranch in the Zululand bush to be told that elephants were in his garden?

Nana, the matriarch, was in front as usual. She saw me, tested the air to get my scent, and then slowly walked over and stretched out her trunk. A little figure was beside her, nuzzling her for milk.

"You're a clever girl, Nana," I said, carefully judging her demeanor and that of the herd behind her. These were wild elephants that for the past four years had been unusually proactive in forging a relationship with me. Even though they knew me well, I still had to be very cautious. "Thank you for bringing your baby to see me. He is beautiful."

A couple of the younger elephants were at the side of the house, tugging thatch out of the roof. This would require some serious repair work once the sun was up, but what the hell, it was worth it for the privilege of being visited by a herd of wild elephants.

A streak of lightning lit the sky in the east, illuminating the beautiful tract of lush African wilderness that I am privileged to own. A storm was brewing far out over the Indian Ocean, and for a moment I was reminded of Iraq. I had been watching the war on CNN earlier that evening, and for some reason the nonstop TV coverage unsettled me.

I knew nothing about Iraq and the politics of war. But what I did know was that in all human hostilities animals have suffered horrifically and often anonymously. Unable to flee or defend or feed themselves, they either were slaughtered wholesale in the initial assaults or died agonizingly from thirst and hunger later, locked and desperate in their cages. Or worse, they were callously shot by blood-crazed soldiers just for the hell of it.

It had happened when the Iraqis invaded Kuwait; it had happened in Kosovo; it had happened in Afghanistan.

In fact, the awful images of the Kabul Zoo crippled in the aftermath of the Afghan Taliban war still haunt me. When the American forces liberated the city from the Taliban, they found the last remaining lion, Marjan, alone in his filthy cage. Starving and dehydrated, he had shrapnel embedded in his neck and jaw and was half-blind from a grenade attack and riddled with mange and lice. It was too late to save him.

But his ravaged, once-proud face glaring into the camera was beamed around the world by TV networks and became an iconic symbol of animals suffering in man-made conflict. Whenever I watched CNN's footage of Iraq, Marjan's accusing stare kept rattling around in my mind.

The same fate awaited the wild creatures of Baghdad. Of that I had no doubt. I knew I had to do something. Anything. I could not let the same dreadful fate happen to the animals of Baghdad. Somehow I had to get there just to see if I could help.

Standing out there on that magnificent African starlit night, watching my elephants contentedly showing off their progeny, I decided for once I was not going to be a bystander. Enough was enough. It was time for me to make a stand, even if I failed.

And if the animals died, I wanted to make sure it would be branded deep on the conscience of man.

Françoise was somewhat understanding but not happy. We had invested a huge amount of money, time, and sweat into our game reserve over the past five years and only now were we starting to reap rewards. It had previously been a hunting ranch and wildlife had been decimated before we bought it, imposed a strict hunting ban, and began renovating and renewing the area. Now the animals had flourished and we had built a small upmarket tourist lodge that blended into an acacia and Tamboti tree forest overlooking a water hole and the river. It is pure bushveld luxury.

Managing an African game reserve is a Herculean task, and Françoise was understandably apprehensive about me suddenly leaving. It was the start of the fire season and we were still vigilantly guarding against poachers. To ask a former denizen of Paris to take charge of a wild, five-thousand-acre tract of Africa was an extreme request. But our staff is loyal and Brendan Whittington-Jones, the reserve manager, was reliable and trustworthy. Françoise has a streak of toughness concealed beneath her feminine French flair, which would see her through, and I think she also knows when there are some things I just must do.

"When are you going?" she asked later that morning, as we sipped coffee on the patio of the lodge watching Gwala Gwalas, beautiful exorbitantly colored Zululand birds, flitting through the bushveld canopy.

"As soon as I can."

That was easier said than done. In fact, I wasn't even sure where to start. How do you get into a country at war? Obviously I couldn't just show up with some suntan lotion and a tourist visa. This trip into Iraq would require not just audacity, but some extensive networking.

As it happened, one of our regular guests at Thula Thula had been an American commercial attaché named Henry Richmond. I knew he was well connected and reckoned that he could point me in the right direction. I put a call through to him, now retired, in Hawaii, telling him my fears for the Baghdad Zoo and pointing out that America could ill afford to allow Baghdad's animals to suffer the same fate as those in Kabul.

Henry was on the same wavelength. As a seasoned mediator he had already sensed that when the fighting stopped, America would have a rough time securing peace. The invasion was, among other things, an initial step in a hugely ambitious attempt to germinate democracy in the Middle East, and they had to get Iraq up and running as soon as they could. So, he asked, what did I have in mind?

I didn't hesitate. I said I wanted to find out firsthand what was happening to the zoo. Could he pave the way for me to get into Baghdad?

After a pause, he agreed to use his diplomatic network, although he warned it could take some time. Permission to enter Iraq would have to come from the coalition Central Command (Cent-Com), which was based in Doha, the capital of Qatar. He would talk to friends in Washington, but I would have to be patient.

Patience, however, is not my strong point. Those awful images of Marjan kept haunting me, and the very next day I phoned Cent-Com myself. Using some serious poetic license, I told them that I had been assigned to take over the Baghdad Zoo. Who would be my contact person?

The people in Doha referred me to the Humanitarian Operations Center (HOC) in Kuwait. I immediately placed a call to the authorities there, repeating my request—but crossing my fingers and adding that CentCom had referred me. An HOC spokesperson told me to put it in writing, and about two seconds later I had banged off an e-mail. I phoned Henry again to assist with expediting the approval.

A few days later my receptionist at Thula Thula informed me that "some ambassador" was on the line from Kuwait. I grabbed the phone and a man with a deep, cultured voice on the other end introduced himself as Tim Carney. He said he had an "impressive string of e-mails" in front of him claiming I might have some ideas about restoring the Baghdad Zoo. Carney had been assigned to become the minister for industrial and mineral affairs in the interim Iraqi administration. The zoo didn't fall directly within his portfolio, but he had a special interest in wild animals.

Jackpot! I quickly explained my concerns and the next thing I knew I was holding a faxed invitation to Kuwait, printed on Coalition Administration letterhead and signed by Tim Carney himself.

The next step, obtaining a Kuwaiti visa, might have been a bureaucratic nightmare, had it not been for the intervention of Martin Slabber, the friendly South African ambassador in Kuwait.

"An invasion is being launched from Kuwait and the country has all but closed its borders," he told me. But Slabber saw beyond bureaucracy and personally took my application to his contacts in the Kuwaiti government, and I was able to leave South Africa the following night.

Though arranging the trip itself may have so far gone smoothly, saying good-bye to Françoise at the airport was one of the hardest things I have ever done.

Once in Kuwait City I contacted Tim Carney, arranging to meet him for dinner that night. Carney, a tall, graying, immaculately groomed American, was a veteran international troubleshooter and had spent some time in South Africa. We immediately found common ground and over dinner agreed that if the animals of the Baghdad Zoo perished through neglect, the powerful green lobby would hound the American administration mercilessly—and with good justification. I stressed as forcibly as I could that the Americans were sitting on a time bomb.

Carney agreed it was imperative to get me into Baghdad as soon as possible but warned me that the city was as volatile as nitroglycerin. The situation on the ground was too dicey for foreign civilians just to barge in. Even the military convoys were regularly attacked. He would pull as many strings as he could, but he stressed that the final decision to grant permission could only come from the military. The place to start was the HOC.

So naturally, the next day found me banging on the HOC's doors until I was in front of Col. Jim Fikes and Maj. Adrian Oldfield, who were responsible, among other things, for issuing permits to get into Iraq. They were thunderstruck by my request. Who in their right mind would want to go to Baghdad at this time on their own volition?

Neither Fikes nor Oldfield wanted the responsibility of letting a lone civilian wander onto a battlefield. They said the chances of being killed were frighteningly high and it just wasn't worth their jobs to sign the papers. They strenuously advised me to fly back to South Africa and wait for the Iraqi border to open.

That was the last thing on my mind, as each hour I sat around twiddling my thumbs meant more animals would perish. While I waited, hoping that the HOC would reconsider, I tried to hitch a ride with the press, pestering CNN, BBC, and FOX, but they were facing their own problems getting to the battlefront.

Then I heard that a certain Colonel McConnell had arrived from Baghdad for supplies and was also sourcing food for the zoo's animals. This was the best news I had heard. It meant that at least some creatures had survived.

I managed to contact McConnell and he confirmed my worst fears. The zoo was in dire straits and the few remaining animals were at death's door, starving and critically dehydrated. He was taking a load of buffalo meat back the next day but admitted this would not last long without adequate refrigeration. I begged to be allowed to accompany him, but it was impossible to get clearance for a civilian. McConnell did, however, send me a copy of his one-page report on the zoo that described the fighting, lawlessness, and looting and the surviving animals' critical condition. The report concluded, ominously: "The zoo is still a very dangerous place." But I naively shrugged off the warning and kept trying to find a way in.

Fortune favors the persistent—or perhaps in my case the thick-skinned—and a chance encounter completely turned the tables. Ambassador Slabber had kept in regular contact and now he requested a diplomatic favor. The Kuwait Zoo had just completed an elephant and rhino enclosure and had applied for a permit to bring animals over from South Africa. Slabber thought that because I happened to be in Kuwait, I might assess whether the enclosure was suitable.

Initially I was reluctant because I didn't want to waste precious time on anything not connected to gaining border clearance. But Martin had been fundamental in getting my Kuwaiti visa, so I hesitantly agreed and was met by one of the zoo's senior veterinarians, Dr. Medoc.

Unfortunately, enclosures did not pass muster. They were too cramped, and I had to tell the Kuwaitis this with as much tact as possible. But as our meeting ended we got to chatting about the Iraqi situation. Dr. Medoc described how the Iraqis had trashed the Kuwait Zoo during Saddam's invasion of 1991. Every single animal had been machine-gunned in cold blood. The Iraqi soldiers had done it for fun, he said.

The shock must have been evident on my face, and I told him I was doing my damnedest to get into Iraq to ensure the animals didn't all die at the Baghdad Zoo as well. Would the Kuwait Zoo donate medicines and supplies to their Baghdad counterpart? It would be a fine goodwill gesture, particularly as Kuwait was keen on establishing solid relations with whatever post-Saddam government emerged. And who better to transport the supplies across the border than me?

Medoc agreed in principle but said final permission would have to come from the minister of agriculture and animal welfare himself. A meeting was set up for the next day.

Again, fate played a strange trick. A few days earlier at the airport, while being held up by the notoriously cantankerous Kuwaiti customs, I had met a Texan named Mike Honey, a senior executive for the U.S. Evergreen aircraft company, which contracted helicopters to the military. My mission intrigued Honey, particularly as it was entirely self-initiated, self-funded, and, in his opinion, bizarrely offbeat. He said he might be able to fly me into Baghdad on one of his "birds," and we kept in contact once in Kuwait City.

The night before the scheduled appointment with the minister of agriculture, I bumped into Mike and told him about the meeting. He asked if he could come along. I shrugged. Why not? Couldn't do any harm.

Imagine my astonishment the next day when it turned out that the minister, Fahad Salem Al-Ali Al-Sabah, had attended the same university in America as Mike. The two men spent the next half hour swapping raucous yarns about the good old days. I despaired we would ever get around to discussing the zoo rescue, but when we did it took barely a few minutes for the minister to listen intently and agree to all of my proposals before turning back to tales of his university exploits. Tim Carney, who was also present, smiled and gave me a thumbs-up.

I now had the authorization I needed. I was no longer just a maverick trying to hustle my way into the war zone; I was on an officially recognized mercy mission. Not only that, but the mission was supported by a strategically vital Arab ally, the neutral South African government, and the interim Coalition Administration.

Despite the fact that they were getting a little tired of this pesky conservationist, Colonel Fikes and Major Oldfield were impressed with my new credentials. Just one small matter—could I get this on an official letterhead from the Kuwaiti government? This meant from the minister Dr. Fahad Salem Al-Ali Al-Sabah himself.

"No problem," said, heart sinking at the prospect of more red tape. Again I contacted the Kuwaiti agriculture and animal welfare offices.

The deputy director, Dr. Mohammed Al-Muhanna, not only got me a letter but also agreed to my proposal to take two of the zoo's staff with me as guides and assistants. One was a trainee junior vet; the other, a trainee in animal husbandry. They would be outside my hotel at 4:00 A.M. ready to go.

Even at the last minute, Colonel Fikes was reluctant to give the final okay. Playing my trump card, I laid it on thick: "This is not the U.S. border we are talking about. It's the Kuwait border. And the Kuwaiti government has given me permission to cross it into Iraq."

Fikes resignedly picked up his pen. He had one final piece of advice: "You are the first civilian in. Keep your head down; it's rough in there."

I finally had my elusive clearance permit. Despite our difficulties, Fikes was a really good man and I could see he only had my own safety in mind. I promised to phone him when I got to Baghdad.

Adrian Oldfield shook my hand when I left. "If you survive this," he said somewhat ominously, "I will take you up on your offer to visit you at your game reserve one day."

I nodded. "With pleasure. And bring Jim Fikes with you."

I hired a car at the airport "for business in Kuwait City," not daring to reveal my true destination and bought supplies. I wished I had a gun, even a pistol would be better than nothing, but getting a weapon in Kuwait was out of the question. I would have to find one in Baghdad.

That night I phoned Françoise and told her I was going in, I don't think she, sitting alone four thousand miles away and knowing I was about to enter a war zone, shared my enthusiasm.

TWO

NOW THAT I HAD FINALLY ARRIVED in Baghdad, I felt as deflated as a punctured tire.

The trashed complex in front of me was the last thing I had expected. Had I traveled four thousand miles, spent countless hours on the phone with officials from four different countries, and bulldozed my way through red tape just to arrive at this?

One glance at the bomb-blasted rubble in the park around the zoo showed with stark clarity that the mountain of bureaucracy I had faced in crossing the Iraq border was merely a pimple compared to what lay ahead.

Seeing the look on my face, Lt. Brian Szydlik nodded grimly. "Not too good, huh?"

He then quizzed me at length about our journey, and I could tell he was impressed we had made it all the way from Kuwait in a civilian car unscathed. We might be mad or stupid, but at least we were serious.

However, our main attraction as far as he was concerned was

that we were taking a major hassle off his hands. The zoo and its pitiful inhabitants were in his zone of command, and it was a non-military problem he needed like a hole in the head.

"You sure you gonna take charge of these animals?" he asked me again.

I nodded.

"The coalition guys in Kuwait told you to do that?"

I continued nodding and tapped my authorization papers.

He beamed and shook my hand once more. It was the first time since I had arrived in Iraq that I felt really welcome. It seemed that all the banging on bureaucratic doors, from South Africa to Kuwait, to get here could even have been worthwhile after all.

"We'll help all we can, but there's still a war on," he said.

"Thanks. We're going to need it."

Brian Szydlik was a professional soldier and damn proud of it. Like all good commanders, he held the safety of his men paramount. He had done what he could to keep the zoo's creatures alive, but in a combat zone this was a distraction he could ill afford in case it endangered the lives of his troops.

As we were speaking, a stocky middle-aged Iraqi man approached us. His hair was ash gray and his face crumpled with exhaustion. But when he smiled you could see humor light up his eyes.

Szydlik waved him over. "This is Husham Hussan, the deputy director of the Baghdad Zoo—or what's left of it."

Dr. Husham Mohamed Hussan's face was a portrait of slack-jawed disbelief as we shook hands and I explained my mission. He could not believe a foreigner had come all the way from the far end of Africa to help his humble zoo. How the hell had I even known about them?

When I opened the trunk of my rental car and showed him the medicines we had brought from across the border, courtesy of the Kuwait City zoo, he grabbed my hand and wept.

I wasn't quite sure what to say. "Has it been bad, my friend?"

He nodded. "Come. I show."

This was what my trip had been all about; at last I would have the truth. I would see it for myself. But nothing could have steeled me for what I was about to witness.

The first thing I noticed was the entrance. Well, I couldn't really miss it—the massive, ornate black-and-gold-painted gates, engraved with lions baring their fangs at each other, had been blasted open and now lurched at drunken angles.

But those were merely the portals to Hades. For once I was inside, the true horror hit me.

The animal cages were foul beyond belief; they had not been cleaned for God knows how long. Evaporated, ammonia-reeking urine formed salty white patches on the ground, while piles of excrement, black and putrid, had hardened in the scorching sun. The stench was pungent enough to turn the strongest stomach.

Black swarms of flies, so dense you couldn't see through them, hovered over the gnawed skeletons of the dead animals that had been tossed into the dens to feed the live ones; the bilious-ripe malodor of death and decay clogged the air like a soiled cloud.

The wall of the lions' enclosure had a gaping hole from a direct hit from a mortar shell, which the Americans had crudely plugged with rubble and wire. If the lions were healthy, that wouldn't hold them for five minutes, I thought, making a mental note to seal the break properly as soon as possible.

Inside the enclosure, the giant cats stared at us listlessly, some barely able to lift their heads. I looked carefully; they were African lions. I was expecting the rarer and slightly smaller Asian subspecies, *Panthero leo persica*.

In another cage a rare Bengal tiger feebly bared his fangs, his once magnificently striped pelt as faded as old string. At the back of the adjacent enclosure, camouflaged in the shade, was another younger male Bengal as scrawny and listless as the other one was.

An Iraqi brown bear, which Husham said had apparently killed three looters who broke into his cage, was doing what we conservationists call stereotyping—dementedly moving backward and forward within his four-walled confines as he went stir-crazy. Another bear lay curled in the corner like a frightened child, distressed beyond belief.

In the adjacent cages a lynx was, like the brown bear, stereotyping. Farther on in a pen some Iraqi boars lay huddled miserably on the only tiny piece of dry land in a flooded, muddied quagmire— courtesy of a wrecked water pipe.

The whole place looked as if a tornado had hit it, then reversed and come back through again for good measure. Rubbish and junk littered the grounds; looters were wandering around unconcernedly helping themselves at their leisure; cages were standing open. The zoo looked and felt like it had been completely overwhelmed. There was an atmosphere of ruined hopelessness, made all the more real for me by the fact that I knew there was no formal rescue team on the way. With the war still going on, no staff, and the city shut down, I realized that there was precious little chance in hell that my presence alone could make any real difference.

Other animals, including baboons and monkeys too nimble for looters to capture, were running free on the grounds. I also caught glimpses of a desert fox, another lynx, and an assortment of dogs whose bodies were scarcely more than fur and ribs. Overhead, parrots, falcons, and other birds that had managed to evade the looters were circling or perched in the eucalyptus trees, squawking noisily.

These were the sole remnants of the zoo's 650 prewar inhabitants. And they had endured only because they had vicious-enough teeth or claws to fight back against the looters. Or wings to fly off.

Dr. Husham, as he was known, said he needed protective clothing to corral most of the animals running wild. I nodded; that would be a priority. But where did one get animal capture gear in a war zone? Perhaps we could borrow some bulletproof vests from soldiers.

We came across a huge bomb crater, too big to climb out if you fell in. Lying near it was a decomposing pony.

"This bomb come before soldiers," said Husham.

I nodded. It was obviously an off-target hit from the "shock and awe" bombing offensive that presaged the invasion.

Dr. Husham then showed us a brand-new enclosure that had been proudly built for the zoo's newest assets—two beautiful giraffes, the tallest and most awkwardly graceful of all creatures. It was empty, the cast-iron gates ripped off at the hinges by a flood of crazed humanity. By some cruel fate, the animals had arrived from Africa the day the war started. Husham told me they were never even off-loaded.

One giraffe, he had heard, had definitely been killed and eaten. The other was probably in some cramped cage, unable to stand, waiting to be sold on the black market.

Two ostriches went the same way, the looters trussing them up and carting them off to an unspeakable fate.

Even now, in bright daylight, a horde of looters were jostling one another outside the buildings, grabbing whatever had not yet been carried off even if it was worthless. We watched, fists clenched tight. There was nothing we, as unarmed civilians, could do.

I had started to walk across a patch of open ground to the lake when Husham grabbed my arm.

"Bombs," he said.

I had been so intent on the hellish scenario before me that I hadn't taken in my surroundings, something I do automatically in the bush as a matter of course. I looked around and saw instantly what he meant. Scattered around was unexploded ordnance, the lethal collateral of war.

"Americans take many," he said, "but some still stay here."

Only the paved pathways were safe. But that didn't seem to deter the looters who stampeded over the grounds like a cattle herd.

A Bradley tank rumbled slowly into the zoo's entrance, its squat menace giving it an imperious air of invincibility. The looters reluctantly moved off, even though they knew the Americans had not started policing them yet.

Husham then led the way to the artificial lake fed by the Tigris

River. The birdcages on the walkway had been ripped open and, Husham told us, most of the inhabitants eaten as if they were chickens. Amazon macaws, European lovebirds, and African gray parrots had their necks wrung and were put in someone's pot.

The lake itself was foul; pumps that sucked the water up from the river had been stripped and looted. Even the giant turbine that kept the lake circulating was now just junk metal. The water was rancid brown, but to my astonishment, there were several paddleboats out in the middle.

I was about to ask Husham what they were doing when suddenly a flock of waterfowl took off, screeching and flapping as they scrambled for height. I heard a thin, triumphant shout echo in the distance and saw a man being hauled aboard one of the boats. In his hand was a writhing mass of feathers.

"Ali Baba," said Husham, using the Arabic slang for looters. They would paddle silently toward the birds, then slip into the water and glide up from behind, grabbing their prey.

I almost retched just at the thought of swimming in that fetid water. Yet these people were doing that daily to put food on the table.

I asked Husham in pidgin English and using a variety of hand signs when he had last had a decent meal. He shrugged: "Many days small food, Baghdad no food—very bad."

He said most of the zoo staff had worked without pay during the buildup to the war. They had only left once the Republican Guard soldiers and fedayeen arrived, ordered them off the premises at gunpoint, and started digging in, preparing for battle. That their chosen battle zone was adjacent to the leading collection of wild animals in the Middle East was irrelevant to them.

The fedayeen had been particularly aggressive, and when he and the zoo's director, Dr. Adel Salman Mousa, argued with the young gunmen, pleading for a little more time to feed and care for the animals, they were told they would be shot if they didn't shut up.

Before they left, Adel, Husham, and the rest of the staff frantically distributed the last of the food and filled the water troughs to overflowing. They did it silently, depressed beyond words. They believed they would never see their animals again.

About ten days later the American tanks arrived and a pitched battle raged in the park grounds, right where I was standing.

I could picture with brutal clarity the horror the animals must have suffered, bullets ricocheting off their cages, turbine-engine tanks at full roar with their steel tracks ripping up roads, missiles whistling from the sky, and cosmic-clapping bombs shredding buildings. However petrifying it must be for humans, it would be unimaginably worse for animals trapped in cages.

As I thought of this, for some reason I looked at the traumatized old brown bear, lying curled in a fetal position. Husham saw my gaze and told me her name was Saedia. She had been with the zoo for thirty years and was blind.

"At least no see bombs," said Husham.

Maybe, I thought. But that possibly meant her hearing was more acute—and her unseeing terror horribly multiplied.

Like most Baghdad civilians, Husham had hidden at home during the brief but vicious conventional military struggle for the city. Each morning he would crack open the curtains and scrutinize the city skyline to see if rockets and bombs were still exploding.

One morning he noticed birds flying in the east, roughly above the area where the zoo was. Falcons, gliding gloriously in the gusting thermals. He rubbed his eyes. Desert falcons flying over the middle of the city? And amid all the gunfire and battle flak?

Husham loved falcons more than any other bird. He told us they were symbolic of his country, Iraq, soaring spiritually and physically above these ancient lands.

Then it dawned on him; those were the zoo's falcons. His falcons! They must have somehow got free. That could only have happened if their cages had been opened.

It was at that moment it hit him. The zoo—his zoo—was being plundered.

He left straightaway, walking the five shrapnel-strewn miles from his home, trying to skirt both American soldiers and rampant looters. There were hit-and-run firefights erupting constantly throughout the streets, so he decided to keep his head down and walk as fast as he could. Every now and again, amid the whining ricochets, a bullet would "crack" close by and he would instinctively duck. But he was fatalistic: it was up to Allah whether he made it or not.

Black Hawk helicopters were *thud-thudding* overhead so low that he could clearly see heavily armed men with wraparound dark glasses staring at him. The gleaming ebony choppers exuded a menace so intense it was almost hypnotic—like a cobra mesmerizing a rat. He dared not look up for long, and hoped those cold-faced men could tell he was a civilian, a man who loved animals, not war.

It took over an hour to reach the zoo. When he arrived, Husham could scarcely believe the destruction. The first thing he noticed was that the locks on every cage had been battered off and the doors ripped open.

Even equipment such as basic gardening tools and the animals' water bowls had been stolen. The glass-walled aquarium had been shattered, and a few exotic fish were lying stiff in the desert sun. Somehow they must have been missed in the mad scramble of the looting.

He counted the remaining animals. There were perhaps thirty in all, those that were too dangerous or spiky or quick even for pillagers—apart from the badger that, traumatized beyond comprehension, had survived by burying itself into the iron-hard ground. Looters had even tried to get into the lions' den, widening the hole by clearing the rubble from the bomb blast. No doubt they had fled when confronted by a pride of starving giant cats.

Some soldiers came up to him and aggressively asked what he was doing. They had a war to fight, and although the order was not to harm civilians under anything but suicide bomber circumstances, they were getting fed up with the anarchy. In broken English he told them he was deputy director of the Baghdad Zoo, and they took him to their commander, Brian Szydlik.

Szydlik was delighted to see Husham; he desperately needed someone to assist with the zoo so he could concentrate on fighting the war. He told Husham the lions had escaped when the mortar hit their enclosure and had been roaming wild in the park after the battle. Szydlik and his men had taken time off from fighting and used armored troop carriers to round the cats up. However, they had been forced to kill three that refused to go back into their cages. One had been shot just outside the tiger's cage, and Husham sighed with sadness. That would be the lioness they had housed with the Bengal tiger in a mating experiment, and the two animals of different species had formed an unusually close bond. She had, in fact, only been trying to get back to her mate.

Seeing Husham's deep distress at the destruction, Syzdlik said the city had gone mad and it was impossible to keep the looters out without actually shooting some as an example. And that they couldn't do.

Szydlik also said some soldiers had fed the lions a pony and a wolf that had been killed during the battle. And when the starving cats had gobbled that up, the soldiers shot a terminally ill gazelle that they tossed whole into the enclosure.

The biggest problem was water. In between patrols, clearing out pockets of Saddam loyalists, and dodging the daily barrage of sniper bullets, the soldiers had ferried a few bucketfuls into the cages. But that was a time-consuming job and Szydlik, repeating the words like a mantra, had a war to fight.

Husham walked about in a melancholic daze. He couldn't believe his people were doing this. He understood the hunger: he, too, had lived through the terrible sanctions. But this was pure thuggery. Why destroy the locks or rip up the cages? Why steal the fridges and fans? Why pull out the basins and toilets?

He shook his head and forced himself to focus. There was much work to be done.

Among the predatory crowds of men prowling the area, he spotted two zoo staff members who came running up when they saw their boss. They were ready to get back to work, even though they knew there was no chance of being paid.

The first priority was water. Dr. Husham was a practical man, a veterinarian but also a superb do-it-yourself improviser. If something broke, he could fix it with just string and chewing gum. But even he looked at the trashed pumps and pipes with dismay. Without parts, there was nothing he could do—and where do you find parts for pumps in a war zone?

He and his two-man staff gathered some pieces of piping strewn around the battleground and, with a bucket a soldier had given him, jury-rigged a rudimentary viaduct system by the lions' cage. One of his men ferried water, a bucket at a time, from the stagnant canal, and they dribbled the precious liquid into the drinking troughs through the pipes.

The lions, crazed with thirst, smelled the water and loped into the cage from the outside enclosure. They had barely had a lick for almost two weeks; even when they escaped, they had been herded back into their cages before they could reach the canals.

Husham described how the stricken lions tried to drink. Their desiccated tongues were too cracked and swollen to lap, so they buried their faces, openmouthed, in the precious liquid. Only when their parched palates had softened a little could they swallow.

Then they drank and drank and drank.

Next the zookeepers watered the two tigers, then the bears, then the rest. Even the badger came out of his burrow, his thirst conquering his terror. Each bucket was lugged up by hand. It was backbreaking work in heat that soared to one hundred degrees Fahrenheit. But they used what they had; muscle, courage, and a bucket.

And that day, that long, hot, awful April day, was all that kept the few remaining animals of Baghdad Zoo alive.

The next morning the three Iraqis started the survival process again. They had all walked an hour or so from their homes through the chaotic city, instinctively ducking gunfire and evading threats from looters. Husham wondered how long they could keep it up; there were not enough hours in a day to water animals that weighed up to seven hundred pounds with just one old bucket.

The Iraqis also managed to scrounge some slabs of rancid beef from a pavement dealer, paying with the few dinars they had between them. The men carried the bloody segments from downtown to the zoo, three miles away, on their backs. This meat was shared among the emaciated carnivores, who gobbled it up with famished ferocity.

The emotional Iraqi showed us the pipe system he had erected—the animals' sole lifeline. His justifiable pride was endearing, and I whistled with absolute respect.

"You've done an excellent job, my friend," I said, looking at the emaciated but still surviving animals. "Well done."

The Iraqi nodded grimly. "Good you are here." The words were said with raw emotion.

We paused for a while and I looked around silently, aghast at the devastation. The task ahead defied description.

I did not tell Husham, but I was at first so dismayed that I considered getting a rifle and shooting each animal on the spot. Under the circumstances, some would say it would be the most humane thing to do. Sickened to the pit of my stomach, I reckoned there was more honor and dignity in death for these once-proud creatures than in this degradation.

I had never seen animals in such appalling conditions. What chance did they have of surviving the next two weeks, never mind the war, with what little we had? And even if by some miracle they did make it, what sort of quality of life could they look forward to afterward?

This was no mere musing. I had come expecting it to be bad, but not for a moment had I considered that the animals would be past redemption, that I would travel so far only to find that I had no choice but to put them down.

Nothing, but nothing, could have braced me for this horror show.

Then the anger set in. This was a crime of cosmic proportions, an abuse of such magnitude against our fellow creatures that it beggared belief. It certainly altered my perception of my own species.

What galled even more was that with pitifully few exceptions—men of integrity such as Husham and Szydlik—no one in Baghdad at the time seemed to give a damn. Sure, everyone said we needed to do something. But those were just words.

The reality was starkly different: a handful of us armed with a leaky pipe and a rusty bucket was all that stood between life and death for some of the planet's most magnificent creatures.

Gradually the fog of depression lifted. I now knew why I had come to Baghdad. I knew an iron example had to be set. As I had instinctively grasped while watching my elephants at Thula Thula barely two weeks ago, some of us had to band together, draw a line in the sand, and say, "This far and no further."

Baghdad was where that line could be drawn. I had to stay; the animals had to survive.

But where to start?

I wasn't exactly sure. But I decided we would have to confront each problem one at a time, like a game of pickup sticks, or else we would be engulfed by the enormity of it all. We needed ripples of little victories to keep morale up, or else we would flounder.

I sensed Dr. Husham and his two helpers were sizing me up, wondering what to make of me. There was no doubt they considered me to be in charge. For a start, I was the only one who could talk to the Americans. I had brought in the supplies. I had some money.

This was a foreign crisis to them—they needed a foreigner to help get them out of it.

Okay, I said, as confidently as I could, our first task was to feed and water the animals with whatever we could. We would do that now.

I then ushered Husham into the hired car with me, and Lieutenant Szydlik provided an escort to an army base near Uday Hussein's palace where meat brought in by a previous convoy had been stored. As much as possible had been kept fresh in two small deep freezes operating off a generator, but the rest had gone bad in the heat. It would have to suffice. There was nothing else.

The rancid meat, buffalo chunks imported from India, was tossed to the famished carnivores and disappeared into a black hole of snapping fangs and claws. Moldy cabbages and vegetables were tossed into the bear cages, to be equally ferociously consumed.

The next step was water. This was critical. Dr. Husham had done amazing work keeping at least a trickle in the cages, but it was not enough to keep large creatures such as lions and bears going for much longer. All the animals were rapidly dehydrating in the intense heat and real summer hadn't even begun. I made a mental note to scrounge some more buckets from . . . well, God knows where; looters had stolen all equipment belonging to the zoo.

I then asked when the zoo staff had last been paid. "Almost two months ago," replied Dr. Husham. His helpers nodded.

"Get the word out that anyone coming back to work will get money," I said. "American dollars—cash," I added for emphasis.

The Iraqi promised to do just that. For what I needed more than anything was strong hands to lug water up from the canals surrounding the zoo with whatever receptacles we could find. It would be backbreaking work in the scorching heat. But that's what had to be done.

I also needed men to muck out the filth-curdled cages and dump the festering flyblown carcasses in a bonfire. Restoring basic hygiene was our third priority after food and water.

"Tomorrow the work starts," I told Husham. The vet nodded. I patted his shoulder; the Iraqi had shown he had grit by the barrelful.

"If it is safe, we will be here," he assured me. "Also Dr. Adel, the zoo director, has come back. I will find him. He will help."

The Kuwaitis and I had planned to bed down for the night in the zoo's three-roomed administration headquarters, but Lieutenant Szydlik vetoed that outright. It was too dangerous: firefights were still flaring throughout Baghdad, and the ferocity of looting intensified exponentially after dark. The city by day was scary; by night it was terrifying.

He told us to follow him as he drove across the park to the Al-Rashid Hotel, which had been commandeered by the Third Infantry Division as their headquarters after the main battle for the city was over. That's where we would be quartered, the only relatively safe place in Iraq.

It was a journey of just a mile or so, but there were so many twisted and jagged cartridges cluttering the road I was convinced we would pop all four of the hired car's tires.

We stuck as close to Szydlik as we dared; any civilian vehicle or unauthorized person in the vicinity was shot on the spot. Buzzing helicopters in the sky maintained ceaseless aerial surveillance. It was comforting to have those sinister-looking Black Hawks hovering above—if they were on your side, that is.

A few minutes later we were at the Al-Rashid.

THREE

THE FOURTEEN-STORY AL-RASHID HOTEL, a rectangular dust brown colossus, towered on the Baghdad skyline like a giant concrete crate. Styled in what is architecturally known as Modern Mesopotamian and built as a showpiece high-rise, it once boasted five stars and was the hub of the city's jet set.

Not anymore. No longer was this some luxury resort with ranks of Mercedes-Benzes and Rolls-Royce parked outside. Instead Abrams tanks and Bradley armored fighting vehicles circled the building in a stifling metallic embrace while their crews in dirty combat gear sweated in the desert sun. Their faces were taut with vigilance and they watched every flicker on the streets through shaded, squinting eyes.

Inside the hotel parking lot and front garden, more tanks squatted on every square inch of space. Scores of Humvee scout cars, which supported the tanks by "painting" targets with lasers, were squeezed in wherever room could be found—some even on the entrance stairway.

The Third ID, the crack unit that had taken Baghdad, had moved in and you knew it.

My hired car couldn't be more out of place among these ugly-beautiful machines, and as we parked up against the hotel lobby entrance, the tank crews stared at us with utter disbelief.

In time this was to become the center of the Green Zone, the most tightly guarded area in Iraq, but at the moment it was where frontline warriors took respite between patrols and firefights. Though it was designated as home base, everyone was on edge.

No attempt had been made to clean up the debris of recent battle. There just hadn't been time. Spent cartridges covered the ground outside the main entrance, and the surface of the turning circle was shredded into tarred gunk by tank treads.

The hotel's walls had been purposefully built to withstand Rocket-Propelled Grenade (RPG) attacks but were pitted from bullet and mortar fire received during the battle to take the building, as were the courtyard pavements.

Lamp poles were bent like snapped toothpicks, while at the gates the bullet-chipped statue of Harun al-Rashid, the legendary caliph of Baghdad known worldwide from the *Arabian Nights* tales, hunched forlornly.

On the pavement, a few meters away from the entrance, the putrid remains of a dead Iraqi fighter lay rotting in the heat. Wherever you turned, the burnt-metallic smell of battle, coppery and caustic, fiercely assaulted your senses.

When American soldiers stormed the hotel they were given a bizarre reminder of how personal this blitzkrieg war against Saddam was. For there, greeting them in the entrance to the marbled lobby, was a cartoon caricature of George H. W. Bush in mosaic on the floor with a "Bush is Criminal" caption inscribed in English and Arabic beneath it. It was so large it dominated the entrance portal. Indeed, it was impossible to walk into the hotel without using the elder Bush's face as a doormat. This was intentional; it was Saddam's "revenge" for the First Gulf War, when the elder Bush had been president. The irony of the younger Bush completing the job was not lost on those at the front lines.

But the elder Bush's parodied portrait was not what I first noticed as I followed Lieutenant Szydlik inside. It was the yeasty-ripe aroma of scores of unwashed men, so pungent it was an almost palpable fog. Khaki-camouflaged soldiers on canvas cots or open-zipped sleeping bags lay around the high-roofed reception area like sacks of dirty laundry, while in the lounge opposite battle-bleary GIs just off patrol and too fatigued to swat the squadrons of whining mosquitoes lay collapsed wherever they could find the space.

Others were sitting around in small groups, either chatting quietly or just crumpled with damp exhaustion, still wearing heavy body armor after a day of skirmishes in the soul-sapping sun.

These were the troops who had taken Baghdad, fighting men from the Third ID. They were among the elite, tough combatants who had spearheaded the strike across the desert, advancing more than six hundred miles in twenty days and obliterating all resistance with almost casual ease. Despite the scene of random chaos here in the hotel, one terse order would have them up and ready for action in an instant.

There had been no opportunity to organize "slop squads" and thus litter was jettisoned everywhere; thousands of discarded Meals Ready to Eat (MRE) ration boxes were scattered on a carpet of concertinaed cigarette butts and glass shards. The massive French windows that lined the huge reception hall and lounge area had all been smashed in, while above us wires hung like blackened noodles from the ceiling. Toilets at the stairwell overflowed in foul ammoniac rivers, and a steel vault door that hadn't opened to a hefty shove had been dynamited and dangled groggily on its torn hinges. All the safe-deposit boxes behind the reception area had been savagely levered open.

Outside the shattered windows, behind a trampled garden and tennis court, was an Olympic-size swimming pool, empty except for a foot or so of soupy green water. Overturned suntanning beds and an empty gym added to the scene of forsaken splendor.

There was no running water anywhere in the city, so when the soldiers commandeered the hotel they knew each toilet in each room on all fourteen floors had one final flush in it. For soldiers who had been cooped up in a tank for three solid weeks, a proper toilet was an unimaginable luxury. Like a rising tide, the bowls filled, and those who still needed to go would move on to the next floor, and so on, up until they reached the top level. Nobody's sure which soldier got the last toilet on the top floor, but it must have been a sprint. When the breeze blew across the desert from the west, you didn't want to be standing in the lee of the Al-Rashid.

Before the invasions, the 379-room hotel had been the buzzing hub of Baghdad and Saddam himself regularly used it as a pleasure dome for entertaining foreign dignitaries. It was also where his sons picked up girls who dared not say no—a decadent oasis where alcohol gushed in an austerely dry Muslim city. At night men and women clad in designer clothes gyrated in the discos to hip-thrusting pop music, light-years removed from the djellabas, burkas, and kaffiyehs on the streets. At least three a-la-carte restaurants catered to those with bulging wallets.

It also was where Iraq's abhorrent secret police, the Mukhabarat, hung out. They were so obvious in their cheap suits and bushy Saddam-aping mustaches that their businessmen disguises were a joke. There was, however, nothing funny about their brutal interrogation procedures and the human shredding machines that were said to be their preferred method of disposing of bodies. Apparently they routinely bugged the hotel's rooms, and stories were told of legions of guests who, having just decided what to order from room service, suddenly found a waiter at their door. He knew their orders before they had called, courtesy of the bumbling Inspector Clouseaus listening to the hidden microphones.

Indeed, Saddam's security paranoia was microcosmed at the Al-Rashid. Each floor had had a round-the-clock concierge sitting at a desk by the elevators to report the comings and goings of every guest to the secret police.

The hotel became internationally famous, albeit probably not in the way its management would have chosen, in the First Gulf War after Peter Arnett's CNN team filmed from its roof the nightly pyrotechnics of Baghdad's administration infrastructure being bombed at will.

This time around, as the war approached, the Al-Rashid was known to be a potential military target and so most journalists booked into the less ostentatious Palestine Hotel on the other side of the river.

However, if the coalition forces regarded an extravagantly opulent hotel as a prime target in their hunt for Saddam, they had good reason. For the Al-Rashid was no mere civilian establishment; it had been specifically designed to be one of the dictator's numerous bunkers around the city, and its thickly reinforced concrete walls were built to withstand rocket attacks. Saddam's final preinvasion propaganda clip of him discussing military tactics with his cabinet was filmed in one of a series of heavily fortified underground chambers that honeycombed the foundation. Lengthy underground tunnels provided a whole host of escape routes.

As we surveyed the devastated lobby, another soldier walked up and Lieutenant Szydlik introduced us to him: Lieutenant Case. They had been at the West Point Military Academy together, and Case was happy to take his friend's word that we were worth looking after.

Officers had taken the bottom floors and after that rooms were grabbed by the crews on a first come, first served basis. The only available accommodations now were on the seventh floor or higher, and we were directed to the staircase.

When we finally reached the seventh floor, chests heaving after the climb, there was a handwritten sign in the foyer near the elevators that was not exactly hospitable: THIS IS DOD PHOTOGRAPHERS' AREA. KEEP OUT.

I assumed, correctly, that DOD stood for Department of Defense. But I had been told by the officer in charge to find a room on the seventh floor and I intended to do just that.

There were no keys and I started testing doors to see which rooms were vacant. This was easy, as all locked doors had been smashed open—courtesy of a sledgehammer conveniently placed against the corridor wall.

Suddenly a voice boomed from behind, "Who the fuck are you?"

It was said with a smile that robbed the obscenity of belligerence. And to my utter astonishment, the accent was South African.

I turned around to see an unshaven, wiry man with a cigarette curling smoke from his bottom lip. He was obviously one of the photographers. Maybe even the guy who had put up the KEEP OUT sign.

"Howzit," I said, giving the colloquial South African greeting. "I'm Lawrence Anthony."

The man looked at me suspiciously, equally astounded to hear an idiom from his homeland. "What the hell are you doing here?" he asked in jovial amazement.

"I'm a conservationist. Come to help out at the zoo."

"The zoo? The one down the road?"

"Ja. It's in a complete mess. They fought a battle right through it. Shot the shit out of the place."

The man laughed as if this were the funniest thing in the world, his chest heaving with crazy mirth. "Everything's a fucking zoo here, man."

I laughed self-consciously with him.

Eventually he put out his hand, stilling chuckling. "Alistair McLarty. Where're you from back home?"

I shook the proffered hand. "Zululand. And you?"

"Jo'burg. Shit, didn't think I'd find another compatriot in this hellhole."

I waved a hand down the corridor. "Which room do you recommend?"

Alistair paused for a moment. "This floor's no good. You'll want to go higher."

He then looked at me for a long moment. He was sizing me up; should the DOD photogs allow me on their floor? In a situation where resources were minimal, you jealously guarded what meager assets you had. This was their floor. They were there first on it, and they decided who stayed there. Or not.

"What do you do back home?" he asked.

"I have a game reserve," I replied. "Thula Thula."

"I've heard of it. That's where they handle problem elephants. Is that you?"

"That's me."

Most South Africans have empathy with wild animals. It's part of the national bushveld psyche.

He stroked his chin, as if wrestling with a dilemma. "Well, okay. Let's see what there is here."

We forced our way into the first room, shoving the sledgehammer-shattered door aside.

"The first thing is to check out the toilet," said Alistair.

He gingerly opened the bathroom door and then slammed it shut with force.

"Whoa! You don't want to go in there!" He shuddered, his face wrinkling with revulsion.

We tried a few more, and Alistair eventually declared that under the circumstances Room 720 wasn't too bad—which meant the toilet wasn't more vile than absolutely necessary. I took that room and the Kuwaitis took the room next door.

Exhausted after the tense nine-hour drive through smoldering battle zones and our first depressing introduction to the zoo, we ate some of the canned food we had brought with us and went to bed.

It was not an agreeable night. The disheveled beds had been slept in before, and dust and grit layered the grimy sheets. The floors were so filthy we left smudgy footprints wherever we walked.

The key choice facing everyone in the hotel was whether to close the windows and steam in the sauna-temperature rooms or open them and be eaten alive by the seething clouds of flies and mosquitoes. Most chose the latter option.

I closed my eyes. Sleep was elusive, despite marrow-sapped exhaustion. I kept getting magnetically pulled to the window by the sounds of fighting that thundered across the city. Tracer bullets and parachute flares incinerated in the sky while tank shells screamed into targets with meteoric ferocity. Firefights erupted every few minutes or so, and just as I fell into a fitful doze, the stuttering hammer of machine guns somewhere on the streets roused me with a start. Radios regularly clattered into life in the hotel around me, and through the open windows I could hear the revving engines of tanks and Humvees seven floors below.

Often in strange places you wake wondering where the hell you are. Not in Baghdad. You knew every minute, indeed every second, exactly where you were: in a damned war zone.

Sweating, filthy, scratchy, mosquito-itchy, noisy . . . it was wretched. Absolutely wretched.

I closed my eyes.

The initial thrill of adventure was by now harshly sullied by the reality of where I actually was. In the middle of a very real, very violent war. This was not part of the plan. Not at all.

God, I'd better not tell Françoise about this.

FOUR

AT EXACTLY 6:00 A.M. I shot out of bed as a terrifying commotion thundered through the Al-Rashid. It was as though a squadron of jumbo jets had flown straight into my hotel room—the bone-shuddering whine of scores of turbocharged engines at full throttle.

I rushed to the window. Outside, seven stories down, drivers of the Third ID were starting up their Abrams tanks for the early-morning patrol. I realized how harrowing it must have been for civilians to watch a formation of these awesomely powerful machines storm their city. Until you got used to it, the crescendo was as disorientating as a panic attack.

I later learned it took twenty-five liters of gas just to kick one of these jet-turbine-powered juggernauts into life. And every morning, the volcanic whining of tanks warming up would be my wake-up call. At the Al-Rashid, that's what passed for room service.

I washed with some of the precious bottled water we had brought from Kuwait. The Kuwaitis were also awake, and after a meager canned breakfast we went downstairs to find an escort to the zoo. It was only a mile or so away, but no civilian car could travel unaccompanied in the immediate area surrounding the Al-Rashid—it would be bombed to smithereens in a blink.

While waiting I found a pile of guest questionnaires on the reception desk, quizzing patrons on whether they had enjoyed their stay at the hotel. I filled one in commenting on lack of room service, food, water, flushing toilets, and electricity. Under "Guest Comments" I complained there were armed men running all over the place shooting at everything in sight and recommended this be reported to the police as soon as possible.

Deadpan, I handed it in to Lieutenant Case saying that unless these matters were dealt with I would consider taking my business elsewhere.

Lieutenant Case guffawed, "apologized" for the inconvenience, and suggested I forward my complaints to a certain Mr. Saddam Hussein, proprietor—but unfortunately he had left no forwarding address.

Case had assigned an armored troop carrier to chaperone us to the zoo, and the distant thud of a mortar bomb greeted us as we left the hotel, followed by the staccato of rifle fire. The Black Hawks circling above dipped their cockpits as they swung toward the firefight, somewhere in the east of the city. The soldiers didn't flinch; this was just the heartbeat of Baghdad—a flare-up here, another one there. They erupted all over the place like minivolcanoes. I marveled at the soldiers' nonchalance, little knowing that within days we would be exactly the same.

Once in the park, soldiers duct-taped the word ZOO across the hood of my hired Toyota. Lieutenant Szydlik radioed all checkpoints instructing that a red-bearded Anglo wearing a khaki baseball cap with the words *Thula Thula* stenciled on it and two Arabs with white and green Kuwaiti Zoo caps, in a new white Toyota with the word ZOO taped on it, were to be allowed access throughout the high-security zone. We were not, repeat not, to be fired upon. It possibly was the strangest order the soldiers had been given since they took the city.

I was also instructed to drive extremely slowly, to stop at least fifty yards from every checkpoint, and to get out of the car with hands exposed and identify myself. I was told not to walk anywhere outside the zoo or hotel grounds. But most important, the Kuwaitis and I had to wear our baseball caps wherever we went. If we lost our headgear, it was possible we would be shot on sight.

Dr. Husham, who had got into the park by clambering over a burnt-out truck jammed in a bomb-blasted gate at the northern entrance on Zaitun Street, was waiting for us. With him were four staff members whom he had managed to contact. I could see they were famished and immediately gave them some dollar bills as advance wages. Abdullah Latif also handed them souvenir Kuwait City zoo T-shirts and caps. He meant well, but given that most Iraqis would not be seen dead wearing Kuwaiti gear, I was not sure how that went down.

I then called everyone together; the five Iraqis and two Kuwaitis. It was time to formulate a plan of action.

I had thought long and hard about what I was going to say. I would base my strategy on two central concepts that formed the core of every project I had tackled, whether in business or the bush: once committed to something, make it go right at all costs; and always complete any cycles of action that you start.

In other words, whatever happens, finish the task you start—easier said than done with fighting and looting rampant all around. But even so, here in a city at war, I already had five people—Husham and his four helpers—prepared to risk their lives just to come to work. This was something precious to build on, and I knew that in order to foster fragile morale I had to keep them productively occupied.

Speaking slowly in basic English, I pointed to the animal cages around us. Every one of these creatures, I said, depended on us. Every single one. It was up to us whether they lived or died.

The American soldiers had said they would help us if they could, but the bottom line was the zoo lived or died under us. We were the last chance. And we were going to make damn sure these magnificent survivors, helpless victims of a brutal war of which they had no comprehension, were going to live.

We lived in a world, I continued, where the environment and animals were viciously abused and soon we are going to pay a terrible price for our neglect. Here in Iraq, we would make a stand that would send a message to fellow humans: that you don't do this to other creatures. More prosaically, I also reminded them that without animals there was no zoo and thus no jobs when the war was over.

I then called upon each of them to speak about their experiences, as a type of catharsis.

A man called Ayed was the first to come forward. "Nobody care about zoo or animals, or people working here, nobody help, everybody fighting, but we try. My wife also she help; she wash your clothes."

I hadn't even thought of that and appreciated the offer, as there was no water at the Al-Rashid.

Husham was next, speaking quickly and animatedly to the others in Arabic and then saying to me. "We thank you; we will be here; we will try."

Then the other Iraqis spoke. They knew each animal well and told of their anguish at what had happened to their zoo, emotionally recalling the names of the creatures they had cared for that had been slaughtered or were missing. It was a type of requiem for the lost animals. Dr. Husham translated their words into rough English, his broken syntax adding a quaint, poetic poignancy.

"Giraffes gone—Ali Baba eat, sure," said one, shaking his head at the utter futility of the slaughter.

"Bomb, lions come out. Soldiers kill too quick, shoot . . . *brrrrrrt*," said another, imitating a machine gun with his hands.

"Why all birds gone? Why Iraqi people do this?" asked another, grappling with the enormity of the trashed cages around him.

After that came the anger. Some of them cursed Saddam Hussein, others the coalition forces. They needed their jobs; their families were as hungry as the animals and their future looked bleak.

Each man repeated the same theme, albeit in different words: It was their zoo and it must be saved. No question about it.

How were we going to do that? I asked.

There was silence. The clarity of our predicament was suddenly and brutally distilled.

I answered my own question. "We will do what we can, right now, using whatever we've got right here in the zoo. And we will make it go right, whatever happens."

The men nodded.

The next question was would they be safe coming to work? Would the Americans and fedayeen busy shooting each other on the streets let them through?

There was nothing we could do about Saddam's thugs, but I pledged to get whatever passage and protection I could from the Americans. My staff, like all civilians, was not allowed even to approach checkpoints and had to come the long way around, through the bomb-blasted gate on the northern perimeter of the park. However, I had no doubt men such as Lieutenant Szydlik would assist us.

Ticking with my fingers, I tabled our priorities.

First we would get what water we could to the cages, as we had done yesterday. That was essential. Water was life.

Next we would feed the animals with what was left of the buffalo meat from Kuwait.

Then we would inspect the animals to determine which ones needed emergency medical attention. I stressed the word *emergency,* as the entire wrecked zoo's inmates needed urgent care. I had brought a limited supply of medicines and antibiotics with me from the Kuwait City zoo—but unfortunately no sedatives—and said I would try to get disinfectant and other basic pharmaceuticals from the Americans.

Hygiene would be the next priority; we would have to scrub the filthy cages until they were livable.

Last, I repeated what I had said to Husham the day before. Any staff members who came back to work would be paid. As I said that I waved a crumpled dollar bill.

"Dollars make them more brave," said Husham, and they all burst out laughing.

I had been waiting for something positive to end the meeting on and decided this was it.

"Let's get started," I said.

That humble gathering of very ordinary men held in the shell of a wrecked office was possibly the most crucial—and emotive—meeting in the zoo's history. Amid the chaos and carnage, without even a chair to sit on, the tiny group of men huddled around me as I outlined in the sand my vastly overoptimistic plan of action.

Somehow, without me even knowing, my simple words—*food, water, care, nurture*; the essence of Mother Earth—touched a chord. We were going to save the zoo, whether we dropped dead in the attempt or not. I could see it in their eyes. Their determination was tangible. Dr. Husham in particular was moved almost to tears.

This was to be our stand. This was more than just a zoo in a war zone. It was about making an intrinsically ethical and moral statement, saying: Enough is enough. You just can't say to hell with the consequences to the animal kingdom. It's all very well getting rid of a monster like Saddam, but that doesn't mean we can forget what we are doing to the rest of our planet. It doesn't excuse a zoo getting trashed just because nobody had the foresight to put a basic survival plan in place for hundreds of animals utterly dependent on humans.

As the men grabbed whatever receptacles they could to ferry water, I walked around the shattered grounds, stopping at every inhabited cage. It was an individual ritual I would go on to repeat daily, calling to each animal—be it a lion, tiger, or timid badger—and as it warily came to the bars I would speak softly, words of encouragement and comfort.

First to come to me was Saedia, the blind brown bear. At last out of her terror-stricken fetal hug, she tentatively approached the bars.

Her eyes were milky opaque, but I sensed somehow she could picture me.

"It's going to be all right, girl," I said softly. "You're going to be safe now. We've got nice food for you. We've got water for you to drink. When it gets too hot, we're going to give you a nice long, cool shower. There're going to be no more bombs here. It's going to be all right."

She cocked her head. I believed she had acknowledged me. At least I wanted—needed—to believe that. I knew from past experience that it was vital to get an acknowledgment, be it as modest as a furtive look or a small body movement.

I moved on to the next cage, then the next, speaking quietly until I got some form of recognition, no matter how insignificant, from each animal.

While this may seem odd to some, anyone working with wild animals knows positive communication is possible and a physical presence, using body language and words, pays absolute dividends. It's uncanny how even the most feral creatures respond to persistent care and communication. This doesn't mean you get into a cage with them; it's no warm and fuzzy Disney movie. It means genuine rapport respecting the fundamental tenets of the natural world. I had no doubt the shell-shocked animals sensed what was going on and that things would now get better. It was this message I wanted to project to them simply by being there . . . acknowledging them . . . letting them smell me. If the zookeepers remained upbeat, that optimism would rub off onto the animals. Those who scoff have no idea of the settling effect on wild animals of a positive, caring frame of mind.

Obviously I had no illusions that this rapport was going to happen quickly. The animals were in terrible condition, listless, starving, and stressed beyond belief, and their sole fixation was food and drink. They, understandably, could barely react to any stimuli other than those basic cravings.

But I knew my persistence would pay off. And from that day on, no matter what happened, I took time to speak words of compassion to them, soothing them and watching for acknowledgment.

The vets by now had done their rounds and came to give me a situation report. The lions would be okay if we could get enough water trickling in. However, the bombed wall of the den needed instant repairs. The giant cats had already escaped on two occasions, and once they got their strength back there was no doubt they would again break out to forage. Three had already paid for that with their lives.

I was aware of this and said that after we had filled the water troughs we would gather debris to plug the hole, binding it with bits of wire we could scrounge from the rubble. I said I would later ask American military technicians to fix it properly.

The two Bengal tigers were also dangerously skeletal, but like the lions they would survive as long as water kept dribbling in. Apart from their raging thirst, they also needed extra water to cool them down in the scorching sun.

The bears were ravenously gobbling vegetable scraps that had been tossed into their cages, the old blind brown bear that I had just spoken to, Saedia, pausing occasionally to gaze vacantly in our direction. In the adjacent cage Saedi, the other bear—the Ali Baba killer—watched us warily as he munched moldy gray cabbage leaves. His water trough was dry as dirt, and I instructed the staff to get containers of the precious liquid into the cage immediately.

In short, the vets said that although all the animals were in awful condition, they were satisfied none were irrevocably on the verge of death. The key question, of course, was how long could we provide food and water?

It was a question none of us could answer.

I drew up a mental balance sheet. On the credit side, I had a few willing workers, some U.S. dollars in my pocket, some meat and vegetables from Kuwait—although much of that was turning rancid—and a trickle of water.

On the debit . . . well, I didn't want to dwell on that. It was simply too huge to contemplate. So I compiled a list of absolute essentials.

First, I needed food for the staff. Without that, they would understandably just grab what we had for the animals. Their families were starving, that much they had made plain, and even the wages I had given them didn't count for much, as shops were either being ransacked by looters or boarded up.

Second, we needed proper buckets to haul water from the canals until we could get the pumps working.

And third, we needed to fix the pumps. Urgently.

The pumps . . . they were the key to everything. Just getting a consignment of water to the cages in the heat on that first day was a forerunner to how cruelly unremitting our workload would be. It was enough to exhaust an ox, sheer backbreaking, muscle-tearing drudgery. We had no proper buckets, so we lugged the precious liquid up with whatever we could find, mainly just rusty cans. It took ages to slake the thirst of a single animal, leaving no time for long-term projects.

If we didn't sort the pumps out soon, more animals were going to die as my ill-fed men dropped from exhaustion. It was as simple, or difficult, as that.

I took Husham aside. He was an impressive handyman, as his jury-rigged viaduct system currently keeping the animals alive attested, and I asked if it was possible to fix the pumps. If so, what did he need?

"Batteries," he said, looking at me as if I were some crazed alchemist. "And a dynamo for the generator."

Batteries? A dynamo? May as well place an order for Beluga caviar. Just the thought of trying to procure something as obscure as a dynamo—a direct-current generator—in a city plunged into anarchy was laughable.

We broke for a canned lunch and I wandered off alone, seeking some respite from the sun's furnace under a giant eucalyptus. I leaned against the trunk and looked up at the sky. Two Black Hawk helicopters walloped past nose to tail overhead, and in the distance I could hear guttural machine-gun staccato.

Hey . . . this was like *Apocalypse Now*, dammit—and in my head I heard the first bars of "The End," the haunting Doors anthem that kicks off the movie, keeping beat with the thudding chopper blades.

An image of the elephant herd back at Thula Thula, which I loved like a second family, flashed so vividly in my mind that for a moment I thought they were standing next to me.

What the hell was I doing here? This was all wrong; this war was supposed to be over. I had known I wanted to make a stand to help the animals of Baghdad, but from the safety of Thula Thula I hadn't realized the full extent of the everyday military hostility in this city. Just a few days ago in Kuwait I had seen cheering crowds on TV welcoming American troops and toppling Saddam's statues.

But this image wasn't reflected here on the ground. In fact, the only area under American control was a few blocks around Saddam's palaces, the park, Al-Rashid, and the conference center—and even that was as dodgy as a sack of rattlesnakes. The rest of the city was a wretched hellhole. Firefights were ongoing, we could hear them all the time, and people were dying violently all over the place.

I also had begun to realize just how dangerous our trip from Kuwait along those desolate back roads had been. It was an absolute miracle we had made it to Baghdad in one piece.

I sat under the tree for several more minutes, daydreaming of home. Then with immense physical effort, literally shaking myself like a wet dog, I yanked my wild-flying thoughts together. There was work to be done. There was no point in feeling sorry for myself.

The younger tiger's cage was just ten yards away and I noticed the majestically striped feline staring quizzically at me. This tiger, Malooh, was the most stressed of all the zoo's afflicted inhabitants, hissing and snarling if anyone got too close.

"Don't worry, fella," I said aloud. "You and me are going to get through all this just fine."

Just saying that made me feel better. I hoped the tiger did as well.

BACK AT THE HOTEL that night, I had supper with the Kuwaitis and then knocked on the smashed door of Alistair McLarty's room.

"Come in, *boet* [brother]," said the South African.

Inside his room, lounging on the disheveled, grimy beds, were three of Alistair's colleagues. They introduced themselves: Bob Parr, Peter Jouvenal, and another man who only gave his name as Nick. They were British ex–Special Service soldiers, hired to film the war as it unfolded at the front lines for the U.S. Department of Defense's archives. They had flown into Baghdad the day after the airport had been overrun and had been at the sharp end ever since. Now that Baghdad had been nominally taken, they roamed around photographing the vicious rearguard attacks from Saddam's fedayeen that were flaring throughout the suburbs. They regularly went in with their cameras to videotape the most dangerous parts of the city: the souks, narrow-streeted slums, and criminal hideouts. They didn't carry just cameras, either. They were also heavily armed. They had to be, as they could not claim to be neutral pressmen. They were contracted to the Pentagon, which made them fair game for guerrillas. If they got into trouble, they would have to drop their cameras and shoot their way out.

It was not the sort of job a file clerk would want. These men were adventurers in the true, swashbuckling sense of the word.

I sat down on a rumpled bed. They were drinking the powdered cool drink that comes in a sachet in each MRE, mixing it with bottled water from their daily ration. The room was strewn with cameras, videos, and photographic equipment, and an assortment of firearms was lying around.

As the evening progressed they started asking questions about the zoo. I mentioned we desperately needed buckets to water the animals, and the photographers said no problem, there were some in the hotel. That's what they used to carry the algae-ridden slush up from the swimming pool to flush the stinking toilets. In fact, being five-star hotel buckets, they were made from shiny stainless steel, unlike the common garden-variety galvanized iron buckets. Would that suffice?

You bet. It was our first major breakthrough, and the next morning I arrived at the zoo triumphantly holding four gleaming buckets, each capable of holding up to ten liters.

Throughout the morning we worked in temperatures steaming

up to 110 degrees Fahrenheit. We were little more than beasts of burden, drawing bucketful after bucketful of stagnant water from the canals, staggering up the banks to the cages a couple of hundred yards away, and pouring the contents into Husham's pipe viaduct. The water was fetid but drinkable for the animals and was also used to speed up defrosting buffalo chunks that were tossed to the carnivores. We had to move quickly, as pillagers stole any food left out too long.

Unfortunately, we didn't move quickly enough. By midafternoon looters had stolen all the buckets. I couldn't believe it; our most valuable—our only—equipment was gone within hours. However, I managed to scrounge a couple more from the hotel, and staff had strict instructions never to let these out of their sight during the day. I took the buckets back with me at night and kept them next to my bed.

The next day a group of helmeted journalists arrived at the zoo, moving awkwardly in bulky Kevlar vests and surrounded by a retinue of armed bodyguards looking menacing in wraparound dark glasses. They were intrigued by what they saw. In between the blood and bullets, here was an offbeat human-interest story. They thought it was good copy; a white African who had gate-crashed a war zone on a zany conservation mission and a group of dedicated Iraqis saving a zoo rather than looting and running rampant downtown. Indeed, the Iraqi zookeepers were probably some of the first Baghdad residents to start reconstructing their city.

One of the journalists, a short, cynical Irishman, asked what I planned to achieve.

"Simple," I said. "We want to save these animals. It's not their fault they're in the shit."

He laughed and shook his head. "They're not even going to save this city. How're you're going to do it with a bloody zoo?"

It was a question I had no answer for. I shrugged: "Perhaps we're just Horatio at the bridge."

He looked at me blankly. He didn't have a clue what I was saying. Horatio was a Roman legionnaire who with two comrades held the invading Etruscan army at bay on the narrow bridge spanning the river Tiber in 510 B.C., allowing the Romans the chance to destroy the structure at the other end and save the city. It was one of the most uneven contests in history, and as I looked at the few exhausted men I had with me that was almost how I felt.

The following morning, newspapers around the world carried reports of the wrecked zoo with picture spreads of bone-thin animals, smiling Iraqis, and me wearing a Thula Thula baseball cap. I never saw the reports at the time but later heard it was a major public relations boost . . . absolutely essential, as I knew all too well that media focus was crucial to galvanizing international aid. Whether we liked it or not, at this pivotal point publicity was our oxygen. I just hoped I could keep things ticking over until our plight affected the conscience of the world.

Later that day a few more zoo workers arrived; no doubt the grapevine message was out that at last they would be paid. Any extra hands were crucial in carrying water to the cages, and I welcomed them with wide arms.

If only I could get those pumps working and our biggest obstacle, water, would be solved.

That was just one of many pressing problems. Dr. Husham again reminded me the staff was close to starving. They saw the animals getting food, and I was sure some of the better cuts of buffalo meat for the carnivores were already being filched for the staff's families.

I couldn't blame them. But even if I gave them more money it would not be of much use, as there was precious little food to buy in Baghdad at that stage.

This posed a serious dilemma. It was pointless trying to run a zoo where the staff was as hungry as the animals.

I said I would see what I could do and at the very least get some MREs from the army. MREs are scientifically programmed food packs with enough nutrition to keep fighting people going under any circumstances, and they would be just what we needed to keep our struggling staff going.

I didn't know if I could officially ask the army to give me a bulk order, but I had no doubt soldiers would hand over any surplus supplies that they could. Before I arrived, some soldiers, sickened by the plight of the starving animals, had fed them with their own MREs. Like every battle, the fight to save the zoo would only be won by grassroots support. And in this regard the ordinary American soldier was magnificent.

However, MREs would be little more than a stopgap. I needed a more permanent source of food.

It wasn't only the staff that was hungry. The supplies from Kuwait were by now almost exhausted, and we were down to the last few frozen chunks of buffalo meat. I decided to keep them for a rainy day, so in the meantime I had to find new outlets for animal food urgently.

The answer to the latter problem was as simple as it was harsh. In ravaged Baghdad there was only one source of affordable meat: the ubiquitous donkey. Even so, war shortages had rocketed the cost of donkeys through the roof and the price was climbing daily. Each one of these gallant and loyal little beasts was now being sold at more than a quarter of an average Iraqi's monthly salary.

We had no other option, so I summoned a nearby worker, peeled off a number of dollar bills, and told him to come back with donkeys.

I never saw the man or my money again. I cursed. If I couldn't trust my own people, whom could I trust?

I walked over to Husham and quizzed him about it, stressing that I only wanted loyal workers. He was adamant I had not given the money to any of our men, and we then realized what had happened. In the general chaos around the zoo I must have confused a looter with a staff member and given him the cash.

I bet he couldn't believe his luck. Husham and I laughed until our stomachs ached.

That afternoon I sent out another worker with more dollars—this time first checking that he was one of us!

A few hours later the man was back. Not only did he have two donkeys in tow but also the zoo's "executioner." His name was Kazim and he was the official ax man, able to kill a beast with one blow and quarter it as deftly as a master butcher. Kazim had slaughtered animals for fresh meat at the zoo for decades, and the Iraqis regarded him as one of the lowlier workers. But he was worth every cent I paid him. For obvious reasons, none of us wanted the grisly job of killing donkeys ourselves.

Before we closed for the evening, the carnivores feasted on fresh donkey meat, the bears on the last remaining vegetables and some MREs. The boars, badger, and other creatures got a mixture of both. We also left out food for the foraging animals, baboons and monkeys that I had spotted hiding around the zoo grounds.

As Husham placed some meat down in the open, little eyes were watching him. A starving desert fox had got the scent of the meat and come out of hiding, desperately waiting for Husham to move off so it could get to the food.

Above me an Amazon parrot screeched loudly, perched incongruously in an eucalyptus tree, an alien in a desert country so far from home. We would never catch it and could only hope that it would return to its cage of its own accord.

The next day the vegetables we had put out for the monkeys and baboon were gone. At least they had eaten.

That night at the Al-Rashid I bumped into Alistair as I trooped exhaustedly up the stairs and he invited me to his room. The other DOD photographers were there as well and we started swapping yarns by candlelight. The men were getting to know their way around bullet-strewn Baghdad like veterans. If there was a deal somewhere, a crate of cold beers going under the counter, some Iraqi rugs or Arabic silverwork on special offer, they would be the first to dodge the gunfire and track it down. Although they had strict orders only to travel in military convoys, they preferred to work on their own, watching one another's backs. It was too cumbersome to move with the military. They needed to be weaving in and out at the front lines of fighting wherever it was happening and as it happened. They even had their own car they had picked up at the roadside for a few hundred dollars. The vehicle had been hired out to some journalists a few weeks before, but after an explosion hit the car and one of them had been killed, it had been abandoned. The one side of the car and the windshield were shattered, but it had a powerful engine that was still thumping and that was all Alistair and his fellow adrenaline junkies needed.

While we chatted, the city's nightly anarchy provided a spectacular pyrotechnic sideshow viewed from Alistair's seventh-story room. It would normally kick off with a stutter of AK-47 or light-arms fire, followed by a searing white illumination flare shot high into the air, billowing down in a blazing parachute, blinding in its intensity. Then there would be the slightly deeper crack of American M-16s seeking out the AK gunmen in the instant brightness. Tracer bullets tore up the sky in pencil-thin fire beams followed by the surly bass *crump* and flash of a mortar bomb or the distinctive double bang of an RPG hitting its target.

Sometimes the flares would be of a different color and the military-trained DOD photographers would remark, "Uh-oh, that's trouble. They're calling for reinforcements."

Sure enough there would then be a *boom-boom-boom* of a Bradley firing. Then silence. And darkness. Supreme darkness, as there was no electricity in Baghdad.

It would all start up a few minutes later somewhere else in the city. On some occasions firefights raged wherever you looked and the sky would flash madly as though some celestial wrench had maliciously sabotaged the heavenly power grid.

Just as an exercise, I attempted to time how many bullets were fired each minute during one of the contacts. It was too rapid even to begin. During some of these exchanges bullets hit the hotel and on two occasions struck windows in adjoining rooms.

I was always amazed how the tracer bullets would appear to float gently through the sky. Only when they were coming toward you did they crack past.

Apache, Black Hawk, and Kiowa choppers whirred incessantly above, blades thudding with astral rhythm. You couldn't see them as they flew completely blacked out, their positions only betrayed by dark shapes obliterating starlight for an instant as they droned through the skies, pilots and gunners scanning the city with sophisticated thermal night vision.

I remembered books on the Vietnam War describing how the press corps would festively congregate on the roofs of their hotels in Saigon each night, whiskey glasses in hands as they watched firefights from the comfort of their five-star seats. The hotels provided a full rooftop bar service, and for many billing themselves as war correspondents this was their sole experience of combat.

It was vastly different in Baghdad. This was no jolly five-star expense account jaunt. The war here was right in your face, close, personal . . . everywhere. I still couldn't come to terms with the fact that I, a man on a humanitarian mission, was taking my life in my hands every time I walked out of the hotel. But that was the reality. It did not matter whether we were foraging for animal fodder downtown or fixing cages in the zoo's open, unprotected grounds; the gunfire never faltered.

Alistair looked at me for a long moment. "Not quite what you expected, *boet*?"

The cameramen were superb company, deprecatingly describing their hazardous exploits and laughing at narrow escapes with raucous black humor. They told me how that day they had surreally stumbled upon the "finest restaurant in Baghdad," miraculously still open in a downtown back alley and even selling ice-cold beer. They promised to take me there soon.

"Is it air-conditioned" I asked.

"Absolutely. They have a generator."

"Well then, don't take me," I said, imagining the bliss of being cool. "Because I will never leave."

From restaurants the topic turned to the zoo, and I mentioned my staff was starving. Alistair looked at his companions and raised an eyebrow. One nodded, then the others, and Alistair instructed me to follow him. We descended the seven floors and turned into a well-concealed narrow corridor leading into a basement. There, as if by magic, sacks of flour, rice, tea, and sugar and hundreds of cans of food suddenly materialized . . . neatly stacked, abandoned by the fleeing hotel staff.

I was dumbstruck; this truly was a gift from the gods.

"Help yourself," Alistair said.

For several moments, I was unable to reply. "You'll never know what this means," I finally said. My voice was raspy.

Alistair punched me lightly on the arm. "Hey . . . you're doing good work. It's okay."

The next morning, the tank commander at the Al-Rashid, Capt. Larry Burris, instructed a burly sergeant named Diehl and some soldiers to pack the sacks onto troop carriers and they ferried the load to the zoo.

The Iraqis hadn't seen so much grub in months. They watched suspiciously as it was off-loaded, unable to believe that it was for them. Then they fell upon the hoard, divvying it up as if it were gold bullion.

It was a defining moment. They now knew I was serious, that they, as well as the animals, would be cared for if I could help it. One came up and gave a little bow of thanks. Husham then said something in Arabic and the Iraqis looked at me, smiles grooved on their faces.

I'm not sure what Husham said, but I was aware that some shadow line had been crossed and it was a precious gain.

However, there was also bad news. Looters had struck during the night, seizing the donkey meat we'd bought the day before. And so we were back to square one. I again dug into my pocket and sent the workers on a foraging party into town, hustling among the gunfire and the looters for more donkeys.

Finding meat was a hit-or-miss affair. The Iraqis merely asked passing pedestrians if they knew of any donkeys for sale, as one would ask strangers for directions. Sometimes we would strike luck in the first hour; sometimes it took days. Indeed, on one occasion later on we had to travel fifty miles out of town. But no matter what, Kazim the executioner was always there with his swinging ax.

Much as I love the noble donkey, feeding them to the zoo's giant cats never worried me. Many conservationists have subsequently queried the ethics of killing one animal to keep another alive, but the Baghdad Zoo's carnivores had always feasted on donkey meat, under the simple premise that donkeys were plentiful and lions and tigers few. It was a straight mathematical equation. The Iraqis did not question it; the harsh reality of nature is that death nurtures life, and conservation politics sometimes must step aside in the face of circumstance.

At that stage there was no other option. Morality was fine in air-conditioned offices of the West, but here in anarchic Baghdad there was a sharp disparity between abstract theory and crisis reality. Even if more buffalo meat were available—which it wasn't—it would be way out of my dwindling-into-a-black-hole budget. Donkeys provided the only affordable protein. The solution to the problem, whether one liked it or not, was clear.

The next piece of equipment we desperately needed was a wheelbarrow to cart food. Each mealtime we had to lug bloody chunks of freshly hacked donkey flesh around by hand, not hygienic and not pleasant, as swarms of metallic black flies covered both carcass and carrier.

I solved the problem temporarily by hijacking a baggage cart from the Al-Rashid Hotel. It was impossible to believe what a difference such a simple tool made. Feeding the animals was now almost a pleasure.

A day later looters broke in and stole it.

That was it. Enough was enough. It was clear to me that something had to be done. Every bit of progress we made was reversed through brazen theft. Unless we confronted the rampant looting problem, the zoo would perish.

FIVE

THE SEARING HEAT scalded my lungs, but I couldn't afford to let up for a second.

Perhaps somewhere in the dim recesses of my mind alarm bells did trigger that a fifty-three-year-old should not be sprinting through a park in a war zone after five people who could well be armed. But such was my anger.

While checking on the cages I had stumbled upon them, a family of looters pillaging at the zoo. Something snapped, and I gave chase.

They had a start on me and for a time it seemed they would escape. But adrenaline does strange things, and I began to close the gap. The family could only go as fast as their youngest child.

Eventually I caught up with them and grabbed the father firmly by the arm.

"Why are you doing this?" I wheezed, each breath knifing my chest.

They looked at me, eyes wide with fear. The mother clutched her youngest child close to her. They didn't understand what I had said.

I pointed to the cages. "Why? This is your zoo. Why do you steal?"

They stared at me vacantly. I then looked at what the man was holding, his booty from the zoo. It was a length of iron, probably wrenched off one of the fences.

My rage exhaled like a popped balloon. Scrap metal. There was a shortage of almost everything in Baghdad—except scrap metal. Just ask the Iraqi army. That was all their tank regiments now consisted of.

I put my hand in my pocket and found a crumpled five-dollar bill. I gave it to the man. He switched from blank resignation to utter incredulity. What was this crazy white foreigner doing?

I pointed at the little girl next to her mother and motioned my hand to my mouth. "Buy food for your children. But don't steal from your zoo."

The words meant nothing, but the gesture was universal. The man bowed his thanks, and the starving family hurried off.

Before the invasion most Iraqis were on government-subsidized food aid. It was one of Saddam's deliberate strategies to keep the population indefinitely dependent on him. But when war erupted, food stocks ran dangerously low and the collapse of law and order into looting was inevitable.

Even so, few were prepared for the rabid barbarism that was to follow. Unlike the family I had chased, many looters were not merely the destitute scavenging for survival. It was not just about food; it was far more primitive. Overnight, ordinary people . . . bank clerks, bakers, students, businessmen . . . morphed into deranged mobs, hell-bent on ripping their city to shreds in a savage, greed-fueled spree.

Perhaps it started with the heady toppling of Saddam's towering statue with its avuncular outstretched arm in Firdos Square. Perhaps it was a first tentative stone thrown at a shop window. But like a wind gusting on sparks in a forest, it soon flared out of control.

They started ransacking the posh Al Mansur district, and those who got there first rampaged with feral intensity. Initially the targets were government buildings and the Americans did not intervene, as they considered such action fair retribution against a hated dictatorship.

This was a crucial mistake, for when the word spread that the soldiers were just standing by, the looters swarmed and started sacking the entire city. There were thousands upon thousands of them rioting in the streets, smashing windows and grabbing TV sets, computers, hi-fis, and CD players. They took everything they could; from office desks, chairs, and filing cabinets to rubber bands and paper clips. If the booty was too large, they used shopping carts to ferry it. Or else they roamed in gangs, helping one another haul off beds and cupboards and freezers and stoves.

Images of the wild rampage were beamed across the world. For those sitting in comfortable living rooms it was a cautionary glimpse into the darkness sprung tight beneath the veneer of human restraint.

Eventually the long-delayed order from the military top command came through: stop the looting with maximum force if necessary. In the worst-hit areas dusk-to-dawn curfews were imposed, particularly in the ravaged eastern sector of the city. The Americans finally fired on some pillagers, and the word got around. The tidal wave of anarchy at last started to recede. In its wake was a city without electricity or running water. The power stations, electrical transformers, pump stations, and water reticulation plants everywhere had been ransacked and stripped bare.

I watched all of this with old, tired eyes. The symbolism was stark. This wasn't only about Baghdad; it wasn't about Iraq.

It was about all of us.

It's what we are doing to our planet. Looting it.

THE PILLAGING MAY HAVE EBBED elsewhere in the city, but not at Al Zawra Park and the Baghdad Zoo. As the park was out of the public gaze, shaded by giant eucalyptus trees, looters could continue their rampage unhindered. Also, the northeastern boundary was wide open to the scavenging masses as gates and blown walls were crudely plugged with burnt-out truck frames and rubble that provided only cursory barricades. The mobs could enter unseen and at will.

It drove me crazy watching these anarchic hordes. I asked Husham if he could get an AK-47 to defend the zoo, something I thought reasonably simple in war-torn Baghdad. But obviously not. He said none of his contacts could source one.

So we judged each case on its merits. If there were only a couple of looters, we would grab iron bars and tell them to move on. If there was a large group we couldn't order off, we would adjourn to the office, where I would swear at the thugs in Zulu. It didn't deter them in the least, but it made me feel better.

I asked for military help, but Lieutenant Szydlik shook his head regretfully; his troops were still fighting a war and had a big patch of turf to control. They had no time to do specific patrols solely to protect the zoo.

However, whenever Szydlik did come across zoo looters he instructed his men to drive them off the premises at gunpoint. It didn't do much good, as they merely waited outside the gates until the Americans left and then came flooding back. The zoo de facto belonged to them.

This frustrated ordinary American soldiers no end. But their hands were tied; much as they wanted to solve the problem with necessary force, they were under orders not to. Their anger was aggravated when at the height of the problem a group of them arrived with some sheep, which they proudly handed over to me "for your starving lions and tigers." While patrolling the perimeters of Baghdad they had met a shepherd, and when he said his animals were for sale the Americans—whom I had never met before—remembered the hungry giant cats at the zoo and reached for their wallets.

They said it was their way of saying thanks for what we were doing for the animals. A bargain, they believed: only forty dollars a ewe.

I didn't have the heart to tell them they had been hugely ripped off. The going rate for a sheep was, even considering the ludicrously inflationary exchange rate, only about five dollars.

Nevertheless, it was a tremendously generous gesture, and those sheep unwittingly played a significant role in upgrading security, because that night looters struck again and stole the entire flock. And that brazen theft, possibly more than anything else, made the American soldiers billeted near the zoo mad. Spitting mad. They had gone to a lot of trouble to get those animals.

"We have got to catch these bastards and lock them up once and for all," I said to Szydlik. "It's got to be a case of 'do not pass Go, do not collect two hundred dollars, go straight to jail.' This whole thing is spinning out of control."

Brian Szydlik at last agreed. As there were no police, courts, and jails operating in the city, he decided to build a makeshift jail outside the zoo grounds to teach the Ali Babas a lesson and at least make a token show of force. His soldiers strung coils of razor wire to form a large square jail around a tree, and guards kept watch. It was only, at best, a stopgap measure, but we somewhat grandiosely dubbed it the Baghdad Zoo Jail.

From then on if we managed to catch looters, they were chucked unceremoniously inside. Depending on the severity of their crimes, they were kept there for up to three days.

For some of the more destitute, the "Baghdad Zoo Jail" was a welcome respite from the rigors of survival in the war-gripped city. They were fed three MREs a day and given fresh water, something sorely lacking at home.

But perhaps more important, during their enforced stay at the zoo the looters saw firsthand that it was Iraqis themselves who were pivotal in the reconstruction of one of their city's prime assets. That perhaps the zoo was something they shouldn't wreck.

The mystery was what the looters actually found of resale value to scavenge at the zoo. After the initial rampage in which any animal without large teeth or claws was carted off and buildings stripped bare, one would have thought the looters would move on to more lucrative pickings. Instead, they resorted to stealing stuff that was virtually worthless—chunks of scrap metal or anything that zoo staff left unattended for a few seconds. A bucket was worth a few meager cents to a looter, but to the lions or bears it was the difference of whether they drank that day or not. And any precious animal food not kept well out of sight was stolen on the spot. This was why it was absolutely essential the looting problem had to be hit on the head once and for all.

At the height of the anarchy I asked several American officers and soldiers for a gun, arguing that we were the only people on duty in the theater (as they called Baghdad) without a weapon. The request was always refused. They said they couldn't go around giving weapons to civilians.

But without a gun we would forever be victims, completely unable to defend ourselves or protect the animals. I kept pestering anyone I could to get me one.

Eventually a captain, who shall remain nameless, disgusted by what he saw happening and our being powerless to stop it, slipped me a 9mm pistol that had formerly belonged to an Iraqi officer killed in battle. The captain did it with no fuss and asked for no thanks, but we both knew he was putting his career on the line for the survival of the zoo.

The difference was immediate. Obviously there was nothing I could do about the larger heavily armed hordes that regularly rampaged through the park, but whenever I saw "manageable" groups of looters I didn't have to back off anymore. I would stride up to them, point the pistol, and gesture angrily at them to move on, and quickly.

They always did and I never had to fire even a warning shot, although I would have had no compunction shooting if any of our lives were at risk; such was the chaos in those dark days.

I like to think of myself as an easygoing guy, but something had to be done. We would lose the zoo if these thugs were not permanently routed. We had tried reasoning with them; we had tried everything. And there comes a time when words are no longer sufficient.

I know this too well, unfortunately. It was a lesson I had learned earlier in my life when I was shocked to discover that there was a price on my head in my native Zululand.

IT HAPPENED about seven years ago. I was at Thula Thula when my mother phoned, her voice scratchy with worry. She had just been given news that was enough to send any mother into a paroxysm of fear. There was a contract out on her son's life.

The South African security police had told her the news. Their informers had penetrated the homestead of a powerful local *induna* (headman) and had firsthand information that assassins were hunting me.

The reason for the killing contract was depressingly similar to most disputes in rural South Africa: land. I was busy establishing the Royal Zulu Widelife Sanctuary, a massive conservancy trust area for the benefit of the local people, and had earmarked bushveld that was too wild for cattle grazing to set the project up. Apartheid was over and at last blacks could legally participate in conservation and tourism. I knew it was absolutely vital to start involving disadvantaged communities in protecting and reaping benefits from wildlife; otherwise our wilderness heritage was doomed.

My reserve, Thula Thula, was the key to getting this project up and running. The bush is thick, and in summer it's a steaming kaleidoscope of different shades of green and gold. The river seldom runs dry even in arid years. The grasses that separate the woodlands are sweet and nutritious—and with that as a platform, I had no doubt the project would be a success.

But according to police information, some tribesmen had decided if I was bumped off, they would be able to seize the tribal trust land for themselves. Even though it legally belonged to five different clans and I was just the coordinator of the project, they believed that once it was consolidated and proclaimed as a game reserve, without me they could stake their own claim. The scenario was reminiscent of the circumstances that lead to the murder of lion conservationist George Adamson of *Born Free* fame in Kenya many years ago.

The police even had the names of the assassins after me. They weren't, however, sure if the *induna* himself was involved.

I know Zulu culture well. I live with it daily. If one does not confront a problem instantly, it can balloon out of all proportion. Blood feuds today still flourish with fierce intensity for reasons no one remembers. There was no other way around it, so I decided I must pay the *induna* an early visit.

A good friend and extremely courageous old man, Obie Mthethwa, said it was too dangerous for a white person to go to the *induna's kraal*—homestead—alone and volunteered to come with me. As Obie was a senior counselor to the chief and well respected in the area, his presence would be invaluable.

Obie also knew who the assassins were by reputation. "*Tsotsis*," he told me, using the Zulu pejorative for *thugs*. "These are bad men."

That afternoon we drove deep into rural Zululand on rutted four-wheel-drive tracks to the headman's home.

In Zulu tradition you never enter a *kraal* unless invited. You stand at the gate near the *isibaya*, cattle enclosure, and shout your name and the nature of your business. Then the host will invite you in at his leisure.

It was a picturesque village with traditional round thatched huts neatly set out on top of a hill. People were finishing their day, herd boys bringing in cattle, mothers calling in children, everyone preparing to retire for the night. The smell of the evening meals wafted across the village.

Obie and I were made to wait almost an hour and it was dark before we were allowed into the *kraal*. That was an ominous sign.

We were then escorted to the *isishayamthetho*, the largest thatch-and-clay hut, traditionally used for important business.

Shadows danced on the walls from a single candle flame that illuminated the simple furnishings, a table and flimsy wooden chairs. I noticed immediately the *induna* was alone. This was extremely unusual, as advisers or counselors always accompany an *induna*. We had seen some of them outside while we waited. Where were they now? What was it he didn't want them to hear?

Then, as is Zulu protocol, we started a lengthy greeting process asking about each other's health, the health of immediate families, and the weather. Only after that is it deemed polite to state the actual nature of your business.

While all this was going on, I maneuvered the back of my chair firmly against the wall so no one could sneak behind me. I had no illusions about what was going to happen and I wanted to face whatever danger came at me headfirst.

Speaking in Zulu, I explained that the police had told me there was a contract on my life and the hit men hired to do the killing came from the *induna*'s tribe.

"*Hau!*" exclaimed the *induna* loudly, the Zulu expression of surprise. It couldn't be his people, he said. They held me in esteem. Was I not the man who was going to bring work for rural people with the Royal Zulu project? Wasn't I myself a white Zulu? Weren't we old neighbors?

I agreed but said my information was impeccable, coming from top policemen who said the people wanting to kill me believed by so doing they could grab the Royal Zulu land themselves. This would not be the case, I stressed, as the trust land belonged to several other tribes as well.

Again the *induna* expressed astonishment and I was starting to wonder if perhaps the police's information had been wrong. The *induna* was either innocent or a virtuoso liar.

At that moment we heard a car pull up outside, followed by the traditional shout of identification. About ten minutes later four men walked in. They had come to report to their *induna*.

The *induna* told them to sit and they squatted on the floor on their haunches, keeping their heads lower than their boss's as a Zulu token of respect.

As they settled down Obie grabbed my arm and urgently whispered into my ear in English, "These are the *tsotsis*, the killers—these are the men whose names the police gave us."

At first they did not recognize Obie and me in the murky candlelight. But as their eyes grew accustomed to the dim shadows the startled looks on their faces betrayed them.

I was wearing a bulky bush jacket and in my pocket was a cocked 9mm pistol. My hand slid around the butt. I gently eased off the safety catch and pointed the pistol through the jacket straight at the closest killer's belly.

Obie was now understandably alarmed. Again he whispered in my ear: "This situation is very dangerous. We have to get out."

But there was no way out. I continued speaking, looking directly at the *induna*, hand on my gun. I said the police had given me names of the would-be assassins and the names were the same as those of the four men who had just walked in. Did this mean the *induna* was in cahoots with the killers?

The accusation was purposefully blunt and sparked an instant heated reaction. The contract killers sprang up and started shouting at me.

I jumped up to face them. Obie also quickly stood up, squared his shoulders, and glared at the assassins.

"*Thula msindu*—stop this noise," he commanded loudly with firm authority. "This is the *induna's* house. He must speak. You must show respect."

The *induna* slowly stood up and then vehemently denied I was on any hit list, but there was no doubting his attitude had radically changed. He was now petulantly on the back foot, accusing me of calling him a liar—a heinous slur in Zulu culture.

"Why is it that these men who the police know want to kill me walk so easily into your house?" I persisted. "Does this not seem suspicious?

"And what's more," I added, "the police know I have come to talk to you. My visit here has been fully reported to them and they await our return. If Obie Mthethwa or I do not get back home this night, they will know what happened here. They will find you and you will suffer the full consequences of your actions."

I knew it was unlikely I would be able to shoot my way out, but I certainly would take a couple of these cutthroats with me. Perhaps that would also give Obie a chance to make a break for it.

I focused on the candle, just a stride away on the floor. If anything started I planned to kick it over and plunge the room into darkness. The *induna* was also looking at the candle, no doubt harboring the exact same thoughts. He then looked at me.

We both knew why.

The *induna* broke his stare first. I could see he was now unnerved—particularly as he believed the police knew we were at his kraal. He had been completely caught out by the arrival of the assassins and the fact that we knew who they were; all his denials before were obvious lies.

The contract killers looked at their boss, unsure of what to do. The four of them could easily overpower Obie and me by weight of numbers, but as experienced gunmen they also knew I had a primed pistol underneath my jacket. If they went for their guns, I would get the first shot off, straight at the first killer. It was now up to their boss what he wanted to do.

The standoff was tense and silent. Nobody moved.

A minute ticked by. Then another.

I finally provided the *induna* with a way out. Looking him straight in the eye, I demanded he give his word of honor that I was in no danger from any members of the tribe. I emphasized that there was confusion and I was not necessarily accusing him of anything, but I wanted a solemn declaration that I remained under the protection of both him and his tribal chief, as was the civic right of any resident in the area.

The *induna* quickly agreed, grabbing the escape route with both hands. He continued to protest his innocence but gave his assurance I would not be harmed by any of his tribesmen.

That was all I needed. The main aim of the meeting had been achieved. The *induna* knew his plan was blown and he would be a fool to go back on his word of honor. He also knew he would be the prime suspect if anything ever happened to me—whether he was guilty or not.

As a parting shot I said our discussion would be reported to his chief at the next council meeting.

We then left. As we got into the car, Obie let out a large *whoosh* of air from deep in his belly. We had just stared death in the face, and I looked at the old man with absolute gratitude. He had the courage of a lion and had put his life on the line for the purest motive of all; friendship.

Driving home through the dark African bush, Obie—a natural actor—recounted the story over and again in the minutest detail, mimicking accents and actions with deadly accuracy. I laughed delightedly, adrenaline still fizzing with the manic relief of survival. I knew Obie would memorize the story with meticulous precision and it would be told and retold around the night fires of his homestead, woven into the rich fabric of his tribe's folklore: of how he and his white friend had called the bluff of one of the most powerful headmen in the area—and lived to tell the tale.

Fortunately, the problem with the *induna* resolved itself permanently a year or so later when his own tribe removed him for incompetence. His replacement today is fully supportive of the Royal Zulu project.

But what that brush with death did teach me was that the best way to deal with any threat was to face it down directly.

It was a lesson that would serve me well in Baghdad.

IN IRAQ, the tidal wave of looting would eventually kick-start Baghdad's post-Saddam economy in a quirky new direction. For amid all the anarchy, booming businesses soon started flourishing in the form of pavement "loot" shops. Goods previously out of reach to all but the wealthiest were now on sale at ludicrously discounted prices.

From a city in which before you could get nothing there suddenly was a plethora. At markets such as those on Ramadan Street, looted food, medical equipment, sportswear, and other miscellany changed hands for a fraction of even production cost. The mind boggled at the variety of the display; from top-range Nike sneakers selling for twelve thousand dinars, or about four dollars, to stainless-steel surgical tools costing just five hundred dinars, or sixteen cents.

More ominously, the going rate for Kalashnikov assault rifle magazines filled with thirty bullets was thirty-five thousand dinars, about twelve dollars. There was no shortage of AKs now, but I had become comfortable with my 9mm.

You could even pick up passbooks looted from the Defense Ministry showing that you had completed your compulsory military service, something not to be sneezed at if you didn't want to spend several years of your life marching in the desert sun. A passbook would set you back seventeen cents.

Unfortunately, included in the bargain-buying spree were wild animals. Several hundred had been taken from the Baghdad Zoo alone, while the figure stolen from underground menageries that proliferated in some of the less savory city suburbs will never be known.

Black-market trade in exotic creatures has always been a problem in the Middle East. Sadly, in the squalid pavement stalls you could purchase, for a pittance, an emaciated, terrified bear cub or a pelican so weak it could not lift its beak.

I knew one day we would have to find those animals. Once we had the zoo up and running, I vowed, we would go for the private menageries where cruelty and barbarism was a way of life.

But this next step happened sooner than I ever expected. The next day soldiers at the hotel told me they had more animals for me. Saddam and his son Uday had been avid wildlife collectors, and their "pets" had been found starving in the palaces.

That the animals—including lions—were still alive was great news. But again the awful mental balance sheet flashed in my mind. The debits and credits of the project were frighteningly mismatched; I had only just arrived, and we were struggling to feed and water the few animals we had in the main zoo.

How the hell were we going to cope with more?

SIX

U DAY HUSSEIN was nicknamed the "Lion Cub" by his syco-
phantic followers, which is a grievous slur on lions. No
wild beast would demean itself by killing as casually as
Uday did.

He was Saddam's eldest son and originally groomed to take
over from his father. If possible, Uday was even more feared than
Saddam himself, secretly loathed for his uncontrollably savage tem-
per. His aptitude for gratuitous violence was the stuff of legends, repeated only in whispers by a brutalized people.

His mother, Sajida, who was also Saddam's first cousin, was
head of Baghdad's elite private school Al Kharkh Al Namouthajiya,
which Uday naturally attended. His classmates recall that although he rarely—if ever—did any work, he always came first.
What a surprise.

After he left school, he graduated from the University of Baghdad's College of Engineering with an average mark of 98.5 percent,
despite barely opening a book. But one may be forgiven for think-

ing this was not in any measure due to an abnormally high IQ. Instead, top marks were attained by the simple expedient of assaulting tutors who failed to rig results.

His sterling grades then paved the way for his appointment as minister of youth, which he used as a springboard to interfere in any facet of Iraqi life that took his fancy, particularly soccer, Iraq's national sport. Players who did not score or prevent goals being scored against them were regularly jailed on Uday's whim. When they returned, their heads were shaved as a mark of their "national disgrace." In 1999 one of Iraq's terrified soccer stars, Sharar Haydar Mohammad al-Hadithi, managed to flee the country and told how he had often been vigorously tortured if Uday considered his game to be below par.

The next year, after Iraq's 4–1 defeat in the quarterfinals of the Asia Cup, goalkeeper Hashim Hassan and defender Abdul Jaber and striker Qathan Chither were beaten and whipped for three days by Uday's bodyguards. On the fourth day they saw the error of their ways and promised not to let in so many goals in future.

When Uday was not inspiring his soccer players, his favorite pastime was trawling discotheques in Baghdad's elite hotels, where his bodyguards would seize women for him. They were taken either to a hotel room or to his riverside "love nest" and raped.

On one occasion Uday walked into a wedding ceremony, grabbed the bride, and raped her in a side room. The groom later committed suicide.

Uday also often was seen strolling around the Baghdad University campus "inviting" attractive female students to his parties. They, too, would often be abused.

Then there's the story of the time Uday and his friends were at the Jadriyah Hunting Club in Baghdad, where the country's most popular singer, Kathem Saher, was performing. Uday was enraged when he saw women queuing up to ask for autographs and fawning over the handsome entertainer instead of himself. So he called Saher to his table, put his foot up, and told the singer to autograph the sole of his shoe. This presented Saher with a chilling dilemma, one that could cost him his life. He either insulted Uday by signing a lowly thing such as a shoe or insulted him by not signing it.

Saher signed the shoe, silently praying that would be considered the lesser insult. That night he fled into exile.

Uday's domestic life was equally unsavory. His wife, Saja, who was his first cousin, left him after six months, fleeing to Switzerland when he viciously beat her up one time too many.

His father regarded these excesses as boyish high jinks until Uday killed Hanna Jajjou, Saddam's personal valet and food taster. Uday was blind drunk at the time and accused Jajjou of procuring women for his father, breaking up the marriage to Uday's mother. He then proceeded to bludgeon Jajjou to death.

This tested even Saddam's patience to its edge. Uday was sentenced to a year in jail and afterward sent into exile in Geneva. That didn't last long, as the Swiss authorities soon expelled him for laundering money. He returned to Baghdad, and although it appeared his father had forgiven him, it was now apparent Qusay, his younger brother by two years, was the anointed one.

In 1996 an attempt on Uday's life was made as he drove around the fashionable Al Mansur district. Gunmen following his car opened fire, and although Uday survived, he was partially paralyzed and could only walk with difficulty.

Most Iraqis believe Saddam was behind the assassination attempt, because no one was ever charged with the crime. This was more than mere speculation. Under the Hussein regime, culprits for any high-profile crime were always found and savagely punished. Whether they were guilty or not was a moot point.

Despite his disabilities, Uday's reign of terror continued. Much of his power stemmed from his control of a large chunk of Iraq's media. His rag called *Babel* was disingenuously described as Iraq's only independent newspaper—it was anything but—and Uday used this as a platform to branch out into highly lucrative projects involving TV, transport, hotels, and food deals. His communications empire included Iraq's most-listened-to radio station, Voice of Iraq FM, and Youth TV, both of which adopted a snappy Western style of presentation, as opposed to the dull style of the state-owned channels.

But Uday's true power base was his leadership of the Sadamyoun, teenagers brainwashed in special schools to worship Saddam as a cult figure. Uday turned it into a militia of about twenty-five thousand members, and it was these fedayeen who fought the most fanatically in Basra, Fallujah, and Al Zawra Park.

In short, Uday was a savage, promiscuous psychopath. He considered himself a "lion" among men, and so what better pets to keep?

IT'S NOT KNOWN when Uday fled his palace, but it was probably around the same time the rapidly advancing American forces took Baghdad's international airport. When the special forces stormed the complex a few days later, it was deserted.

Well, almost. Bemused SF soldiers cautiously entering an unkempt patch of garden to the right of a massive entrance hall (where a decapitated statue of Saddam Hussein greeted them) came across a thick steel pen. It was about fifty yards long, thirty yards wide, and the fences were at least a story high.

In the cage, crouching together under the shade of a spikytrunked palm tree, were three lions. And judging by their prolonged snarling, they were not happy.

However, Uday's lions, a male and two females, were luckier than their counterparts at the Baghdad Zoo, as food was immediately available. The soldiers found some sheep, emaciated to the point of death, locked in an enclosure nearby, and these unfortunate creatures were shot and thrown into the giant cats' cage, where they were gobbled up within minutes. Soldiers also fed the lions blackbucks they found corralled in another pen. Blackbuck, a small indigenous antelope, is considered a delicacy and was also apparently Saddam's favorite meal. A herd was kept at the palace to feed the Iraqi aristocracy.

It was soon discovered that the loudest-growling lioness was heavily pregnant. Perhaps that was why she was more belligerent than the others, and the soldiers named her Xena after the fantasy warrior princess. The second female they named Heather; and the magnificently large male, Brutus.

The Special Forces, or Green Berets, as they are often known, soon adopted these three fierce felines as their mascots. So Husham and I decided to leave them where they were rather than move them to the zoo's enclosures. Their pen was not cramped by Iraqi wildlife standards. They had a sandy outside area among a few shady palm trees to stretch their limbs, and as the palace was close to the zoo, it was logistically simple to ferry food over each day. Indeed, they were being well cared for by the soldiers, who even had a notice up on the metal fence proclaiming: SPECIAL FORCES LIONS. DON'T MESS WITH THEM.

This was advice to heed. Uday's cats were far more bellicose than the listless lions in the zoo. When I first approached them, they leaped up to the fence, baring their wickedly pointed cuspids with curled lips. They seemed to have no fear of humans, possibly for reasons that we would only learn of later.

Not only were the lions considered SF mascots, but to my incredible good fortune, the American soldiers took a liking to me as well. I was known as the lion man of Africa who had come thousands of miles to rescue these cats. This reputation was unwittingly a major coup for the zoo. When you're accepted and backed by the crack Green Berets it certainly helps your street credibility.

The American Special Forces are arguably the best warriors in the world—I say "arguably" only because the British Special Air Service also claims that title. Suffice it to say that these superb soldiers are exemplary of George Orwell's pithy observation on the fragility of democracy: "Good people sleep peaceably in their beds at night only because rough men stand ready to do violence on their behalf."

Thankfully for us, the Green Berets took us under their wing. They were among the few able to travel anywhere in the ransacked city at will, and when they had the time they sometimes used their awesome survival skills to forage essential food and supplies for the zoo. They did this purely as private initiative. As far as they were concerned, a crazy conservationist trying to rescue animals in a war zone couldn't be all that bad.

However, it was soon discovered that Uday's pride wasn't the only one in the vast Hussein royal residence complex that snaked along the banks of the muddy Tigris. The next day SF soldiers led Husham and me into Uday's palace through a maze of unimaginably opulent rooms and halls as high as cathedrals to a quadrangular garden. There in the middle was another fenced enclosure.

This was a different situation altogether, and as I entered the compound my stomach heaved at the rotten stench of ripe decay. The source was easy to identify: the decomposing carcass of an adult lioness stiffly sprawled near the fence, smothered with a seething shroud of buzzing flies.

Also in the enclosure were two cubs, about three months old. They came to the fence as I approached and, to my astonishment, I noticed a pair of skeletal dogs with them—a German shepherd and a Labrador retriever, with ribs jutting out like coat hangers. The hounds eyed me warily as they circled the cubs. The pen otherwise seemed deserted, so I opened the gate and walked in.

The gate clicked closed behind me. I had walked about twenty yards into the center of the enclosure when something roused in a dark corner . . . something getting up. It was a young male lion.

In the shadows there was another movement. Another lion. And from the opposite direction, barely visible in the shade, two more started padding toward me.

Shit! How many more were there? For a brief instant a terrifying thought jolted through my head; this was how the biblical Daniel must have felt in the lions' den.

I quickly assessed the situation. There I was in a closed cage with four starving meat eaters. There were not many leisurely options open.

I knew it was potentially fatal to turn and flee, for that almost always triggers an instant charge. The safest bet was to retreat slowly and not make eye contact. If you stare at a dangerous wild animal, it can interpret this as a threat and the eye contact may prompt an attack. A mellow backing off was always the best way to withdraw.

But it wasn't easy being mellow just now. Instead, I judged the distance and, believing I could make it, recklessly turned and fled for my life, yanking the cage door open with a strength I never knew I had.

Fortunately, the lions hadn't charged. Perhaps they were too starved and listless to muster the energy to give chase.

There was no explanation why the starving lions had not already killed and eaten the dogs. We guessed it was because the animals had huddled together through so much terror during the bombing raids that they had bonded in a way only nature could fathom, forging some mystical affinity that transcended the torment of hunger. Indeed, even in their sapped state, the two dogs were nuzzling and cuddling the cubs—testimony that nature is not always red in tooth and claw.

I decided that we would have to relocate these lions—along with two cheetahs cooped in an adjourning pen—to the Baghdad Zoo as soon as possible. The emaciated animals were in far worse condition than the pride being cared for by the Special Forces, and their cages were rank beyond belief.

But how to move them all?

We had enough drugs to tranquilize just one animal. That left us with the extremely dangerous dilemma of confronting three others face-to-face inside the enclosures. And as the agitated youngsters were almost as big as cougars, some serious persuasion was going to be needed.

Lions have a savage reputation, and to the uninitiated they are probably the most fearsome of all wild animals. This reputation is rooted more in folklore than truth, and I, along with other wildlife veterans whom I know, would much rather come up unexpectedly on a lion in the bush than a black rhino or a big male buffalo in a reed bed. In fact, a startled bush pig is more likely to do you serious harm.

Like anything else, once a person has some understanding of

lion behavior, they can be relatively predictable. In the wild they can spend up to twenty lethargic hours a day sleeping and resting, as they only hunt every three days or so, and generally want to be left alone to get on with their lives.

The problem was that these particular lions had just experienced a horrific aerial bombardment, as Uday's palaces had been a prime target, there was a rotting lioness in the enclosure with them, and they were starving and frightened. All of this made the situation extremely volatile.

The big question was: would the lions retreat when we came in, or would they challenge us?

Husham and I discussed our options, but they didn't look good. I was again forced to consider the last resort of simply shooting them all. The situation felt hopeless. But as we watched and talked, carefully studying the lions' behavior and temperament, we decided that a rescue attempt was perhaps possible. Our decision was based simply on the fact that despite one halfhearted mock charge at the fence where we were standing, the lions generally backed off or kept away whenever we approached the fence.

I looked at the lions and a feeling of pity and desperation came over me. These poor creatures, I thought, owned and abused by a cruel dictator, caged in alien surroundings far from their natural environment, afraid and intimidated, and yet there was still fight in them. They still had spirit.

Suddenly my mind was made up. "We can do this," I said firmly, hoping to inspire as much confidence as I could. "We must do it."

Husham and Abdullah nodded, and I was heartened by their positive attitude.

The ever-helpful Lieutenant Szydlik provided a truck with a crane and the zoo staff found some rusty transport cages that had been too heavy for the looters to carry off. So we were in business.

However, the main problem would be coaxing the felines into the mobile cages. Dr. Hussan and I had an on-site chat and came up with an idea that edged upon lunacy but—with a lavish dollop of luck—could work if everyone kept their nerve.

The plan was simplicity itself. Each lion had a cage that led into the communal open area where I had first stumbled onto the dogs guarding the cubs. At the back of each cage was a small door, about a meter high. If we placed a transport cage directly behind the slide-up door and drove the lions into their cages, then toward the open trap door, the cats would have nowhere to go but straight into the mobile cage.

That was the theory. Of course, only a barking mad idiot would have sanctioned such hairy tactics; there was a great deal of chance involved, but these were desperate times.

In the courtyard the zoo team found a junked fence gate—basically just a tubular steel frame meshed with plastic-coated chicken wire. This would be our shield, our sole buffer against about 150 pounds of spitting, snarling razors and daggers. I was hoping for something less flimsy, but it would have to do. It was all we had.

The radio in a troop carrier parked a few yards away clattered into life. It was an officer from Lieutenant Szydlik's base camp instructing the soldiers with us to return as soon as possible. One of the GIs walked over.

"Did you hear that?"

I nodded.

"We've got to move quick, man. Let's load these cats and go."

"How much time have we got?"

"Two hours max—even that's stretching it. But we may not get this crane again. This could be your only chance."

"Okay, let's get cracking."

We held a brief team talk and Dr. Husham translated the plan into Arabic for the other zoo employees.

I then asked two soldiers to stand at the fence with their M-16 rifles cocked and ready. Their job was to ensure the team was not attacked from behind by other lions and to shoot if this happened.

But, I stressed, lions often mock-charged and it was vital the soldiers fire warning shots first. Only at the last instant should they shoot to kill.

"How will we know the difference" one soldier asked.

"When I start screaming, shoot, and not a moment before," I replied, "and please don't hit us."

Husham and Abdullah Latif, one of the Kuwaitis, grabbed a side of the fencing each and, with me standing between them issuing instructions, we cautiously advanced toward the closest cat, a lioness.

The rest of the zoo staff formed a semicircle about five yards behind us—the "bull's horn" attack formation used with devastating effect by the great Zulu warrior Shaka. Slowly we inched forward, making no sudden movements, and the lioness started backing off warily, moving into her sanctuary, the cage.

So far, so good. Now to drive her out the small back door and into the transport cage. Abdullah and Husham gently edged the fencing into the cage and steadily pushed it toward the feline who was now barely three feet away. The lioness—hissing and baring her sword-sharp fangs—kept retreating, finally finding nowhere to go—except through the trapdoor into the transport cage. Once she was through, the door was immediately snapped shut.

Whew . . . I expelled a noisy blow of relief, buckets of adrenaline dumping into my system. This was freaky stuff, and the possibility that somebody could get badly hurt, or killed, was frighteningly real. A derelict piece of fencing was a screwball defense against angry lions. But we had nothing else, and if we left the cats where they were, they would probably die.

"We were lucky that time," Husham said.

He was right. I knew what he was talking about. I had come to within a whisker of being attacked by lions in Africa several years beforehand after inadvertently driving slap bang into the middle of a pride of hunting lions.

It had happened on a dark night when Françoise, some friends, and I had been cruising slowly along a road that was little more than a dirt path when our tracker's spotlight picked up a lion crouched in the bush. Then another, and another. We realized that we were surrounded by a huge pride of lions, spread out through the veld around us. Up ahead, our headlights shone briefly on a herd of impalas. We were caught in the middle of a hunt, and all hell was going to break loose at any moment when the attack began. We stopped and, as is customary to deny advantage to either predator or prey, turned off all the lights and waited.

As we were watching and listening, the trap was sprung from behind the herd and the bush came alive with impalas and lions running frantically in all directions around us. I looked over and saw a large male impala hotly pursued by two lionesses darting toward us. The panicked buck bounded straight at our open Land Rover, jumping higher and higher as he got closer.

God, I thought, he is going to jump into the vehicle, followed by the lionesses.

I braced for the impact, and as I did so the buck and two lionesses hit the side of the Land Rover next to me in a screaming, tumbling crescendo of raw violence.

The heavy impact from the trio slewed the vehicle over on its suspension, and in the ensuing melee blood from the dying animal sprayed onto my face and jacket as the lionesses' massive teeth ripped open the impala's neck.

The impala was forced down and under the vehicle, and as more and more lions arrived and started trying to get at it beneath the Land Rover, the vehicle started rocking like a boat in surf.

Hearing a loud roar off on my right, I turned to see the huge alpha male loping in from the other side to claim the kill. For a split second I thought he was going to take the shortest route and climb over us. At the last moment he went under instead of over. Savagely shouldering the females out of the way, he dragged the buck out into the open right next to me. Suddenly he became aware of my presence, stopped, and looked straight up at me. His huge face was barely a yard or so away from mine in the open vehicle, his mouth and mane covered in blood and gore, his hunched shoulders snaked with wriggling cords of muscle. He stared straight at me, his eyes glistening like polished opals in the spotlight, and a chill shot down my spine. I averted my gaze and, moving very slowly, felt in my pocket for something to defend myself. All that was there was a cigarette lighter. Great. Perhaps I could singe his whiskers. . . .

To my relief, he broke the stare and continued feasting.

Fortunately, twenty-two lions (we counted!) will make short work of even a large impala buck. Soon all that was left was a chewed skeleton and the giant cats moved off.

But it was too close for comfort, nevertheless. A golden rule in the bush is that even though they generally are unlikely to attack you without provocation, you don't get too close to dangerous animals. Keep out of their immediate space and they will leave you alone.

HOWEVER, HERE IN BAGHDAD we had no option but to break the rules. We had to invade these lions' space—almost an invitation to attack—if we hoped to force them into the transport cages.

I didn't want us to be lulled into a false sense of security after the first, easy transfer and so called Husham aside, and we discussed ways to fine-tune the capture technique for the second lion. Whatever happened, he and Abdullah could not let go of the piece of fencing, the sole bulwark between us and the lion. If that went spinning, the cat would be onto someone at sonic speed. A charging lion is as fast and lethal as a runaway train, and as young as these were, it could be a deadly attack.

Getting the second lion into his cage proved relatively easy at first. But not for long. Just before entering the cage, the infuriated animal suddenly turned and hurled himself at the flimsy fencing. It was so sudden that Husham and Abdullah nearly dropped their shield. Quick as lightning the cat started clambering over it. Husham and Abdullah reflexively thrust the fencing upward, spilling the cat off the top. As he landed he went low, slithering like a snake. But Husham and Abdullah were fractionally faster, smashing the gate down to the ground a blink beforehand.

The lion then scrambled up the barrier again as the two men held fast with grim determination. I rushed to help them cling on, for if the berserk cat got through the chicken wire he would be among the staff in a flash.

It was a crucially close call; we were jerking the gate up as the lion attempted to scale over, then desperately yanking it down as he tried to scamper under. At times we would have to let go with one hand, arm muscles searing as we doggedly gripped onto a wafer-thin barrier being battered by a cyclone of rage.

And the racket! The lion was roaring at full decibel while the staff were either screaming in terror or yelling encouragement.

Out of the corner of my eye I saw a TV crew set up and start filming. I groaned out loud. That's all we needed—crazy men being filmed trying to capture hungry lions. Or even worse, a real-life lion attack being beamed into a million living rooms.

Then the lion backed off for a moment. He lay crouched on his stomach facing us, ears flat, snarling and switching his tail—sure signs he was on the verge of attacking again.

"Leave the fencing," I hissed urgently to Husham. "Let's wedge it against the wall to trap him and wait for everything to calm down."

The pandemonium was just what I had been dreading. The whole aim was to relocate the animals with as little trauma as possible. Well, as little as possible under the desperate circumstances. I was also very concerned about the possibility of inducing capture myopathy, a condition brought on in an animal by the stress of game capture that often leads to death. We needed to stop for a while.

We slowly retreated out of the cage. In the enclosure one of the other cats, a lioness, had climbed high into an Albizia tree while another attempted to dissolve into the shadows on the far side of the den. Both had obviously been spooked by the ruckus, and there could be problems in capturing them later as well.

The good news was that during the mayhem zoo workers had nabbed the two lion cubs by the scruffs of their necks and they were now in a cage with their friends the dogs, ready to go.

I sat cross-legged on the ground, mentally going over our seat-of-the-pants capture system again and again, step-by-step, trying to visualize improvements. The Iraqis, meanwhile, used the break as prayer time, prostrating themselves toward Mecca. It was Friday, I suddenly realized, and the muezzin was calling the faithful to pay homage. The fact that these men were prepared to work—indeed, to risk their lives—at this holy hour was powerful testament to their dedication. I hoped they were praying for a successful capture.

Half an hour later we returned to the cage and this time I insisted on absolute silence and fewer people in the "bull's horn" behind us. Only I was permitted to speak, and that was solely to give instructions. Fewer people meant less commotion and less claustrophobia for the lion. I also wanted fewer of my men in the firing line; I was profoundly aware that the fencing was all that held back an enraged wild animal equipped with fangs as sharp as butchers' knives.

By now the lion appeared to have calmed down, and as Abdullah and Husham began nudging the fencing gently forward again, he turned, bolted out through the trap door, and was captured. The prayers had worked!

The third lion was the easiest, as his brother and sister were already in their separate transport cages and he was eager to join them, scudding through the trap door quickly as Husham and Latif approached.

The last lioness, which had been up a tree watching the pro ceedings with interest, suddenly climbed down and ran into the main cage by herself. This was going to be easy, I thought to myself.

A few minutes later I regretted my optimism. For once in the cage, the lioness swiveled and faced us, slashing at the fence while Abdullah and Husham held on with bone-white knuckles.

Then she backed into a corner and refused to budge, roaring at the two men. Suddenly someone behind us, thinking they were helping, leaned over and threw a bucket of water over the poor creature. She went ballistic, jumping at the fence and slashing dementedly.

"It's no good," I said, by now concerned at the feline's frenzy. "This one we must sedate."

Dr. Husham agreed and went to fetch a hypodermic syringe and the last ampoule of our drugs.

On his return, a dapper gray-haired man who had been watching in the background stepped forward and took the syringe from Husham. As the team jammed the yowling cat between the gate and cage bars, he reached over and at arm's length injected the lion. Within minutes the animal was out for the count and gently carried into the transport cage.

This was Dr. Adel Salman Mousa, the zoo's director, whom Husham had told me about. Although he had visited the zoo several times before, we somehow had always missed each other. But today some American soldiers back at the zoo had told him we were at the palace and he hurried over to meet us. Husham introduced him to me—and the look of gratitude on Adel's face now that he had some outside assistance for his beloved zoo reminded me of why I had come to Baghdad. I knew right away that we were going to become friends.

The cheetahs were far weaker than the lions and, despite putting on a token snarling show, were relatively easily rounded up. All the animals were then transferred to the zoo as rapidly as possible, as the soldiers were now needed for night patrols around the city's Red Zones—the danger areas where safety catches on weapons were always kept off.

The lions, although emaciated, had had full run of the open-air enclosure and were in a redeemable condition considering their dire circumstances. But the cheetahs had been cooped in tiny pens and were in a terrible state. The zoo vets immediately got them food and water, then inspected them thoroughly. They were smothered in lice and mange and so wasted they would have died within days. One also had a nasty leg injury and was limping. The vets sprayed the wound with antiseptic, as any infection in the foul cage she had been cramped up in could be life threatening.

To my surprise, the rescue of the palace cats had gone perfectly. A few men had got into a den with four angry young lions and virtually barehanded corralled them into transport cages. And not one had even been scratched. And a good thing it was, too, for we had no first-aid kit and didn't even know where the nearest hospital was.

AFTER THE SUCCESSFUL ROUNDUP of the palace animals, soldiers alerted us to another menagerie that was caged in equally horrific conditions at a building they labeled "Uday's love nest."

The so-called love nest was in fact a smallish cottage on the banks of the Tigris where it was said Uday seduced his legions of "conquests," willing or otherwise. We were given vague directions on how to get there, and the next day I took the two Kuwaitis, Adel, and Husham, with me to investigate further.

After driving in circles on the riverbank for a while, we eventually discovered the cottage's secluded entrance. The steel gates were locked, so we smashed our way in with a hefty crowbar and drove cautiously up the winding road until we reached a Western-style building with a peaked tile roof, unlike the usual flat-roofed Middle East house. It looked very ordinary compared to all the opulent palaces surrounding it. In fact, the only thing extraordinary was that the front of the building had caved in—the aftermath of a B-52 bombing raid that also left a massive crater in the front garden.

On the far side of the premises I saw a series of cages, and I set off to inspect them. However, I had barely covered a few yards when I sank almost to my knees in thick mud. The entire garden had been turned into a quagmire thanks to a burst underground pipe that was still spewing water up through a bubbling sinkhole. I was stuck fast—for a moment I thought I was in quicksand.

Abdullah, seeing me marooned in the muck, wisely skirted around the marsh and arrived at the cages first.

"Monkeys," he shouted. "All dead."

Somehow I managed to extricate myself from the glutinous sludge and sloshed over to him.

It was a wretched sight. Six or seven emaciated green monkeys lay huddled against one another on the floor, killed by thirst. They had been locked in the cage and left to die.

I shook my head, disgusted beyond belief. It would have taken Uday Hussein or his staff perhaps a minute to open the cages and let the animals free before fleeing themselves. Instead they had condemned the poor creatures to suffer the most awful death imaginable.

Once again it hit me with bitter clarity exactly what we were up against. To callously allow animals to perish so horribly beggars description.

Sadly, man has an obsession with keeping wild animals as pets or ornaments. Indeed, the illegal trade in animals is so vast that only drugs and arms trafficking are more profitable. It is cruel beyond words; all captured exotic animals are denied their freedom and a normal life for the amusement or financial gain of their barbarous owners and with few exceptions end up living miserable lives. Worse still, they are clearly treated as objects rather than living creatures. They can be abandoned as soon as they become inconvenient to their owner.

Surveying the scene, I heard a whimper and looked up. A baby monkey was sitting on top of the cage, the sole survivor of the family. He was the only one small enough to squeeze through the bars and find water. I imagined his anguish as he watched his parents and siblings slowly and agonizingly wither in front of him, not knowing what was going on or how to help.

I remembered I had a couple of apples in the car and walked back to get one, circling the mud. I offered the apple to the baby monkey and he gingerly came toward me, taking the apple and stuffing it into his mouth as fast as he could. These monkeys were tame, I thought. They were pets, which made their cruel abandonment even more treacherous.

We then explored the house, taking great care not to disturb anything, as we were worried the shattered roof might cave in completely. We also meticulously checked for booby traps wherever we went.

In one room we could see pictures of Uday Hussein and decided to take some as souvenirs, but we soon changed our minds, as the bombed building was simply too unstable to venture farther inside and I was concerned about booby traps.

As we came out, the baby monkey was waiting for us and, tempting him with another apple, I was able to coax him into the car. He would get a good new home at the zoo.

Driving out, I noticed another large cage, and we stopped to investigate. Inside were three ostriches and four or five peacocks. They stared at us with dull, listless eyes, sure signs of dehydration. "Water," I shouted. "They need water."

Husham strode off and returned minutes later with a bucket, which we filled from the broken pipe and ferried to the birds.

I have never seen any creature drink so much. Bucket after bucket after bucket of water went down their long, withered throats like huge bubbles until I thought they would burst.

Next we watered the peacocks, which also gulped each bucketful down as if it was their last. Dr. Adel found some bird food in a shed and we filled the feeding troughs.

We couldn't take the birds with us in the vehicle, so I told Adel and Husham we would later return and walk the birds to the zoo past the checkpoint, which was only a couple of miles away.

I alerted the American soldiers at the checkpoint about what we planned to do, but it took us so long to prepare the birds for the journey that by the time we were ready the guards I had spoken to had changed shift. Consequently no one was prepared for what was undoubtedly one of the craziest scenes in war-torn Baghdad at the time. . . .

THE YOUNG SOLDIER at the roadblock guarding Saddam's palaces yanked off his aviator sunglasses and rubbed his eyes. He was seeing things; he was sure of it. There coming up the street were three ostriches, running full tilt at him.

Every soldier manning a roadblock was understandably edgy.

Stories of suicide bombers pouring through Iraq's sievelike borders were commonplace. Four marines had already died at Narjaf, and every checkpoint in the country was on hair-trigger alert.

And here some giant fowl were charging him. Was this some new tactic? Were these suicide ostriches?

But hang on, there were some Iraqis behind them, holding on to the stampeding creatures' wings with grim determination. And behind them was an armored troop carrier with an ostrich neck sticking out the top. What crazy mirage was this? Was the bird actually driving?

The Iraqis were yelling something incomprehensible. The poor sentry didn't know what to do. He cocked his gun.

"Halt," he shouted with as much ragged authority as he could muster under the surreal circumstances. But he could see there was no way these birds were going to stop, nor could the Iraqis hanging desperately on to them. The soldier had the presence of mind not to fire. This was too crazy even by Baghdad standards.

The soldiers in the truck behind were now close and he could just make out what they were yelling: "It's okay, man. We're taking these buzzards to the zoo."

Then they whizzed past. The men at the roadblock watched, weapons still cocked, surprise grooved on their sweat-streaming foreheads. One of the soldiers leaped off the troop carrier to explain. The ostriches had been found at Saddam's eldest son Uday's riverside love nest and were being transferred to the Baghdad Zoo. But they were too large to all fit all into the vehicles, so zoo workers had planned to walk them the two miles or so to the cages. However, the birds had been cooped up in confined spaces all their lives, and suddenly finding open road in front of them had been too much of a heady drug. They started stretching their legs in glorious exhilaration until they were at ecstatic full gallop. It is a credit to the zoo staff they didn't let go, or they would never have seen the birds again. They would have ended up as ostrich steaks or starved exhibits on the black market.

"Where are they from again?" asked the soldier at the roadblock.

"Uday's love nest. The zoo guys found a whole freaking menagerie there."

I think the guards spent the rest of their day scratching their heads. But one thing was for certain: almost all the soldiers in Baghdad now knew there was a zoo in their midst.

Tragically, that was the only lighthearted moment of "Operation Uday's Love Nest." For that night—the first time in perhaps months that these animals got proper food, care, and attention—a despicable gang of looters raided the cages. Fortunately, they didn't get the ostriches, but the baby monkey and peacocks were seized. The heavy-duty locks on their cages were smashed to scrap. The beautiful birds had their necks twisted and were sold as meat.

The little orphan monkey that had survived so much and seen his family die horribly was probably destined for the black market, spending the rest of his life in a cramped cage. But he, too, may have been eaten.

Once again I appealed to the soldiers to help guard the zoo; once again they regretfully said they were too busy fighting Ba'athist fanatics.

Other creatures rescued from the palace hellholes fortunately fared better. All were now getting watered and fed regularly, and their skeletal rib cages were slowly starting to flesh out a little. I was considerably cheered by the fact that they seemed to be recovering so well.

Consequently we decided to reunite the dogs and lion cubs. We had separated them for obvious reasons, but they pined for each other so intensely it seemed more humane to put them together again.

The reunion was an absolute eye-opener, the dogs furiously wagging their tails and the cubs scampering up to greet them. One needed an arctic heart not to be moved at how fiercely protective the two bitches were, rushing up to guard the cubs if anyone came near the cage.

The incredible story of this unlikely bond between canine and feline spread and many soldiers made long journeys to Al Zawra

Park to see the "lion dogs." This was priceless publicity, as anything that elevated our embattled zoo onto the conscience of the outside world was vital to its survival.

However, I later learned that keeping dogs in lion dens was not that unusual among private big-cat owners, of whom there were a number in Iraq. They believed by mixing dogs with a newly born litter it was possible to tame the cubs. The cubs would witness humans handling the dogs and come to trust them as the hounds did. If some dogs got devoured in the process, so be it.

That still doesn't explain why in this case the lions had decided, almost mystically, to starve rather than eat their friends. It was an unusual but welcome case of sympathy in the harshest conditions.

However, there was some disquieting news concerning the male and two females—one about to give birth—adopted by the Special Forces that by now were always referred to as "Uday's lions." Most Iraqis considered these three to be serial man-eaters. According to local legend, they had feasted upon an array of Uday's opponents, ranging from political activists to unfortunate love rivals—just as the equally sadistic Ugandan dictator Idi Amin had thrown anyone who crossed him to his pet crocodiles.

True or not, these stories were so embedded in Baghdad's folklore that most Iraqis considered them fact, particularly as owning man-eaters was something typical for the psychotic Uday. On several occasions I was asked to shoot the entire pride.

I obviously refused, emphasizing that there was no proof, but privately I also confessed to harboring some niggling suspicions. The zoo lions, I recalled, had been lethargic and disinterested when I first approached them. No so with Uday's three cats, Xena, Brutus, and Heather. Whenever I came near they rushed up to the fence, aggressively eyeballing me. I wouldn't go as far to say they only viewed me as a tasty snack, but they certainly had no fear of humans.

These concerns were passed on to the military and SF soldiers who subsequently dug up every suspicious mound in the palace grounds to see if they could locate buried human remains. None were found, to my huge relief.

At the time nobody at the zoo paid particular heed to the man-eaters legend, as there was a load of other tasks, not least the extra mouths to feed. It made little difference as long as the three lions were in cages.

However, it would return to haunt us with a vengeance later.

SEVEN

I T WAS ONE OF THOSE EVENINGS that makes you want to pull up a deck chair, pour something long and cold, and appreciate being alive.

The sun had just set and the cool star-studded evening soothingly doused the dying fire red desert rays. Even the incessant blood-sucking mosquitoes that made life a misery had returned to base for a brief respite.

I was chatting to the Third ID commander, Capt. Larry Burris, a frontline leader of the audaciously swift American advance to Baghdad, and some of his troops relaxing near their tanks parked outside the Al-Rashid when loud volleys of gunfire rattled through the sky.

Panicked, I dropped to the ground, hugging the grass for cover. If I could have dug a hole and crawled into it, I would have.

Then silence.

I looked up to see several quizzical pairs of eyes upon me. All the soldiers were still standing next to the tank. One or two sniggered.

I got up, feeling somewhat foolish. Obviously military etiquette means you don't dive for cover.

Half an hour later another spurt of bullets shattered the heavens. I steeled myself and resolutely stood my ground.

I suddenly realized I was alone. All the other men had hit the dirt, rifles at the ready. I was unsure what to do; should I do a belated dive, like a character in a cartoon comedy, or show that hey, I had meant to keep standing all along?

"Get down! Get down!" screamed one of the soldiers, and I quickly dropped to the ground.

When the firing stopped, the grinning Americans got up. One took pity on me and explained the diving procedure: If you hear shots as "bangs" the gunmen are aiming elsewhere, but if you hear the bang and a simultaneous "crack" overhead, then lead is flying your way. You had better take cover. Fast.

That was during the first week I arrived and it was an invaluable lesson that I had plenty of opportunity to put it into practice. Twice during those early, tenuous days there were full-scale battles with Saddam's die-hards in the heavily guarded streets around the Al-Rashid. On one occasion, it was so ferocious I feared that the insurgents would break through the so-called steel cordon and storm the hotel. I was in the foyer with psyched-up soldiers awaiting orders and asked an officer what was happening.

"I don't know, and I'm sure as hell not going out there to find out," he replied.

The deafening gunfire, interspersed with the screeching of tires and screaming metallic "clangs" of vehicles crashing, eventually fizzled out and all of us in the foyer exhaled loud sighs of relief.

"Okay, that's it. We'll find out what happened when the checkpoint shift changes," said the officer, putting his M-16 down.

I heard later that it was an attack on the checkpoint just down the road in an almost suicidal attempt to break through to the Al-Rashid. But by morning all evidence of the attack was gone.

Equally terrifying was when the alarm went out that suicide bombers were poised to penetrate the building through underground tunnels. This really touched a nerve, as the hotel was riddled with secret chambers built as bunkers for Saddam. The Americans had fine-combed what they believed to be the entire network, but there was always the worry that a semtex-wired fanatic would find an unwatched manhole covering some unchartered drain and obliterate the building.

Fortunately, the alarm proved to be false—or else the bombers had heard the Americans coming and scampered away. But each day those of us in the hotel lived with the knowledge that there could be something lethal emerging from the sewers below.

Those were indeed helter-skelter times. I was once discussing the awesome firepower of an Abrams tank with a lieutenant when he casually asked if I would like to go for a drive and fire the main gun. That, he said, was the only way to experience such cataclysmic potency with a simple touch of a finger.

I was stunned. Here we were in a main street outside the city's premier hotel and I was nonchalantly being offered the chance to fire a shell from one of the most fearsome weapons in the U.S. Army.

"It's okay," said the tank man. "I've cleared it with my superiors. We'll shoot high."

To my eternal regret, I had to get to the zoo urgently and said no. But it did show what state of mind the city was in—that you could fire a live tank round in a main street and no one would even blink.

The bizarre thing was that with the anarchy came a weird sense of freedom. There were simply no regulations or rulebooks. No police, administration, government, officials, traffic lights, shops, water, electricity, sewerage, or refuse removal. No businesses were functioning, and nobody went to work. There was no constitutional order whatsoever. Civic anarchy ruled.

This meant that to survive I had to rely purely on my own moxie. Everything I did was based solely on whether I could pull it off. I structured my day entirely as I saw fit. How I got food and drink for myself, the staff, and animals was totally up to me. I had to find a way to make it happen or all at the zoo would starve; it was as simple as that. The only way to do that was to wheel, deal, loot, beg, trade, and barter with as much chutzpah as I could muster.

For the first time in my life I was living off my wits through absolute necessity, on the edge of survival. And there is no better way to sharpen the mind than to find every code you live by, everything you have always taken for granted, has simply been chucked out the window. You wake up—smartly!

In today's strictly regulated world, laws don't only tell you what you can't do; they now also tell you what you *can*. But in Baghdad in those wild early days, there were no laws. What you did or didn't do was totally up to you. And I hate to say this, but it was exciting, in an exhilaratingly primordial sense—even though it is no way to live for long.

However, amid all that palpable tension, I knew something had to crack soon. We were all operating at breaking strain. And sure enough, a day or two after the "ostrich run" from Uday's love nest the two men on loan to me from the Kuwait City zoo came storming up.

Both were highly agitated. Abdullah Latif let rip in Arabic and I put up my hands: "Whoa, I can't understand."

I called over Husham, who attempted to translate the words erupting in a torrent, but I soon got the gist of the problem. The Kuwaitis wanted to leave Baghdad immediately. Apparently rumors were rife that the Kuwaiti army was about to invade Iraq under the protection of the Americans and exact bloody retribution for Saddam's brutal invasion of their country twelve years ago.

When the Iraqis stormed Kuwait in 1991, the highly disciplined Republican Guard—probably the toughest troops in the Middle East—had been at the forefront. But once the tiny country had been seized, Saddam sent in his conscripted army, which pillaged extensively. The Iraqi commanders made no attempt to discipline their ill-trained troops, as it was a matter of policy to frighten the Kuwaitis into submission. And now many Iraqis believed the time for revenge had come.

Obviously this was just wild talk. The coalition would never countenance another invasion, let alone allow the Kuwaiti army to go on a reprisal rampage even if the Kuwaitis had wanted to. But rumors, once they're in motion, gather an inexorable momentum.

It was well-known around the zoo that Abdullah and his colleague were Kuwaitis, and even Husham agreed that their lives were in danger and it was imperative they flee the country as soon as possible. They wanted me to come with them, pointing out that the security situation in Baghdad was much worse than we anticipated and I also was in serious danger. Our trip, they stressed, was only meant to be a fact-finding mission—something we had achieved.

I understood their predicament, even though I didn't agree. This trip had progressed into more than just a fact-finding expedition. It was now a full-scale rescue mission.

"When do you want to go?" I asked.

"Tonight, must drive out tonight," Abdullah replied. "Daytime too dangerous."

I shook my head. If I left now, I might as well do what had originally crossed my mind: shoot all the animals. There was no way the zoo would survive without our help and our collaboration with soldiers.

But the Kuwaitis were adamant; they had to bolt right away. And their only way out was in my hired car.

I thought about that for a moment or two. The car might be their only getaway, but it was also mine. If I gave it to them there would be no escape for me, a major worry considering the violent circumstances we were living under. Military convoys refused to ferry civilians, and all air traffic to and from Baghdad was also purely for military purposes. Without my car, I would be trapped in the war zone for God knows how long.

But it was also true that if I left, the project would collapse. That was the stark reality of it. At that time I never even knew how many people would arrive for work each morning. Every day was based on wildly blind optimism that we would be able to stay out of danger, source food, have enough hands to lug water from the canals, and keep out as many looters as possible. And as none of the Iraqis could communicate effectively with the Americans who were still fighting a hit-and-run street war, there was little doubt the zoo rescue would implode without me there to act as an intermediary.

I considered again my reasons for coming here. For me, this was more than just about saving a zoo. It was about making a moral and ethical stand, about saying we cannot do this to our planet anymore. This realization had a profound impact on me, and I decided that an example had to be set. A responsible, influential stand had to be made against mankind's irreverence for other life-forms. I decided then and there that Baghdad was to be the place it started.

It was to be my line in the sand. This far and no more. I couldn't leave now that I had started the rescue operation, no matter how dangerous.

I handed Abdullah my keys. "I am staying. Thank you for what you have done."

He again signaled frantically that I must come with them.

The closest cage was a Bengal tiger's. I pointed to him. "If I leave, he will die."

Abdullah went silent and then nodded. He understood. We shook hands and they left. I hoped they would make it safely. They were both brave men and had been a great help.

I never saw them again, but months later I received a receipt from the rental company. The car had been returned in one piece, and my two friends had made it home.

With the Kuwaitis gone the reality of Abdullah's warning struck home and I realized how precarious my security situation at the zoo actually was. About a mile south of the zoo inside the park was a military base. To the northwest outside the park were the tanks at the checkpoint where I first came in and met Lieutenant Szydlik. In the north and east there was no military presence at all for miles. This area, soon to become known as the Red Zone, was completely open to the park and zoo. It was a gaping security hole through which Adel, Husham, and the workers came to work every day. And if they could get in, so could anyone else.

I was the only western civilian in the entire lawless area, unprotected and exposed, and I felt very alone. The questions I received from looters or intruders who were brazen enough to stride up to me and ask, "You American?" compounded my fears. Husham, always at my side, would quickly answer that I was a South African and that South Africa was neutral and had sent me to help Iraq. His answers in Arabic were always sprinkled with the words "Nelson Mandela," the only part of the discussion I ever understood.

In an area where soldiers only ever moved around in tanks and armored vehicles or convoys of heavily armed Humvees, my sole protection was the goodwill that was generated by Husham and the zoo staff actively spreading the word that I was a South African. I believe it was the only thing that kept me alive.

IT WAS ONLY 10:00 A.M., but already sun rays shimmered like high-octane gas fumes. Even in April, early spring, the heat wilted energy into apathy and you continuously craved ice water, an unheard-of luxury at the time. All drinking water tasted as though it had been tapped straight from a warm geyser.

It was a day or two after the Kuwaitis had left and I was outside the trashed three-room bungalow that was the zoo's headquarters, contemplating which of the gazillion tasks to prioritize, when a Humvee with four soldiers clutching M-16s came skidding up.

A man dressed in newly ironed combat fatigues hopped out of the passenger seat and introduced himself: Capt. William Sumner of the 354th Civil Affairs Brigade.

"I am the zoo man," he said, smiling.

I let this sink in for a while, then grabbed the officer's hand and shook it hard. I could scarcely believe it. The zoo now had an accredited representative. Someone out there in the sacrosanct halls of administration had actually decided that what we were doing was . . . well, worthwhile. We at last had a direct link to the hallowed powers-that-be. We were officially a blip, albeit tiny, on the radar screen of bureaucracy.

Up until now, almost everything that had been achieved was thanks to the goodwill and compassion of ordinary American soldiers who had the common decency to do what they could under extreme circumstances. From Lieutenant Szydlik to patrol-fatigued soldiers who gave up their time and rations, people helped because it was the right thing to do. Whenever I thanked them, they just said it was "because of the animals."

But now, through Captain Sumner, I finally had the ear of the administration. Not that this was any guarantee we would get our way—the zoo was still drastically low on the priority list—but at least we could aim requests at the right targets.

Sumner had previously been assigned to the Baghdad Museum when the furor of the apparent looting of priceless artifacts erupted. At first it had been thought the museum, which exhibited exquisite Mesopotamian antiquities, had been ransacked during the frenzied first days of Saddam's defeat. Sumner had been part of the investigating team that discovered, to their utter relief, almost all the irreplaceable items had been stored for safekeeping by museum staff instead of being stolen.

I found his job description as "military curator" for both the museum and zoo amusing. Only the army could give a guy two such diverse tasks, from sourcing ancient tablets in the cradle of civilization on one day to scrounging food for tigers the next.

Captain Sumner was a military man moonlighting as a youthful professor. He came from Germantown, Maryland, and had degrees in political science and archaeology and planned to "get a bunch more" once he returned to civilian life. But in times of war he's a dedicated soldier. In other words, he's a contrasting mix of deskbound academic and man of action. Tigers or tablets, it's all in a day's work.

His family has a staunch military tradition, with ancestors fighting gallantly in America's conflicts as far back as they could remember. A reservist for the past decade, he was scheduled for duty when war flared in Afghanistan after the Taliban refused to surrender Osama bin Laden. But as Captain Sumner's daughter was "inconveniently" on the verge of being born, his file was moved to the bottom of the pile.

When war broke out in Iraq, his daughter was a happily, gurgling one-year-old and so Sumner was back at the top of the call-up pile—as was only right, in his estimation. Barely had Baghdad fallen when he was attached to the military government, and being an archaeology graduate, he was the obvious choice to investigate the museum debacle.

At the same time his colonel called him over and said, "By the way, I've got a zoo thing for you as well."

The "zoo thing" was a less obvious choice for an archaeologist. And little did Sumner know what it would escalate to.

His first job was to find out what, if any, administration was in place at the zoo, and while he was doing so Lieutenant Szydlik's soldiers, still camped at Al Zawra Park, told him about the "loco lion man."

At our first meeting, Captain Sumner and I soon found we were speaking the same language, even though neither of us harbored illusions that the zoo was of much consequence in the military's overall scheme of things. At the time just delivering basic services such as lights, water, and sewerage to a beleaguered city of 6 million souls was a sorely sobering challenge. Nurturing a handful of barely living wild animals was not something that would automatically leap to the top of any administration's things-to-do-list.

But in Sumner, Baghdad Zoo at least had an officially appointed champion for its cause.

He assessed the root problem rapidly. Looting. We could buy or wrangle as much food for the animals as we liked, but if it was stolen each night, the project would collapse. The zoo's creatures would die. Simple as that.

The risk of confronting armed looters who were quite prepared to settle arguments with bullets was obvious, but we took them on knowing what was at stake.

However, did anyone in the administration have the cojones to do the same?

Sumner had, as we found out almost immediately.

It happened one morning when two looters snuck into the zoo by rowing paddleboats across the sewage-riddled lake. We spotted them and Sumner grabbed his M-16, fired a warning shot, and ran screaming at them. This is military technique: you yell like hell at someone at the top of your voice to disorient them.

The chase was on, with Sumner and his soldiers sprinting over mounds of bombed rubble, vaulting fences and hurtling through animal pens, while animals roared in alarm as buckets and pipes went flying.

Sumner could have fired at the fleeing thugs, as he was always in range, but he wasn't going to hurt anyone unless he had to.

Despite the wild melee, they managed to cut the looters off from both the exit gate and their paddleboat. Eventually the looters were cornered and forced to lie spread-eagled on the ground, whimpering in fear, with Sumner still screaming at them.

By now everyone at the zoo had gathered around to witness the thieves' humiliation. Some of the staff laughed derisively. It was the most effectively degrading punishment we could have imagined.

Except Sumner had a better idea. Instead of showing the looters into our makeshift "Baghdad Zoo Jail," he instructed his men to lock them in one of the largest cages and give each one a scrubbing brush. For the rest of the day, the looters scrubbed. And scrubbed, until the cage was as clean as it was going to get.

Husham's broken English resulted in him referring to these thugs as "lootiman," and as the information boards outside the zoo cages gave English, Arabic, and Latin names for each occupant, I suggested we pin up: "Lootiman / Ali Baba: *Humanus horribilis.*"

Eventually Sumner let them go. They never returned. And with these "work as punishment" tactics, looting began to decrease.

I took an instant liking to Captain Sumner. He was a hard worker, honest as the day is long, and totally committed to the zoo. We could have been unlucky and got some average jobsworth. Sumner was anything but that. His wry sense of humor, philosophical outlook, and huge work ethic set him apart from some of the more regimental officers we came across.

To cap that, Sumner was a master haggler and his specialty was exotic guns. Iraq had been at war, internally or externally, low- or high-intensity, for almost thirty years. For a firearms aficionado, it was a candy store. And during the advance to Baghdad Sumner took full advantage of that, amassing an impressive assortment of unusual hardware captured from Iraqi soldiers. These he skillfully used as barter with gun buffs from other divisions for fridges or batteries or whatever other essential equipment we needed. Indeed, the industrial deep freeze still thumping away in the zoo's administration office is courtesy of a deal involving a World War II Tommy gun. This was my kind of guy.

Almost as soon as he arrived, Sumner appointed me administrator of the zoo. Our friendship also boosted morale among the zoo staff, and Sumner probably was the first American in uniform to earn the absolute trust of ordinary Iraqis. This was a profound compliment. At the time, just weeks after the city had officially fallen, there was understandably much mutual suspicion across the divide.

However, even with Sumner firmly on board another major problem loomed—one that could hamstring the project as surely as the looters. It was money. Or lack thereof. Of my original stash, fifteen hundred dollars had disappeared, either at the zoo or at the Al-Rashid, and was nowhere to be found. And we weren't going to last forever with what I had left.

I was single-handedly financing the zoo's desperate regeneration attempts, and no other help was visible on the horizon. Buying donkeys, scrounging food from pavement stalls . . . each day or so was tantamount to widening the gaping hole in my pocket. In addition I was footing the staff's wages and paying exorbitant black-market rates for piping and any other essential equipment we needed from the shadow economy. Every emergency that cropped up—which happened with regular monotony—cost me money one way or another, and there was no way to get more in.

Sumner promised to try to get some funds and place the staff on the ORHA (Office for Reconstruction and Humanitarian Assistance, later called the Coalition Provisional Authority) payroll, but he first had to get that passed by newly arriving administration clerks coping with a host of other issues affecting the ravaged city. Cutting red tape for the low-prioritized zoo could take forever, and time was a luxury we did not have.

In the interim, I kept paying out. This wasn't because of innate generosity. I would have been more than happy to shift the burden onto someone else with a bigger checkbook. There simply was no one else.

EIGHT

A FEW DAYS AFTER the "ostrich run" I called the team together. Previously our energies had been focused on foraging food, moving animals from Uday's palace with dangerously rudimentary equipment, and lugging water—one damn bucketful after another—into the cages.

Our next task, I told them, was to completely clean the cages. These were not only foul beyond belief, crusted with slime and excrement and gore, but the festering filth was a putrid fly magnet also.

Indeed, it was impossible to walk past a cage without thousands of flies buzzing your eyes and ears. Apart from the appalling hygiene issue, the insects were driving everyone bananas, as they usually attacked when you were burdened with raw meat or water and thus couldn't swat them off. And you didn't even want to think about what those disgusting midges had been feeding on.

We'd already given the cleanup duties occasionally to looters as punishment. It was the kind of job that you wouldn't wish on an ordinary worker, but it had to be done. I knew the only way to tackle it was to set an example and get cracking right away myself. So I stripped down to a pair of shorts, grabbed a bucket and a scrubbing brush, and got down to work. Adel, Husham, and the others joined in.

It was a horrid task. The filth had scabbed solid and wouldn't dislodge. While we scrubbed, squadrons of flies and mosquitoes blitzed us mercilessly, gorging on our sweat and biting any patch of exposed skin until we were all covered in fiery red bumps.

Dr. Adel said we were whistling against thunder unless we could find some industrial-strength detergent and insecticide. I agreed and sent some of the staff into town to see if they could buy any. But with most shops still barricaded tight against looters, it was futile. Even the loot-laden pavement stalls mushrooming all over the city didn't have any.

So I decided there would have to be another way. I would have to use my bartering skills.

"Tell everyone to take a break," I instructed Adel. "I'll get cleaning stuff for us."

He looked at me as if I was mad.

DESPITE THE WAR, I soon discovered that with persistence and innovation you could scrounge the most amazing things necessary to persevere in Baghdad. As in all survival economies, trade was based almost exclusively on barter, and by now I had become an expert forager, swapping goods or services for whatever I could rustle up as exchange. Consequently I knew there had to be a "deal" where I could source industrial-strength detergent. I just had to nose around.

My trump card in most bartering situations was my satellite phone. I found this out by chance. I was pilfering food and utensils in Saddam's abandoned Al Salam Palace kitchens when a soldier confronted me. "No access here," he said. "It's all off-limits now."

Damn, I thought. They're starting to get a bit organized. Previously security at the palaces' kitchens had not been too intense, and so once or twice I'd been able to keep the zoo fed courtesy of Saddam's stockpiles.

Despite my pleading with him he was adamant—no entry!

While we were talking I saw his gaze switch to the satellite phone hooked on to my belt. After a pause he said, "Does that phone work?"

"Yes. I can ring anywhere in the world." I suddenly grasped the significance of what I had just said. "When last did you speak to home?" I asked the soldier.

"Months ago."

I felt terrible but knew what I had to do. I asked if his family would like to know he was safe. "And what about a girlfriend? Do you have one?"

He nodded.

"Well," I said, "I could let you use the phone, but it doesn't work right here. To get a signal you have to go around the corner, about fifty paces away."

He knew exactly what I was getting at. "How do I dial?"

I showed him and as he walked off with the phone, I bolted through the kitchen door in a flash, grabbing desperately needed food and supplies, which I stacked in the back of a Humvee belonging to one of Captain Burris's men, knowing that he would drive them to the zoo for me.

Half an hour later I retrieved my phone from the palace guard. He smiled knowingly as he handed it back.

My sat phone was probably one of the only civilian communications systems working in the city. Once it was known that I was happy to let homesick soldiers use it, my popularity at the Al-Rashid Hotel and the Al Salam Palace, earmarked as the future coalition administration center, soared.

My ability to keep essential supplies flowing to the zoo also increased exponentially. I now passed through roadblocks in record time, got regular supplies of bottled water and MREs, and was allowed into off-limits areas and soldiers even gave me lifts wherever I wanted to go.

The downside was my phone bill. During those first six turbulent weeks it rocketed to seven thousand dollars as battle-begrimed GIs whispered endearments across the stratosphere to families and sweethearts. But the goodwill it generated had no price.

Thus I wasted no time in getting the word out to anyone within earshot that I urgently needed pesticides and detergent—adding that, by the way, my sat phone was working just fine.

I didn't have to wait long. And on this occasion I didn't even need to lend out my phone. Instead, it was thanks to my old friends the photographers.

It happened the evening after our abortive first attempt to clean the cages. I was describing the Herculean task we faced in restoring basic hygiene to the DOD photographers when they suddenly looked askance at one another. Then they nodded. They had made some silent decision.

Alistair McLarty stood up first. He said there was another secret storeroom in one of the hotel's bunkers, even bigger than the one we raided when I first arrived in the war zone. That was merely a pantry; this, said Alistair, was a veritable supermarket. Perhaps I would find what I needed there.

The photographers had discovered the storeroom some days back while exploring the building's underground innards and had kept it quiet so they could sneak out some of the goodies for themselves. But now . . . well, I hoped they reckoned that I was a worthy cause. I was one of them. I wondered if I hung around long enough what other unknown treasure troves would be revealed.

Alistair led the way down the stairs into the maze of cellars, passing through various vaults that had been specifically designed as bombproof command centers. He knew his way around, and we arrived at a thick steel door that he creaked open.

It was indeed a storeroom—massive, half the size of a sports field, stocked for a siege with crates of food ranging from canned sardines and baked beans to rice and maize meal sacks. There was also enough booze to float a battleship, with top-name brands like Moët & Chandon champagne and Johnnie Walker Black Label.

But as far as I was concerned, the biggest bonanza was finding large barrels of high-potency industrial detergent and disinfectant, as well as stiff-bristle brooms, mops, and scrubbing brushes. It was better than stumbling upon diamonds.

I took what we needed as well as extra food supplies for the hungry zoo staff. Both the hotel and the zoo were government institutions, which meant they had belonged to the Hussein family, so I regarded this as just an "interdepartmental transfer."

It was indeed a heady form of wealth distribution. And when I arrived at the zoo the next day, courtesy as usual of Sergeant Diehl and his Humvee, the stunned Iraqis were silent for a long moment. Then they said I was a magician. Where had I conjured up all this stuff?

I shrugged. "I found it on the side of the road," I said, which sparked delighted guffaws. The food was divided equally and then we got back to work.

IF WE HAD THOUGHT lugging water in searing heat from sewage-ripe canals was backbreaking, we hadn't bargained on cage cleaning. It made water duties look like a walk on the beach.

We started with the lions' cages, herding the animals out of the pens into the open-air enclosure. We then flooded the cement floors with liquid detergent, got down on our knees, and started scrubbing.

The first wash made no discernible difference whatsoever. The grime was so deeply epoxied, no elbow grease could make a dent.

So we sloshed the floors with more buckets of water and industrial-strength soap and began once again. This time we also drenched everything with insecticide, which Husham had quite amazingly sourced from a street stall. The effect was immediate and the flies dropped like . . . well, flies. They covered the floor in a disgusting carpet of tiny corpses, millions upon millions of them. There wasn't a square inch of cement visible. There were too many to sweep out, so we sluiced them out the cages down the stairs and into the drains in solid black jets. When too many thick-matted rafts clogged the pipes, broom handles were used to free the gunk. Husham dubbed it "the river of flies."

The next day we began again and slowly the glue of filth began to loosen its steel grip and grudgingly wash free. By the end of the following day the cages were almost clean.

Once the lions' cages were at least what I considered to be hygienic, we started on the tigers' cages . . . then the bears' . . . and so on, until each inhabited den was reasonably clean. With an uncompromising hygiene program now in force, I knew the weeping wounds and mangy sores that had been festering on most of the animals would slowly begin to heal.

I also used this period of muscle-sapping manual labor to instruct staff on the importance of completing cycles of action. The buzz phrase was "put order into confusion." For some of them it might have been the first English sentence they heard, and they heard it often. If they started something, they knew they had to finish it before beginning something else. They had to focus solely on the job at hand.

This was imperative for the zoo's survival. For if any of us, including myself, stood back and looked at the bigger picture we would despair. It was simply too mind-blowing to envisage—too impossible to contemplate headway. But no one dared say that.

Thus I stressed again and again the merits of completing cycles of action, completing a single job at a time, no matter how minor. On one occasion, while squirting flies with insecticide, we came across a gang of young looters and I instructed Husham and his team to finish what they were doing. They could chase the looters off later, which they did.

Gradually this policy began to pay off. By completing one task at a time the zoo staff was starting to see progress, albeit in minuscule fractions. We were sourcing enough food to keep the animals alive, although we still could not buy donkeys in advance, as looters without fail stole them. Sometimes we couldn't get a donkey and the carnivores went without food for a day, but never two days. And somehow, no matter what, we kept that critical trickle of water flowing into drinking troughs.

However, the war was always with us. Most of the Iraqi zoo staff who walked to and from work braved a daily gauntlet of bullets, looters, and murderous fedayeen keen to slit the throats of anyone associating with foreigners. Despite being senior-ranking veterinarians, Dr. Adel and Dr. Husham also trekked the hazardous miles from their homes, taking the same chances as the humblest laborer.

We never knew who would pitch up each morning, and we never blamed those who deemed it too dangerous to make it that day. If there was a firefight on the street by your house, it was better to stay at home.

Understandably, our nerves were raw from the terror of the daily grind. And when one morning a massive *ka-boom* thunder-clapped close by, I led the way in diving for the floor, shouting for everyone to do likewise. Outside the window we could see rubble and grit spew up in a lethal fifty-yard cloud.

For several minutes we lay on the cement, waiting for a second blast or retaliatory gunfire. None came. When all was quiet apart from a ringing in our ears, we warily got up and went outside. The mortar blast had been on the far perimeter of the zoo, with the wall taking the full brunt. Fortunately, nothing inside the grounds was damaged. I pried a piece of shrapnel out of a tree as a souvenir.

On another occasion while at the hotel we heard an explosion in the park. The DOD photographers rushed out to investigate.

It turned out that the explosion was near the zoo and through the murky film of dust they noticed a group of children huddled about one hundred yards away. Some were sobbing; others looked dazed, as if drugged, staring at the smoldering heap of rubble rendered by the blast. Most were bleeding. The photographers called out to them, asking if they were okay.

The children looked at them fretfully and then ran off.

It later became clear that the kids had been playing with unexploded ordnance and something had detonated. It seemed one child may have been killed, but if so, the body was dragged off before the soldiers arrived. Few questions were asked at Baghdad's sardine-can mortuaries in those turbulent times.

However, it was a somber reminder of the dangers we encountered every moment of our lives. The next day Adel and I called the staff together to warn them again not to stray off the paved sidewalks.

This was easier said than done, as there were no functional toilets and our only latrine was the sand outside. While I am used to a "bush toilet," in Baghdad there was no paper, nor were there any leaves in the desert, so sand was all we had. We all walked gingerly off the beaten track, and not just because of unexploded bombs.

To compound matters, almost everyone in Baghdad except the locals suffered from diarrhea. There was no respite; it was just a matter of varying degrees. Good days meant no runs; bad days, continuous dashes outside. And so it was for almost my entire stay in Baghdad.

I now know why ancient Arabic law stipulated slicing off a person's right hand if he or she had committed a crime. With only a left hand for wiping, it meant you would never be properly clean.

I WAS UNDER STRICT MILITARY ORDERS not to remain at the zoo overnight, and when darkness fell I would grab a lift from the nearest Humvee and head back to the Al-Rashid. After long days in the sun, there was not much to do in the evenings except chill out— although with summer galloping toward us, *chill* was hardly the right word.

Our main meeting place at the hotel was a makeshift coffee shop at the reception desk that had been renamed the Baghdad Café and was run by Sergeant Diehl, a tough, no-nonsense tank man and highly respected character in the Third ID.

For many of us, the Baghdad Café was the highlight of those grim early days, and it happened totally by accident. In one of his letters home soon after the Third ID had commandeered the Al-Rashid, Diehl—or Sarge, as everyone called him—wrote that there was no decent coffee to be found anywhere in Iraq and he was craving the stuff. His wife told her sister, who told a friend, who told another friend . . . and pretty soon when the post arrived Sarge had enough caffeine to keep him wired for a decade. So he decided to stop brewing ersatz mud at his tank and set up the Baghdad Café at the reception desk. Here select customers could get the only decent cup of coffee, Colombian or Brazilian or otherwise, in Baghdad.

Under Capt. Larry Burris, the Baghdad Café soon became a gathering point for many of the officers, both commissioned and noncommissioned, and while Sarge kept brewing his great coffee I learned more about the war from those informal chats than anything I will ever read in history books.

Obviously the American tanks were far superior to the Iraqi ones, but according to these guys, their superb thermal night-vision technology and laser sights was the deciding factor. That, possibly more than anything else, was what won the war so quickly. One battle with the Republican Guard at Al Najaf started at midnight and was over in a few hours because the Iraqis couldn't see a thing while everything was clear as daylight for the Americans on their computer screens. It was tantamount to playing video games in an amusement arcade against blindfolded opponents.

I don't know what soldiers in other wars called killing. In this one the phrase was "pink misted," which describes it exactly. The Abramses' and Bradleys' firepower was so awesome that humans were simply vaporized at huge distances. And so accurate that once the computerized cannons were locked on, day or night, they couldn't miss. Basically all that remained was pink mist.

The Baghdad Café was a shrine of sanity in otherwise crazy times, and I have many fond memories of it. I will certainly never experience such camaraderie again, and I don't think coffee for me will ever taste the same.

Those informal chats regularly went on long into the night, but when the sun rose we would all be up. After a quick MRE for breakfast, I would catch a ride to the zoo—often with Sarge—and our perpetual quest to feed and water the animals would begin anew.

The slog was merciless, and endlessly lugging bucketfuls up from the canals was not only backbreaking but also extravagantly time-consuming. Searing summer days were approaching, and I knew we couldn't keep up with the voracious tempo at which the parched animals were drinking for much longer. This was eased slightly when Husham managed to connect a pipe into the city's main conduit that ran underneath the park. The system was obviously not pumping, but there was sufficient water lying dormant to feed a small hosepipe. We now had fresh water for the first time.

But we needed to get a pump working; that was what occupied much of my waking hours.

LESS THAN TWO WEEKS had passed, but it seemed like an eternity since I had crossed the Iraqi border. There was a colossal amount of work to be done, but even so, I breathed a sigh of relief. We were operational, albeit barely.

It was around this period when an American officer visiting the zoo told me President Bush had just announced the "end of major hostilities." It was the first I had heard of it, as we had no access to TV.

"All we now need," the officer said caustically, "is for someone to tell Saddam and the Iraqis. It seems they haven't got the news yet."

For us at the zoo, time was agonizingly measured in twelve-hour increments; who would be at work that day; would we get donkeys that day; would we manage to ferry enough water that day. And, more ominously, would anyone get hurt or shot that day.

It was impossible to look further than that.

Every morning I would hold my daily ritual of visiting each animal individually, talking to them in soothing tones and reassuring them. I repeated again and again that we would get them food and water, that they were now safe. There would be no more bombs or bullets in their home, and people who really cared for them were in charge. The subadult palace lions were gradually starting to get some flesh on their skeletons, and the chronic mange on the two cheetahs we had rescued was slowly starting to clear up—a sure sign they were on the road to recovery. The terrified badger was now intermittently coming out of the hole he had dug in the cement-hard soil to escape the bombs. By now they recognized me, and even blind Saedia would look up when she heard my voice. This doesn't mean I was establishing some mystical bond; rather, it meant that hugely traumatized animals were getting used to routine, care, and order in their lives.

As we began our third week, Lieutenant Szydlik arrived at our office—for want of a better word—in his armored troop carrier. "Good news," he said, and for a moment I thought they had caught Saddam Hussein.

Szydlik laughed, eyes glinting. Every American soldier in the country was on the lookout for the Iraqi tyrant still on the run. But no, this time it was something a little less hostile. Another conservationist had pitched up at a roadblock on the far side of the zoo. Would I go and escort him through?

I was surprised. I knew news of the zoo's plight had leaked out via journalists who were swarming into the Palestine Hotel a few miles away, but there had been negligible contact from any of the international animal welfare bodies. I had presumed at the time that I was on my own because Baghdad's wild animals weren't actually in the wild and thus weren't as sexy as globally warmed polar bears.

I walked through the western sector of Al Zawra, and on the road outside a bomb-shattered gate that had been plugged with a burnt-out truck was parked a gaudy orange-and-white Chevy sedan.

It was a taxi. The door opened and an elegantly handsome man dressed as if he had just come from the sidewalks of Paris emerged languidly from the car.

His name was Stephan Bognar and he was from WildAid. He shook my hand with warmth. I got into the car to escort them through the roadblock and into the zoo.

Al Zawra Park. COURTESY BRENDAN WHITTINGTON-JONES

In the Red Zone near the zoo, a building shows damage from Abrams tank fire.
COURTESY GRACIA BENNISH

ABOVE: Lawrence Anthony just inside the zoo entrance with Capt. William Sumner, a fine officer and a good friend. COURTESY BRENDAN WHITTINGTON-JONES

BELOW: The Al-Rashid hotel in better days. COURTESY GRACIA BENNISH

Brutus at Uday Hussein's palace. Checkpoint bomb smoke rises in the background.

Saedi, the bear who killed three looters.

ABOVE: Zoo staffers and volunteers, including (in the back row, from left) Ali the taxi driver, Lawrence Anthony, Dr. Adel Salman Mousa, Capt. William Sumner, Brendan Whittington-Jones, Dr. Husham Mohamed Hussan, and (in the front row, second from left) Ahmed. COURTESY BRENDAN WHITTINGTON-JONES

BELOW: Last Man Standing—the last occupant of Luna Park—finally arrives at the Baghdad Zoo. Brendan Whittington-Jones, left, steadies the makeshift transport cage. COURTESY BRENDAN WHITTINGTON-JONES

Farah Murrani holds one of the Special Forces lion cubs born
at Uday Hussein's palace. COURTESY GRACIA BENNISH

ABOVE: Some of Saddam's young Arabians run in Al Zawra Park.
COURTESY GRACIA BENNISH

BELOW: One of Saddam's Arabian mares and a stable hand at the Baghdad University stables before transfer to the zoo. COURTESY GRACIA BENNISH

The Tiger. COURTESY BRENDAN WHITTINGTON-JONES

A volley of gunshots rat-tatted high above the roof of the taxi as we approached the entrance. Nothing too serious; this was Baghdad, after all.

Stephan and I ducked, and he looked around wildly, trying to see where the shots came from.

"No one told me this was a war zone," he said, alarmed.

I laughed nervously. Gunshots, explosives, and the *crump-crump* of mortar fire were Baghdad's music—the songbirds of war.

"Most of it is farther away. You'll get used to it."

Stephan then told me he had supplies in the taxi's trunk and he had brought a wallet full of much-needed dollars.

Manna had arrived in the nick of time.

STEPHAN BOGNAR, I quickly learned, was not afraid of hard work, and he was soon paying his way, mucking out the cages with the rest of us, although we marveled at how even in the sweltering heat he always looked immaculately groomed. He checked into the Al Hamra Hotel, part of the fortified Palestine Hotel complex that housed the international media, and I introduced him to the checkpoints so they would know he was one of us.

The look of astonishment when I first walked him around the zoo was a picture.

"There is a lot to do," he said.

"We have already come a long way," I replied, "but there is still a long way to go. This place was an almighty mess, and I am really glad you are here to help."

A Canadian, he had been in Israel recruiting agricultural specialists for a project in Cambodia when he received an SOS message from WildAid headquarters in San Francisco instructing him to hotfoot it to Baghdad.

But he told us he had been delayed by a "minor" security problem after he asked his Palestinian taxi driver to transfer his luggage from one Tel Aviv boardinghouse to another.

The owner of the establishment watched as an Arab took out

some suitcases not belonging to him from a room rented by a foreigner and put them into a taxi. He reported the matter as "suspicious" to the Israeli security police, and within minutes Bognar and his driver found themselves being grilled by steel-eyed cops. This was in a land where suicide bombers queued up, and Stephan was hard-pressed to talk his way free. It didn't help when he said his next destination was Iraq.

But Stephan was used to flying by his fingernails and had been in scores of scrapes during his years as a WildAid undercover investigator into the shameful black-market exotic species trade.

However, Stephan's scant regard for authority sometimes posed problems in a military zone. Once, when stopped at a roadblock by a soldier who said Stephan would have to wait while they radioed ahead for entry permission, Bognar told the young GI to "stick your radio up your arse."

The soldier was livid and reported it to his commander, none other than Capt. Larry Burris, who was in charge at the Al-Rashid Hotel.

Burris came storming into the zoo with another lieutenant, and they weren't messing around.

"Where's the fancy Canadian guy?" Burris asked me abruptly.

"What's up?" I asked.

"We're gonna teach him some manners," said Burris, his voice cold with menace. "He told one of my men to stick his radio up his arse, and nobody speaks to my men like that. Where is he?"

I told Burris I didn't know, then asked, "What are you going to do?"

"We've got plans for him," said a grim-faced Burris. "And when we're finished we are going to lock him up in the Al-Rashid tennis court in the sun."

I promised to find Stephan and bring him to Burris's tank. But I decided to make a last-ditch plea on the Canadian's behalf.

"Larry, I know what he did was not right and I'll get him to apologize. But I really need him right now. I need every hand we've got, so please don't lock him up. It will just make things more difficult, not only for me, but for them." I gestured at the animal cages.

Burris was a fine guy and, despite his blazing anger, relented. He knew my predicament. "Okay. But tell him not to come anywhere near me. And if he arrives at one of my checkpoints again he is going to be strip-searched and made to wait all day. That's if they don't beat the crap out of him first."

When I later saw Stephan I told him Burris and the Third ID were on the warpath. "From now on you go through checkpoints at you own risk. You don't mess with these guys, and I strongly suggest you go back to the checkpoint where you gave them lip and apologize."

To his credit he did, and I breathed a huge sigh of relief. Without the goodwill of Burris and his men, we couldn't survive in Baghdad. They gave us accommodation, food, water, and security and took a genuine interest in what we were doing. Aggravating them could have seriously jeopardized—if not aborted—our entire mission.

On another occasion, against all local advice, Stephan ordered a hamburger from one of Baghdad's more dubious street vendors. Eating this food takes guts, literally, and within an hour he was comatose in his hotel room with chronic food poisoning. Luckily for him, his taxi driver, Mohammed Ali, was nearby and brought him to a military hospital where he was put on an emergency drip.

Ali, a tough former Iraqi commando who had seen frontline action during the First Gulf War, then returned to Stephan's room at the Al Hamra Hotel and guarded the Canadian conservationist's money and sophisticated photographic gear until Stephan was well enough to be discharged. Ali's exceptional loyalty was noted and he later became an integral part of the zoo team. A burly man who knew Baghdad like his own backyard, Ali had initially been a taxi driver plying his trade between the city and the Jordanian border. His spiderweb network of contacts, on both sides of the law, would later prove immensely beneficial to us, and he managed to source food and supplies that we believed were unattainable anywhere in the city. We later discovered that if Ali couldn't get us something, it meant no one in Iraq could.

But even Ali couldn't get what I wanted most: a pump to ease our endless quest for water.

One night, while drinking coffee strong enough to stop bullets at the Al-Rashid with a bunch of soldiers, I casually remarked that I needed some heavy-duty batteries to start the zoo's pumps.

A man with sergeant stripes on his arms whom I had never met before nodded. "You're from the zoo, huh?" he drawled.

I nodded.

"Well, I've got two spare batteries in my Humvee that I may just be able to loan ya."

Gold dust. Without us even asking, a gang of soldiers deposited the batteries at the zoo the next day, and Husham got to work, pirating parts from whatever bits of broken machinery he could scrounge.

Several days later he told me it was ready. Well . . . except for one thing; he still needed a dynamo to charge the batteries. Without that, the entire contraption was useless.

Once again we faced frustrating reality. Where in God's name do you find a dynamo in a ransacked city?

What happened next was unquestionably a miracle. During one of his jaunts downtown foraging for animal fodder among the pavement stalls now springing up with looted goods, Husham discovered what we had been praying for: a dynamo. At first he couldn't believe it, blinking his eyes to make sure he wasn't seeing things.

But this was no mirage. Nestling alongside pillaged Nike sneakers and Ray•Ban sunglasses was a machine more precious than anything else for sale.

And exactly the fit we needed. In fact, it may even have been the zoo's original one stolen by looters; we didn't know. Nor did we care. Dollars again changed hands and Husham connected the final piece to the pump's jigsaw.

He pressed the starter button. The batteries sparked, the motor spluttered a few times, and with a tubercular cough it started ticking over. A few minutes later a trickle of water beaded at the pipe's nozzle, then a thin stream, then a gush as the pump got its momentum cranking and began to suck water from the canal as voraciously as a thirsty camel.

Suddenly, like a wildcat strike, water started spouting everywhere. Then the sprinklers sprang to life, spraying water all over the sun-baked soil. The pipes leading to the canal were so perforated from being ridden over by tanks and armored vehicles that anyone standing nearby was soaked to the bone.

As if on cue, everyone ran into the heavy spray, shouting and wildly applauding the beaming Husham.

Then we turned the water onto the animals, especially the shaggy-coated bears and Bengal tigers that particularly felt the heat. Each creature got a long, cool shower, with dirt and grime sluicing off in solid chunks. The bears even changed color, from sooty black to chestnut; the tigers, from brown to orange and golds.

For us, the men of Baghdad Zoo, the look of bliss on the creatures' faces was reward from heaven itself.

NOW I HAD ADDITIONAL HELP, I could start planning ahead further than twelve hours at a time and begin cementing some basic administration into place. Even though the Iraqi staff received regular rations, some of the food destined for animals was still being hijacked for their families. Although understandable, this posed a major problem and Stephan and I decided a daily communal meal should in future be cooked at the zoo to ensure everyone was eating at least once a day. It was vital the staff know that even though our primary mission was to save the animals, we still placed humans first. This may sound obvious, but chronic insecurities die hard in a country as brutalized as Iraq.

Stephan also offered for WildAid to pay ten dollars per month to all staff members while he was there. This may sound small, but when you consider that professionals in Baghdad such as Adel and

Husham probably only earned thirty or forty dollars monthly, it was well received.

I also asked Stephan to be responsible for feeding Uday's lions, which were still being caged at the palace. Stephan was happy to do so, and so I introduced him to the SF soldiers who had taken such an interest in Brutus, Heather, and Xena. This took another immediate problem off my back. Stephan soon became part of the team and made a valuable contribution in difficult times.

Finally we got some good news. The Coalition Administration decided to share some of the Hussein family's billions with the people of Iraq and everyone was to receive an instant payout of twenty dollars, the equivalent of a month's salary to most citizens. Thanks to Sumner's persistence, the zoo staff would be among the first to receive the gift.

We heard the members of the media were scheduled to arrive at the zoo with the paymaster to record the big event, and on the morning of bonus day we worked feverishly trying to spruce up everything as best we could.

Unfortunately, Kazim, our butcher, decided to have a private celebration and arrived at the zoo staggering drunk—most unusual for a Muslim man. Shoving his way forward, shouting and singing, he had everyone's attention when for some bizarre reason he pulled his white caftan over his head. This graphically revealed to all, including the cameras, that perhaps Kazim had some Celtic blood in him, for he wore nothing under his desert kilt.

To make matters worse, he got his head tangled in his clothing and, unable to see where he was going, stumbled around like a vaudeville clown, basically stark naked. This certainly provided some lighthearted entertainment for the rest of us until Adel led him away.

The Coalition Administration also announced that in a bid to get civic services up and running, all municipal workers—which included zoo staff—would be placed on an official payroll as soon as bureaucratically possible. With this announcement most of the zoo employees returned to work, including an amiable old man who knew just a single phrase of English: "I am Salman; I work tiger, lion, thirty years." He would repeat that whenever he saw a white person, which in my case was up to twenty times a day.

Salman was, frankly, not all there, and I am amazed that he had survived working with lions for so long. I once watched him walk into the giant cats' outside enclosure and bend down to pick something up, as if on a Sunday afternoon stroll. To my horror I noticed a couple of lions about forty yards away loping rapidly toward him. I screamed at him to get out, but he couldn't hear me, and as I sprinted for the gate I somewhat absurdly reflected on the statistical life span of an aging, deaf, slightly bonkers lion keeper. He couldn't have shuffled any slower if he tried as the felines, ears flat in classic hunting mode, sped up behind him.

Somehow Salman reached the gate first and sluggishly closed it with scarcely a heartbeat to spare. He was completely oblivious of what had just happened.

We swiftly changed his duties to keep him as far away from the lions as possible, but he would still absentmindedly keep pitching up at the enclosure. I am sure he is back there today—that's if he hasn't been eaten.

Even though we now had an almost full staff complement, the daily search for fresh meat was becoming more and more arduous. At times we'd have to travel far into the desert to find donkeys for sale, and with the lions from the palace we now needed at least two a day.

This increased food load presented another problem all of its own. We urgently required our own transport—otherwise our animals would starve. I badgered Pat Kennedy, the chief of staff of the ORHA, to provide a car, but he regretfully refused, saying every vehicle was needed for the war effort. I pointed out they were daily removing scores of shot-up and abandoned cars from the streets of Baghdad.

He looked at me incredulously. "You mean you want one of those?"

"You bet."

The next day we had two beat-up old jalopies, but at least the engines turned over. Things were looking up.

As with everything else at the time, we had to rely on our wits when it came to obtaining fuel. There was a depot at the far end of Al Zawra Park and we would drive up and say we were from the zoo and desperately needed gas.

We would then be asked for authorization. We never had any.

Without fail, the soldiers at the pump would look around to see if the coast was clear, unscrew the cap, and fill the car up to the brim.

They knew they could get into serious trouble for fueling unauthorized vehicles, but whenever we thanked them, they would shrug: "You're from the zoo. That's for the animals."

Some sleepless nights, when the frustration got to be too much, it was people like those soldiers who kept me going, ordinary people who couldn't stomach what had happened to the traumatized creatures we were caring for and did what they could to help.

But the most magnificent gesture of all was one afternoon when a soldier drove a truck up the zoo's office, asking for me.

"You're the South African?" he asked when I came out.

I nodded.

"I gotta take a leak, which I'm gonna do by that tree over there," he said, pointing to a eucalyptus. "When I arrived my truck was empty, and I intend to leave with it empty—please check that."

I looked at him uncomprehendingly. He surreptitiously motioned to the truck and walked away, unzipping his pants.

In the back was a brand-new generator still in its wrappings; something we needed more than food, gas, or even gold.

I quickly called the rest of the staff and we off-loaded it. It was damn heavy, but we were so excited we would have lifted a battleship if we had to. This would at last provide power for deep freezes and desperately needed security lights at night around the office.

The soldier came back and climbed into the driver seat.

"I want to confirm that your truck is as empty as when it arrived," I said to him. "Thank you. Thank you very, very much."

He nodded and drove off. I had never seen him before. I never saw him again. I still get goose bumps when I think of it.

Later that afternoon I mentioned to some South Africans doing VIP bodyguard work that at last I had a generator and now all I needed now was some deep freezes.

The next day they arrived with two brand-new freezers in the back of their SUV.

"Where did you get those?" I asked, scarcely able to believe my good fortune.

"We liberated it from one of Saddam's huts," said one bodyguard called Jeremy, referring to the palaces.

At last we could freeze surplus animal food that beforehand would have gone rotten in the heat. It's almost impossible to describe how fantastic that was.

Scores of these professional bodyguards by now were starting to arrive in Iraq with lucrative assignments to protect foreign civilians doing reconstruction work for the Coalition Administration. Much of the rebuilding of Baghdad was done in extremely hostile sections of the city, and the military didn't have the manpower to protect the hordes of foreigners now in the country. The press referred to the coalition-contracted "hired guns" such as Jeremy as mercenaries. Jeremy and his mates, however, called themselves executive bodyguards. But there's no doubt their preferred description was "warriors."

The South African contingent mainly came from the crack Reconnaissance Commandos, or Recces, as they were colloquially called. They were serial adventurers, but they would do anything for you if they considered you a friend.

I was fortunate to have them on my side, as they were a tight-knit group; intense camaraderie fused in the fire of many battles together, and they didn't readily accept outsiders. But they respected what we were trying to do against overwhelming odds at the zoo, and one day Jeremy put his arm around my shoulder and said to the others, "Listen up! This is Lawrence from the zoo; he is my brother from another mother."

That was their colloquialism for "he's okay by me," and after that I was totally accepted.

From then on they drove past the zoo each day to see if we were okay, and would often stay for hours. There is no doubt that the dire looting problem before Sumner arrived would have been even more serious without their presence. Jeremy actually offered "as a favor" to shoot a couple of looters dead, just to teach them a lesson.

"It's the only way," he said. "Let us kill a few for you, and the word will soon get out. Your problems will be over, man."

I realized he meant exactly what he was saying, and politely declined,

"Then don't come complaining when you get into shit," he said.

However, he did me give me their emergency satellite phone number with instructions to call anytime if we were in trouble.

I also told Adel and Husham to let it be known on the street that "mercenaries" were guarding the zoo. These tough men were on many an occasion our scarecrows, frightening away troublemakers— and they looked the part with multiple bullet belts, back-turned baseball caps, T-shirts bearing the logo of their favorite rugby team, tight black shorts, and sneakers without socks. They were wild men, all right.

Jeremy was a particularly interesting case. Over the months, I got to know him well and we often had long discussions sitting outside the zoo in the early evenings. He considered the "warrior cause" to be the highest calling and absolutely scorned the "effete" lifestyle of today's men.

"They're the living dead," he said. "Just look at them. Boring jobs, boring lives, boring wives. I'd rather be dead."

He also believed devoutly in reincarnation. "I have been a warrior for ten thousand years and I always died on the battlefield. This life will be no different."

For them, Baghdad was a battlefield where no rules applied. At night the Special Forces would arrive at the hotel to collect them for an undercover mission and they would kit up and go out. This generally meant pulling on a T-shirt, short pants, a baseball cap, and a pair of sneakers without socks. By comparison the SF troops were always immaculately dressed in full combat uniform.

There was no love lost between the two groups, though. The Special Forces looked upon the mercenaries with total disdain, and in return the "mercs" made it loudly clear that as far as they were concerned, "SF" stood for "Sick Fucks." They delighted in purposefully keeping the punctual SF team waiting just to bait them.

On one occasion I was in the mercenaries' room as they prepared for a mission.

"Where's the knock-knock?" Brad, a stocky, well-built fighter, kept repeating agitatedly as the others filed out. "Where's my fucking knock-knock?"

"Behind the bed," Jeremy called back casually. "I kicked it off earlier."

Brad reached down between the bed and the wall and with a grin brought up his "knock-knock." It was a sawed-off shotgun with lead slugs almost the size of bananas that was used to shoot out the locks of a house they were storming. That's how Brad "knocked" on a door.

They were certainly a different breed of men, but they helped us incredibly at the zoo. Make no mistake, when you are in a war the toughest, bravest warriors are the people you want on your side.

NOW THAT I HAD DEEP FREEZES I devised another plan to bolster security. Although the bodyguards helped when they could, we needed a more permanent military presence, as there were still gangs of insurgents roaming the city and launching hit-and-run attacks. I had been trying for some time to get the army to step up patrols on the zoo grounds, without success, but with two deep freezes now chilling in the office, I quickly got the word out that we had plenty of frozen bottled water on the premises.

It worked instantly. All of a sudden there were scores of soldiers pitching up in Humvees, tanks, and armored cars to exchange their daily warm-water ration for frozen bottles to get a long icy drink, something not inconsequential in Baghdad at the time. This increased military activity at the zoo was certainly noted by the fedayeen. The plan had come off perfectly.

After WildAid the next international organization to pitch up was Care for the Wild International (CWI). Their chief executive, Dr. Barbara Maas, phoned me from England and asked what the zoo needed.

I immediately rattled off a wish list starting with meat and vegetables and, most important, a dart gun. About ten days later she arrived in a military convoy with a load of much-needed supplies, although Kuwaiti customs had confiscated the dart gun, deeming it to be a "dangerous weapon."

This caused real mirth in Baghdad, where bullets were whistling around the streets like in a bad gangster movie. Perhaps they considered the dart gun to be a Weapon of Mass Sedation.

However, Barbara's timely arrival with food was an absolute godsend, and she certainly had courage by the bucketful to come in to Iraq when she did.

For us, working twelve hours a day, seven days a week, among the mayhem that was Baghdad at that time, there was no respite. The situation we faced was critical, and we were far from the next level we were striving for; that of "mere" emergency rather than the current dire conditions.

Then came Luna Park.

NINE

W E GLARED at each other. Both of us were sweating pro-
fusely, and it was not just from the heat blasting off the
desert.

I leaned forward, poised on the balls of my feet, my fists
clenched and white-knuckled.

"This is private property," he hissed at me in Arabic. "You have
no right to be here."

The sentence was translated for my benefit. I took a step forward. The man did not step back.

"Are you the owner of this disgusting place?" I asked.

The translator put the words back into Arabic.

"I own this park. What are you doing here?"

"I have come to shut the zoo in your park down."

"Why?"

"Because it is the most disgusting place on the planet."

We were now shouting. The TV cameramen, anticipating a fist-
fight to erupt at any second, crowded around us.

I gestured at the TV crews, without taking my eyes off the Iraqi's face. "You see these cameras? You are now internationally famous for the worst abuse of animals on earth."

The man stared back, eyes screwed into slits with naked hostility. "This is private property. You have no right to be here."

"We are going to close your zoo down," I repeated; then choosing my words carefully—officiously—so that the interpreter would not mistake them, I continued, "You will only be allowed to reopen when you conform to international standards of animal care."

Then I flipped and shouted, "In other words, when you bloody well know how to look after animals properly."

"I have a veterinarian who does that."

"Go and fetch him for me."

"Why should I do that?"

"Because I want everyone to know who he is! The whole world will see he deserves to be struck off the roll!"

The man turned on his heels and strode off.

"Come back here," I shouted after him, and to my surprise he stopped and turned around.

"So you understand English! Come back here! These animals can't fight back, but I can."

He looked at me with a sneer and shrugged elaborately.

I went crazy. "That's it!" I shouted, completely losing it and starting after him. "I'm going to beat you up right now!"

Sumner grabbed my arm, pulling tightly. "Leave him, Lawrence," he said, and then again much louder, "Leave him." He then shouted at me, "Leave him! He's finished!"

I turned to Sumner angrily. "When we have got the animals out we are going to bulldoze this place flat or else this bastard is just going to start again."

Sumner nodded. A few of the soldiers clapped.

"Thanks," I said to Sumner later. "It would have been a mess if I had got hold of him—but I would have enjoyed it."

Sumner looked at me strangely. "I never knew you were capable of such anger."

"Me, neither."

But then, none of us had ever seen such barbarism as this before.

I HAD BEEN AWARE that there were several rogue zoos operating in the city and had heard that one somewhere in western Baghdad was particularly awful. But we were too bogged down with the main zoo to take on any extra problems, pressing as they were.

Then reports, filled with revulsion, started filtering through, some from Iraqis, others from soldiers who had seen this hellhole of a "zoo" and were shocked to the core at the conditions in which the animals were being caged. Something had to be done.

As a preliminary precaution Sumner and I approached the military's legal department housed at Saddam's main palace to get advice on the legitimacy of closing down a privately owned zoo in an occupied country. Military lawyers weren't sure, as it had never happened before, and so looked up Iraqi legislation on animal cruelty. It was basic in the extreme, in effect stating vaguely that you shouldn't do it. Under Saddam's ruthless regime, where human rights barely nudged the moral barometer, animals didn't rate at all.

But that vagueness, argued the lawyers, would work in our favor, as we could interpret it how we liked. They all agreed the key comparison should be with zoos allowed to operate in the United States. If a zoo such as this would not be allowed to operate there, we should shut it down.

The zoo was called Luna Park. Even before the war there were press reports that told grim stories of staff poking the hyena with sticks to "make it more lively" and encouraging visitors to throw chewing gum and chocolate bars to the bear and monkeys. There was much suspicion that it also was a vital jigsaw piece in Iraq's diabolically cruel animal black market, possibly as a type of halfway house, bringing buyers and sellers together.

Luna Park was located deep in the Red Zone, where the war had never really ended. It was called red because soldiers had to keep their weapons' safety catches off, ready for instant battle. Consequently Sumner anticipated serious problems raiding it. He asked for twelve soldiers and four Humvees to escort us in, and despite sniping fedayeen regularly attacking Westerners in the area, there was no problem finding volunteers.

Sumner's role in providing security for the zoo's growing number of "Noah's Ark" operations was, literally, a matter of life or death. But he did it so subtly no one appreciated just how much planning and effort went into each raid. Here he was taking unarmed civilians into some of the most chaotic security areas in the country and he only had a handful of soldiers to provide cover. He was the classic commander, efficient, unflappable, and totally in control. However, the gnawing concern that he might lose someone during one of these hazardous missions was always with him.

Before setting off, we loaded the remaining animal transport cages from the Baghdad Zoo that had been too cumbersome for looters to carry off. Adel and Husham were coming along to give on-the-spot assessments of the animals. Stephan Bognar, Barbara Maas, and several press and TV crews also joined up.

The convoy took the long route, skirting the southern sector of the city so as to not alert Luna Park's owner. This was going to be a surprise assault, not a courtesy call.

An hour later we arrived at the complex on Palestine Street. A garishly painted mural at the gate depicting animals cavorting on spacious savannah greeted us as we stormed in. A large cutout of Mickey Mouse was bolted on the archway, just above the Humvees that skidded to a halt at the exit to block anyone escaping.

But this was no Disney in the desert. Far from it.

The first cage we came to housed a huge bear, squashed into a claustrophobic eight-by-eight-foot den. His head was bald from chafing against the iron bars. His only access to water was through a bowl outside the cage, which meant he had to learn to squeeze his paws through the bars and try to flick the liquid into its mouth. The bowl was dry.

In fact, it was more than dry; it was filled with dust. No one could tell when the animals had last been fed or watered. He had been locked in that hellhole for five years.

In a slimy green pond nearby, a male swan floated like a feathered blob of flotsam. Next to him was his dead partner, her long neck lying in the algae-infested muck like a broken stalk. Swans mate for life. He had apparently been attempting to revive his dead spouse for days.

A few yards away a pelican was tethered to a pole in the desert heat, unable to reach the water—her natural element. Her feathers, once surf white, were now sickly gray, and her elastic pouch dangling from her bill was wizened and empty.

In a nearby cage a camel had collapsed in the sun. His enclosure was the same size as the bear's. There was scant room for him to move.

A striped hyena that was stressed out of her mind kept running round and round her tiny pen. In other coops there were badgers, mongooses, jungle cats, foxes, pigs, birds, and monkeys, all as emaciated as concentration camp survivors. The dogs were too weak to wag their tails.

We found a gazelle lying on a piece of corrugated plastic—her only luxury, if you could call it that. She was barely able to lift her head.

Other animals, including a piglet, lay dead and stinking in their cages. The staff had been too idle to remove them.

In other cages that constituted a makeshift aviary, an assortment of scrawny, bedraggled birds sat staring vacantly.

Sumner and I mulled over the words of the military lawyers. There was no way a disgusting hellhole such as this would be allowed to operate in any civilized society. The question the lawyers had hypothetically posed answered itself with brutal precision.

"We're gonna shut this shit house down," shouted Sumner so we could all hear. I smiled. So did the soldiers. It would be a pleasure.

At that stage the man purporting to be the park owner stormed up and our confrontation erupted. As it turned out, he was an employee, not the owner. That dubious privilege belonged to an individual named Karim Hameed, whom we would meet later.

We were fortunate to have both Stephan and Barbara there, as they both had animal husbandry skills. Husham and Adel issued instructions to the reluctant Luna Park staff, while William and I stayed together and coordinated the overall rescue with William, keeping a keen eye on security. Farah Murrani, an Iraqi vet who spoke fluent English and who would soon become a vital part of our team, translated and coordinated the movement of animals to the vehicles.

We started organizing the removal of the animals. However, the cages we had brought from the zoo were barely suitable; most had at least one trolley wheel missing, so soldiers had to hold up a side while others pushed on the remaining wheels. Some had no functioning wheels at all, the ball bearings seized solid, and had to be maneuvered as clumsily as a cupboard in a small room.

We also had no drugs or even a dart gun. So we loaded the smaller creatures first: the pelican, the widower swan, an owl, two Egyptian vultures, two porcupines, two rhesus monkeys, four goats, four ducks, two birds of prey, the gazelle, three German shepherds, three spaniels, three terriers, two Maltese, and a small Pekingese.

The little Malteses were so dehydrated I poured water through the wire mesh directly into their mouths. They soaked it up like sponges—and were still thirsty. It was absolutely pathetic watching them desperately trying to grab at the bottle with their teeth, terrified I would snatch it away.

Next we took, barehanded, two snarling desert foxes, a wolf, and a jackal. As we had no protective clothing, this involved some skilful maneuvering, with one man opening the cage door while another quickly pushed the transport cage into place. Others then rushed to the back and banged on the bars to ensure the animals bolted forward into the mobile cage, whose door was instantly slammed shut. The starved animals were snapping at anything they could, and the threat of rabies if anyone got bitten was very real.

The rhesus monkeys also posed problems. These simians bite at the slightest provocation, and to avoid their slashing incisors one man had to grab the flailing arms at the same time as another grasped the legs and carry the monkey spread-eagled to its new cage. What made it worse was the Luna Park staff had no keys to the cages, so we had to smash the locks off with a crowbar. This spooked the animals even more, and you could hear them screaming with eerily human voices above the noise of the hammering. It was a miracle no one got bitten.

There was some room in the last Humvee, so we decided to take the camel as well. He appeared to be tame and a rope was looped around his neck as he was guided out of his squalid den. In front of the cage was a patch of rough spiky grass, jutting out of the desert sand like brush bristles. The camel flopped onto the grass and started writhing like a snake. He was so riddled with fleas and mange that his skin was on fire—but he had never been able to scratch himself in his cramped cage. The ecstasy on his face was infinite.

We then gave him some water and he drank. And drank. And then he drank some more. I thought camels weren't meant to get thirsty, but this one couldn't get enough.

With much pushing, cursing, and shoving, the camel was loaded onto the Humvee.

Then we went across to the bear. The rescue cage was ready and I looked down at the animal huddled in the corner.

"What's the problem?" I asked the zoo workers nearby. "Let's get the bear."

As I spoke he reared up to his full height on his hind legs. Bears are not indigenous to Africa and so I'm not familiar with them. As this giant stood up, his head banging the cage roof, I couldn't believe it. I had never seen a bear actually stand up before—the two at the zoo were always crouched—and this one was as big as a mountain, towering and growling at us. My God, I thought, there's no way we're going to fit this monster in.

"Whoa! Forget the bear," I said. "We'll come back for him later."

Eventually our convoy left, looking like Noah's Ark on wheels as it meandered through the city. It brought Baghdad's chaotic traffic to a standstill. Even though camels are a common sight in Iraq, no one could have claimed to have previously seen one standing imperiously next to a mounted machine gun in the back of a Humvee.

People stopped and stared, and then laughter and clapping spontaneously erupted as children pointed excitedly to the pelican and the vultures and waved at the soldiers. Fathers lifted sons onto their shoulders, and mothers and daughters jumped up and down to get a better view. It was a magnificent sight, the first time I had seen such joy on Baghdad's streets.

It suddenly made everything worthwhile. These animals, abused beyond belief, were having an impromptu parade of honor. Even the battle-tempered soldiers were smiling as they constantly scanned the perimeters, ever vigilant for a sniper attack or ambush.

At the Baghdad Zoo the animals were off-loaded into cages the staff had prepared and given food and water. It all went smoothly, except when they got to the camel. He had no intention of going anywhere.

The soldiers even reversed the Humvee up to an embankment so he wouldn't have to jump off, but he still refused to budge. Perhaps he thought he was going to go on another victory parade; perhaps he feared he was being transferred to another hellhole cage. Whatever, he sat down and rejected any attempts to eject him point-blank. No amount of cajoling or tugging on his lead would persuade him otherwise. The Humvee, he had decided, was his new home.

Dr. Barbara Maas, who had cradled the surviving swan during the trip back to the zoo, was adamant that the "softly-softly" approach would work and tried to get the camel to stand up by dangling a piece of lettuce in front of his nose. But the animal wasn't interested in the slightest. He sat and stared at the lettuce leaf with dignified but absolute disdain.

The rescue had taken longer than anticipated and the soldiers were now growing impatient. They needed their Humvee for operational work and told me so in no uncertain terms. After twenty minutes with the camel still eyeing the lettuce as if it were a piece of dung, the soldiers gave me an ultimatum: either the camel moved voluntarily or they physically turfed it out.

Adel and Husham had been watching all this with some mirth and came running over. They told me they, as Iraqis, understood camels and it was imperative we got Barbara out of the way.

I knew they were going to do something that would upset her, but I wasn't sure how to get her to move on. So I asked her to check if the foxes were okay, but she didn't fall for that. She was determined to entice the camel out with that lettuce leaf. But if the camel thought it was unappetizing before, he was even less likely to go for it now, as it had shriveled like a green dishrag in the sun. We also weren't sure if lettuce was even camel cuisine—it's not exactly something you find every day in the desert.

The soldiers were getting more and more agitated. Suddenly Husham had an idea.

"Barbara," he said. "Have you touched camel?"

He knew full well she had. In fact, she had even had her arms around the animal's neck for various press photo shoots.

"Yes, of course," she replied.

"Oh no!" he gasped with theatrical horror. "You get mange. Your hair fall. You go bald. Quickly wash hands in office. Very important."

Barbara understandably sped off like a gazelle, every now and again glancing over her shoulder with a ferocious frown as if she knew something untoward was about to happen.

As soon as she was out of sight Husham and Adel jumped onto the back of the Humvee, grabbed the camel's tail, gave it a firm twist, and administered a hard kick up his butt. He shot up with alacrity, and before he could sit again, they yanked him down from the Humvee with the neck rope.

Problem solved. When Barbara returned with hands scrubbed pink, the camel was happily adjusting to his spacious new enclosure. The zoo had a designated camel den, but a bomb had hit it and there was possibly some unexploded ordnance still embedded in the ground. He was consequently placed in the elephant enclosure, although thankfully the zoo had not housed any jumbos before the war. The staff piled in bales of alfalfa and filled the water trough. The camel drank for several minutes and then ate until every morsel had been finished. It was a sight to behold, as his teeth were angled forward like the prow of a ship and he was humming with pleasure as he munched away. Sumner in particular grew attached to the camel, spending hours clipping his matted, filthy coat to help cure the mange.

"This is a fine camel," Sumner said to anyone who would listen. "He doesn't hiss or piss and crap all over the place. He's just a friendly guy."

Dr. Adel started mange treatment, and the good news today is there is one happy, well-fed, humpedback ship of the desert residing at the Baghdad Zoo.

IT WAS NOW A RACE against the clock to rescue the other animals still holed up in their cages at Luna Park. These included the huge brown bear, a striped hyena, a bobcat, two badgers, and some pigs that couldn't be squeezed in during the first raid.

As we were planning the next sortie, my Thula Thula game reserve manager, Brendan Whittington-Jones, arrived from South Africa. I desperately needed backup and Brendan was a competent manager and absolutely dedicated to animals, so I had asked him to come and help out.

"How do I get there?" he asked when I phoned him.

"Go north and turn left," I told him. "You'll find it."

He had a torturous journey getting to Baghdad, spending a mind-numbingly dull eighteen hours at the Dubai departures lounge trying to catch a flight to Kuwait, which he alleviated by downing some "Guinnae—plural of Guinness"—at the airport's famous Irish bar.

I had also given Brendan strict instructions to get the dart gun Barbara Maas had brought in, which was being held at Kuwaiti customs. This proved to be a major problem, as the officious Kuwaitis dug in their heels, refusing to release it.

The stalemate lasted for three days and Brendan, who was itching to leave Kuwait and get to the action in Baghdad, summed it up to me perfectly: "Here we were in the middle of a military zone with cruise missiles and depleted uranium shells, and the Kuwaitis were worried about a dart gun that could fire tranquilizers at one hundred yards."

Finally an American officer at the coalition's Humanitarian Operations Center lost patience, went to the customs offices, and when no one was looking quietly grabbed the gun. He gave it to Brendan and rushed him to the military airport outside Kuwait City to catch the next flight to Baghdad.

They were just in time. On the runway was a C-130, a massive, squat, oddly beautiful monster, shimmering in aviation gas fumes and with propellers the size of roof beams. The C-130 is a military cargo plane specifically designed to make passengers as uncomfortable as possible. The seats are a cramped crisscross of webbing, and if you don't instantly get deep-vein thrombosis, you never will. You strap yourself in with a seat-belt buckle that looks like a blunt can opener.

The pilot handed out earplugs with the texture of bubble gum and his sole briefing to Brendan and other passengers was a laconic: "If there's a fire, or if we go down, follow me."

The flight was ninety minutes of restless tedium edged with fear that a surface-to-air missile might come hurtling out of the sky. It was virtually impossible to talk as the engines were too loud, and Brendan gave up trying to read as the vibration from the turbines was too jarring. Once over Baghdad's airport the plane literally dropped out of the sky, swiveling down to avoid enemy fire and popping passengers' ears like corks. For obvious reasons, pilots flying in Iraq don't have the luxury of leisurely landings.

Baghdad Airport was a maximum-security area and no unescorted civilians wandered around unless they had a death wish. There were signs all around warning that this was a shoot-to-kill zone. A shoot-to-kill zone, of which there were many in the city including the Al-Rashid hotel, meant just that. No warning, no pity. If you violated the rules you died, no question. Unfortunately, we couldn't dispatch anyone to meet Brendan, and as he couldn't walk outside onto the road to find a lift, he had to wait in the VIP terminal—a dusty shot-up building with every window blown out. All around were battle-weary soldiers napping on stretchers or eating MREs and listening to music. He eventually bummed a ride to the hotel with a group of British soldiers, who were astonished to find a conservationist, let alone a foreign civilian, in the war zone.

An hour or so later we met up as I was coming back from showering at the swimming pool. The pool's shower was the only place in the hotel—possibly even in Baghdad—that had running water, as it was tapped directly from an artesian well. Each evening there would be a snaking line of tank crews waiting their turn to soap off. To conserve water we would strip and lather ourselves up while still in the queue. And then for a few ecstatic seconds the sweat and grime and stink would sluice off our bodies. The water was ice-cold, as it was piped from deep in the earth. It made you want to yell, such was the intense pleasure after a day in the dust and the heat.

To while away the evenings prior to Brendan's arrival, I had built him up to be some sort of bush superman, a cross between Crocodile Dundee and Tarzan. The legend grew to such an extent that soldiers at the hotel now believed Brendan to be a modern-day caveman. They asked if he was like Steve Irwin, the Australian Crocodile Hunter, who was a major TV star back in the States. Well, I said, Brendan was way, way ahead of him. In fact, I told them Brendan complained that on TV Steve Irwin was given three or four camera takes to catch a reptile whereas Brendan, who operates in the real world, only gets one.

So when he arrived, he had a tough reputation to live up to. But to Brendan's relief there were no crocodiles in either the zoo or that section of the Tigris for his reptile-wrangling skills to be put to the test.

I was delighted to see him, as his presence would take huge pressure off me. He has a degree in zoology and wildlife management, plenty of bush experience, and just by looking at him you know things are going to get done. What you see is what you get; a solid, capable, friendly guy with a great sense of humor.

That afternoon I showed Brendan around the hotel and introduced him to the DOD photographers and Captain Burris and his men. I also briefed Brendan on security, instructing him to obey the military at all times and outlining what one could and couldn't do at the Al-Rashid and the zoo.

We then went over to the zoo and I took him on a grand tour, introducing him to Adel, Husham, Stephan, and the staff. We visited each enclosure and I recounted the history of the individual animals inside, describing what we were doing to keep them alive. I also told Brendan how I spoke to them individually each day, and he nodded. He knew what I meant.

The animals were still scrawny, but they were in far better condition than they had been when I first arrived. Both the tigers' pelts were starting to get a little gloss, while the male bear, Saedi, no longer spent his days aimlessly pacing up and down his cage. The lions also were far more alert and active than they had been when I initially found them dehydrated and starving, and they watched us with interest, hoping we were bringing food. Their healthy appetites were a good sign.

The two dogs were still living with the lion cubs in their own cage, barking as we approached, and Brendan was as intrigued as we were to see the incredible bond between canine and feline formed in such dire circumstances. The two cheetahs were also putting on weight, and the nasty leg wound on the female had now closed up. She was no longer limping.

I was about to comment on how well the animals were doing compared to when I first arrived, but Brendan got in first.

"Shit," he said, looking around. "There's some work to be done here."

And there I was thinking how much progress we had made!

However, the best news was that with Brendan's arrival we now had a dart gun. With this vital new piece of equipment, we could launch the next rescue raid on Luna Park.

Sumner wasted no time and the following morning our military escort arrived and we were off to the vile private zoo—giving Brendan an impressive baptism of fire of what we were up against. Once again, the man purporting to be Luna Park's owner whom I had threatened to thump accosted us, shouting that we were on private property and were thieves and trespassers—or whatever other insult he could muster. Sumner warned he would be forcibly removed if he made a nuisance of himself, and he stormed off, muttering furiously.

Adel, Husham, and Brendan took control and decided to kick off the rescue by sedating the striped hyena. The press had again come along for the ride, and in front of TV crews and flashing cameras Adel prepared to fire our brand-new dart gun at a hyena.

The first inkling Brendan and I had that darting the animals might not work as well as we hoped was when we saw Mohammed Ali rigging up the gun. Ali was a taxi driver, and while his driving prowess was legendary, no one was aware that his skills extended to animal sedation. I was about to ask Brendan to assist but figured Adel was a vet and knew what he was doing. We watched apprehensively.

Dr. Adel was indeed a dedicated veterinarian, but due to sanctions in Iraq he had not fired a dart gun for more than a decade. If he needed to tranquilize an animal, he merely clipped a syringe onto a pole, stuck it through the cage bars, and jabbed the creature. Perhaps that's why he asked Ali to pressurize the gun for him.

Anyway, the big moment arrived and Adel squeezed the trigger. *Bang* . . . or rather *phffft*. The dart barely made it through the barrel. It sort of dribbled out and then fell onto the floor. We couldn't have planned a more ignominious start if we tried—and in the full glare of the press. Seeing the mortified look on Adel's face, I asked Brendan to go over and get the pressure right.

Brendan cranked the gun up and with the next shot Adel was spot-on target, his reputation restored.

The slumbering hyena was loaded into a cage.

Next came the African badgers. Barbara and a zoo worker called Jaafar Tahb showed bravery beyond any call of duty by going into the badgers' den to coax them into the transport cage. Anyone who knows African badgers will tell you that they are among the toughest, meanest creatures around, with teeth that will rip an arm open. They are also totally fearless, willing to attack animals several times their size if they feel threatened.

However, one of the badgers was injured and Jaafar managed to get her in without much trouble. But the other was mad as hell, spitting and baring his powerful teeth. Jaafar is a former Republican Guard soldier, and although barely five feet tall he is as hard as granite. All he had for protection was a pair of rubber gardening gloves, but he was as deft as a picador and, after some wary circling, pounced and snatched the furious animal by the loose skin on his neck. Jaafar then bundled the writhing hunk of muscle and fur into the cage.

After that the pigs were herded in with relative ease.

Finally only the bear remained, hunched in his cramped quarters. But by now all the vehicles were packed to capacity, so Sumner reluctantly decided we would again have to leave the bear behind. The Last Man Standing, we dubbed him, as a reference to the Bruce Willis movie. We left plenty of food and water in the cage, enough to tide him over until we returned later in the week to close Luna Park down for good.

Sumner, glancing anxiously at his watch, instructed the convoy to depart. You didn't want to loiter too long in that part of town, even with an armed guard, when the sun goes down.

On the way back to the city center we had to pass through a tunnel. Just before we entered, the cry went out: "Sniper!"

In a heartbeat all the Humvee gunners had their weapons

trained on a group of fleeing bystanders. Other soldiers leaped from the vehicles and took up strategic positions around the convoy.

The men moved in practiced synchronization. Guns were swung to cover all angles, ensuring they could return fire from every conceivable direction. All the while they scanned the crowds, updating one another through their radio mouthpieces on anything looking even slightly suspect. If a suicide bomber or gunman came at them, within seconds he would be riddled with more holes than Swiss cheese.

I was in the back of Ali's taxi and carrying only my 9mm pistol. As soon as I saw what was happening, I told Ali to stop and back away from the convoy. The soldier in the nearest Humvee decided otherwise and, swinging out of the vehicle and waving his M-16, started screaming at us to get closer so he could protect us, which we did.

All the other civilians just kept their heads down. No one spoke for a few slow, terrifying minutes. Finally we cleared the tunnel.

Those few moments gave us an idea of what soldiers patrolling the city faced every day. Most of them were barely out of their teens and they were fighting the worst possible type of war imaginable: a war where the enemy were indistinguishable from civilians, wearing no uniform and emerging silently from the shadows. A war where suicide bombers rushed at them with lethal semtex belts, where IEDs (Improvised Explosive Devices) placed randomly on streets could go off at any minute, blowing patrols and innocent bystanders to smithereens.

In comparison to the average soldier's daily life, the difficulties we faced at the zoo hardly seemed worth complaining about.

STEPHAN TOLD US that he had been called back by WildAid and would be leaving shortly. I asked Brendan to go across to Uday Hussein's palace with him and to familiarize himself with the feeding procedures for the SF lions, which he would be taking over.

A few days later I also left for Kuwait on a C-130 en route to the

United States to raise awareness of the dire situation facing Baghdad Zoo.

It was the first time I had been out of Iraq since driving into the war zone almost two months earlier, completely unprepared for the wreckage and chaos I would encounter. I had originally come in on a reconnaissance mission to find out what was needed and wanted to hold the zoo together while things settled down. I thought the war was over and all sorts of help would be forthcoming, that I would merely help coordinate things and make sure the animals were well looked after. How wrong can you be!

Once in the States I made contact with David Jones, coordinator for the influential American Zoo and Aquarium Association (AZA). AZA had done more than any other organization to assist the Kabul Zoo after the Afghanistan invasion, and their expertise and fundraising skills were vital if the Baghdad Zoo was going to survive in the long haul.

Jones, impressed with what had been achieved with virtually no resources and against serious odds, pledged to assist us. They had already begun fund-raising for the Baghdad Zoo via mail shots and the Internet.

While I was away, Brendan, Sumner, and the team in Baghdad were getting ready to rescue the sole remaining occupant at the Luna Park, our Last Man Standing.

This time they decided simple tactics would work best. They would merely dart the bear, load him in a net onto a flatbed hemmit truck while unconscious, and then speed back to the zoo, hoping like hell the eight-hundred-pound animal didn't wake up while stuck in rush-hour traffic. Indeed, the beauty of the plan was that they didn't even need a transport cage.

Brendan made sure the dart gun was fully cranked beforehand and Dr. Adel hit the bear's flank straight on with a full dose of Telezol. They sat back, expecting him to drop within minutes.

Half an hour later, to everyone's astonishment, the animal was alert as ever, eyeing the people surrounding his cage as quizzically as they were eyeing him.

They decided to give him another shot of tranquilizer. The next dart only semipenetrated the animal's tough hide, injecting just a half dose—but Adel believed that would be enough.

Not so; after another thirty minutes the bear was still as wired as a caffeine addict. He did vomit a little to indicate the drug was at least in his bloodstream, but he showed no inclination to doze off.

Adel nodded sagely and explained to everyone that Iraqi brown bears were bred in the harsh mountains of northern Iraq and were far tougher than their wussy European counterparts. That seemed to be the case—well, with this bear anyway.

After another half hour, with the bear still wide-eyed and wondering what all the fuss was about, it was decided to give him a third dose. This time the dart struck true, injecting another full dose of sedative. After a few minutes he lay down and rattled his teeth.

They weren't sure whether that was the drugs working or a death rattle, but things looked promising.

Not for long. Every time the bear's head lolled, his teeth rattled and the noise seemed to wake him up again.

Eventually one of the Luna Park employees watching the fiasco sauntered over and told Sumner that the previous zookeepers regularly spent their evenings guzzling beer with the bear, often getting the creature blind drunk.

In other words, the bear was a junkie. The drugs he was being darted with probably just gave him a bit of a buzz.

This was useful information, and now knowing the bear was highly tolerant to toxins, the vets decided to dart him for a final, fourth time. They were running out of time and options, and no one knew when—or if—another convoy could be arranged.

The soldiers also were understandably not happy about hanging around in this dodgy area of town longer than necessary, and so the rescue team had to move fast.

But even the fourth attempt failed to drop the animal. In that searing heat—over 115 degrees Fahrenheit—with almost four times the normal dose of Telezol fizzing in his system, Last Man Standing was still grumpily stomping around the tiny cage with a string of darts hanging from his butt in perfect symmetry.

Brendan decided there was nothing for it but to write this off as a bad day. One person distracted the bear as others rapidly plucked out the darts, and the rescue team left, hurrying home before darkness descended.

By now the tough Luna Park bear was becoming famous, much to the red-faced chagrin of the rescue team. In fact, he was being touted as the only creature in Iraq that had withstood the might of the U.S. Army. Sumner was even receiving phone calls from generals who had nothing to do with the zoo asking how the bear was getting along, while soldiers would come up to us in the street and ask if we knew of this bear that no one seemed able to rescue. We knew, all right.

But most disappointed of all were the DOD photographers. The story had become confused on its way along the grapevine, and they had heard Sumner and Brendan had hit pay dirt, getting hold of a truckload full of cold beer. They sped back to the zoo, tongues drooling in anticipation.

Not only was there no beer, but there was no bear, either.

TEN

I HAD HOPED to be back from America in time for the next rescue attempt, but my tight schedule of talks and meetings was relentless.

To make matters worse, Last Man Standing certainly wasn't being cooperative. And as Brendan and Sumner scratched heads on how to rescue the recalcitrant bruin, pressure started to mount from the soldiers themselves to "do something." Troops stationed in the western quarter of the city often popped into the squalid park to give the animal MREs from their own rations and check the water supply, and they were becoming increasingly vocal that no creature should be allowed to live in those dire conditions. Consequently there was no shortage of volunteers when the rescue team needed helpers.

Brendan and Sumner decided the best way to move the animal would be to get a bigger cage, and as bear cages were somewhat thin on the ground in war-torn Iraq, they contracted some of the taxi driver Ali's friends to build one.

Ali had by now became a friend and a trusted member of the team. He was a strong-willed, no-nonsense kind of guy who could get things done, but more important, he knew the city and its people and was on the information grapevine. Ali plugged us into Baghdad, and with him we could go almost anywhere safely. I sometimes still think that the reason we didn't have a suicide bomber or insurgent attack at the zoo was because of Ali's connections. I believe he knew a lot more about what was going on than he let on.

It took four days of feverish welding and cost seventy thousand Iraqi dinars—about seventy dollars—but at least the zoo now had a bear-proof transport cage. "Cage" was perhaps a generous description, as it looked more like an exhibit in a trendy art gallery. It also bore little resemblance to the specifications Brendan had requested. But it would work; or to be more prosaic, it had to, as it was all we had. The brown bear, of which the North American grizzly is a subspecies, is, after the polar bear, the largest of its genus and can weigh up to fifteen hundred pounds. Thus the cages we had used to move the lions were way too small.

The First Armory Division was now in charge of Baghdad, as my friend Capt. Larry Burris and the Third ID had been transferred to Fallujah, a militant-infested city in the heart of the Sunni Triangle.

I was extremely sorry to see them go; they were fine friends, loyal companions, and had played a significant informal role at the zoo in the early days. Without them the Baghdad Café closed forever; I still miss it today. Before they left, Capt. Larry Burris called a few of his officers together and presented Brendan and me with their regimental medal for bravery. Larry told us the Third ID only presents the medal on active duty and we were privileged and honored to accept it. Today mine hangs framed on the wall at Thula Thula.

THIS CHANGE OF LEADERSHIP radically affected rescue missions, as one of the first acts of the new command was to draw up a stringent set of convoy rules. Due to the increasing number of suicide bomb attacks by Ba'athists and foreign al-Qaida-linked combatants, from now on there had to be at least four soldiers and a combat medic manning each Humvee. The minimum number of patrol vehicles on the road at any given time also had to be four; thus the days of me and Sumner cobbling a few gung-ho soldiers together and launching a surprise rescue raid—often acting on ad hoc information—were over.

Sumner drew up a revised rescue plan under the new transport regulations, but despite his meticulous attention to detail, the mission started off as a comedy of errors. The military convoy he requested set off to Luna Park as arranged but somehow neglected to fetch Ali's newfangled cage from the zoo. Although Sumner's own Humvee was available, he was prohibited from driving the cage or the zoo team to the western sector alone thanks to the new travel restrictions. The result was the military escort was cooling its heels in one part of town and the rescue team in another.

No one was quite sure what to do, so Brendan and Ali sped off in the taxi to tell the soldiers that sorry, everything had gone seriously pear-shaped and they would have to postpone for another day. However, the soldiers were fired up for the mission: they wanted the bear out of his hellhole, no matter what it took. Their commanding officer, Captain Little, sensed the mood and declared he wasn't "postponing nuthin'." He ordered his men to drive back and collect the cage.

A convoy was quickly formed and it followed Ali's orange taxi weaving through Baghdad's nightmare traffic back to the zoo. The soldiers loaded the cage onto the hemmit flatbed in record time and the armored procession started to snake its way back through the maze of motorized anarchy to Luna Park.

It was not a good trip. The convoy was much larger than our normal "in-out" rescue operations and the going was considerably slower. Children also came running up to wave or chat with the soldiers. The Americans had to keep shouting, "Back off! Back off!" not something they wanted to do with kids. But due to the ever-present threat of suicide bombers, every civilian, no matter what age, had to be treated as suspect.

At Luna Park the greasy owner, Karim Hameed, came running out, rubbing his hands and uttering the predictable question: "How much are you going to pay me?"

He had arrived at the Baghdad Zoo earlier demanding compensation for the animals we had confiscated. Sumner told him at the time that while there was no compromise on Luna Park's closure, Hameed was welcome to present an invoice to the American administration. Personally I thought he should just be shoved into the tiger's cage, with or without an invoice, but luckily for Mr. Hameed, Sumner has a little more milk of human kindness than I do.

Anyway, this offer seemed to mollify the despicable zoo owner, for he must have known that most of his starving animals would have been dead by now if we hadn't taken them. To make some money out of that eventuality was not a bad economic proposition. He was obviously aware that even with more resources and our constant input, the Baghdad Zoo was only just surviving on a hand-to-mouth basis. The fact we had seized his animals could just be his lucky day.

That was three days ago and Sumner had no desire to get embroiled in another argument with Hameed; he wanted the bear rescue to crack on as swiftly and painlessly as possible. So he assured the Iraqi his claims were being processed and he would be paid out in due course, although certainly not the figures Hameed had quoted. In fact, his payout demands were causing some much-needed mirth at military headquarters. For example, Hameed was asking ten thousand dollars for five goats. A goat cost five dollars at Baghdad's pavement stalls; by Hameed's creative accounting, inflation had rocketed by some 4,000 percent.

The soldiers leaped off the Humvees and went straight to work. They snipped the front bars of the bear cage with hefty bolt cutters and wheeled up the transport cage, wedging it flush against the newly created hole. Some food was then placed in the carrier cage as bait and everyone waited for the animal to rush in.

And waited.

The bruin barely acknowledged his eager rescuers. No amount of cajoling or tempting food would sway him. Brendan then sprayed water into the transport cage, hoping the shaggy-coated animal would move there to cool off in the searing heat.

But the bear dismissed the temptingly refreshing cascade. He was chilled out enough where he was. His look of supreme disdain spoke volumes. This was, as Brendan told me later, the bear equivalent of giving you the finger.

It had now become purely a waiting game, and with nightfall approaching, time was not on security-conscious Sumner's side. As the shadows lengthened, it would soon be too dangerous to hang around in this seedy part of town.

At one stage there was great excitement when curiosity got the better of the creature and he briefly lumbered into the transport cage to have a quick look-see. However, the overeager soldiers on top of the cage jumped the gun and didn't slip the drop door evenly. It jammed, and the screech of grinding metal chased the bear out.

You could have heard the collective groan from miles away.

Finally, after placing vegetables, honey—even MREs—in the mobile cage to no avail, someone discovered week-old scorched rice scrapings in a fire-blackened pot used by the Iraqi staff. These were added to the growing pile of food treats as a last resort—and to the astonishment of all, the bear sniffed the air for a few seconds and then rushed in to devour the scraps.

Everyone held their breath; the silence was absolute.

Brian Kellog, a muscular soldier now in charge of dropping the door, kept his cool and did his duty expertly; the gate slid down with a smooth metallic hiss and the bear was secure. Kellog, who came from the elite Ranger unit, was unquestionably the man of the moment. He was joyfully pummeled to the point of bruising by the ecstatic rescue team.

At long bloody last, and all it took was some burnt rice scraps.

The bear that had caused so many headaches was now chauffeured to the Baghdad Zoo, and his hulking presence on the back of the hemmit again brought the street hordes to a halt.

But it was not over yet. After he arrived at the zoo the staff off-loaded the makeshift cage and had barely pushed it a few dozen yards when the rubber casing popped off a trolley wheel. They adjusted the angle of the cage to put the pressure on the remaining good wheels and carried on shoving. Then the next rubber casing burst off.

Then the next. The men who were pushing were now straining up against the cage with their fingers inches away from the increasingly angry bear.

It was going to be a photo finish. Everyone wondered whether the wheels would seize before they got the bear to its new home . . . but the screaming bearings held. Just.

The door was pulled up, and the tough old brute ambled into his cage, a relatively spacious den with an outside area, shade cloth on the roof, and fresh water inside. Gone were the days when he had to flick stagnant liquid into his mouth from a filthy bowl placed outside the bars. Or be taunted by cruel crowds or fed liquor by bored staff.

Indeed, he now has a regular shower every afternoon to cool off. His fur is as sleek as an otter and he is putting on weight. Whatever one thinks of cages in zoos, he lives in luxury compared to the diabolical den that was his home at Luna Park.

The story did not end there. When I later called David Jones of AZA to tell him we had evacuated all the animals from Luna Park and planned to bulldoze it flat, there was a stunned silence on the other end of the line. AZA had Luna Park at the top of its list of "Worst Zoos on Earth" and had been trying for eighteen years to shut that abomination of a place down. Without knowing this, we had just gone and done it. Never again will those awful cages imprison wild creatures.

THE NEXT ABUSED BEAR to be rescued from black marketeers was quaintly named Wounded Ass for the simple reason that she had a suppurating abscess exactly there.

The zoo team discovered the horrifically treated creature through Farah Murrani, who as newly appointed head of the Iraqi SPCA (Society for the Prevention of Cruelty to Animals) was digging around the murky underworld of animal trading and heard Saddam Hussein's former private vet now ran a practice in town. According to Farah's sources, he had an injured brown bear at his surgery that was caged in appalling conditions.

This was around the same time as we were attempting to rescue the Luna Park bear, and as my aforementioned American fundraising trip was looming, I asked Farah and Brendan to investigate further in the name of the Iraqi SPCA.

The Iraqi SPCA was founded by myself, Brendan, Sumner, Adel, and Farah. It was the first humane society for animals to be established in the country. In fact, it is doubtful whether the creation of such a society had been even fleetingly considered during the endemic brutality of the Saddam regime. And Farah, as the first-ever chairman, took her duties seriously.

A slimly built, highly intelligent woman, she had graduated from Baghdad University several years previously and set up her own veterinary practice in the city. She is a Christian, which means she can treat animals many Muslim vets won't, such as dogs, which are considered unclean. That's why canines are kept in Arab zoos as objects of curiosity.

Her practice was doing reasonably well until the Mukhabarat arrived and ordered her to evacuate her surgery immediately—and permanently. She still has no idea why, except possibly because the Russian embassy was across the road and perhaps the Mukhabarat wanted her offices for surveillance purposes. She wasn't paid a cent in compensation. In a blink her business was ruined.

Although it was not uncommon in Iraq for officialdom to wreck lives as casually as a cat claws a bird, for a young woman on the threshold of an exciting new career this was a soul-shattering experience. She was too unnerved and disillusioned to open another practice and didn't work for nine months.

Then the war erupted. This was no surprise in Farah's life. She was in her midtwenties and had only known seven years of relative calm in her country.

A few days after Baghdad fell she met a group of American SF soldiers at a friend's house. They spoke of a crazy conservationist from South Africa who was trying to get the Baghdad Zoo back on its feet, and she said she would like to help.

The SF troopers came over to the zoo, told me all about Farah, and asked if as a special favor to them, I would take her on the staff at the zoo. I agreed immediately and they went off and came back with her.

As soon as we introduced ourselves, she burst into tears. I wasn't quite sure what to do, as you tend to forget how traumatized everyone was at the time once you got used to the permanently tense situation. However, she soon regained her composure, and it didn't take a genius to realize she was a quality person and we were extremely lucky to have her with us. Her honesty, integrity, and capacity for hard work were exemplary.

However, what really interested me in that initial meeting was that Farah spoke excellent English. I desperately needed a reliable interpreter. Although my communication with Adel and Husham had been forged through hard times and was honest and good, it was still done in pidgin talk. I also knew that as a post-Saddam Iraqi administration slowly came into being, I would increasingly be dealing with officials who at best knew only a smattering of English.

Farah could be a vital communication link, and she was a qualified vet to boot. She also was prepared to work for free. What more could you ask for?

She said she needed to take care of some things and would be back in about ten days to start. True to her word, she returned, and I was very pleased indeed to have her on the team.

Apart from that, for some weeks I had been toying with the idea of setting up an Iraqi SPCA based at the zoo, and as a committed and qualified animal carer Farah was the ideal person to kick-start it.

I introduced her to Adel and Husham. At first they were non-committal; Arab society is relentlessly male oriented and a woman in the workplace is not encouraged.

To compound matters in their eyes, Farah is about as opposite to a traditional Iraqi woman as you can get. She dresses in jeans and blouses—even shorts sometimes. She wears makeup; her raven hair has a bleached streak. On a hot day she is not averse to sipping a cool beer. In fact, she is so far removed from a subservient Arab female that Iraqi men think she is foreign, something she encourages by speaking with a fake Jordanian accent.

But perhaps the biggest aspect of her feminine independence is the fact that she openly smokes. This requires a major leap of chutzpah and courage in Arabia, but courage is something Farah is not short of. For while Iraqi men smoke like bonfires, they forbid their women to do so in public. Indeed, an ironic joke among Iraqi women goes like this: A husband comes home early one afternoon to find his wife in bed with another man. "Look at you," he says. "See what's become of you. If you carry on like this soon you'll be smoking as well."

Despite her modern style, with her contacts in the veterinarian world, her extensive family connections, her courage, and her cheerful capacity for hard work Farah soon more than proved her worth to the zoo. And eventually led us to Wounded Ass bear and Saddam's ex-vet.

His name was Dr. Nameer and although the Baghdad Zoo staff knew of him, they had had no professional contact due to his "exalted" position. Or former position, now that his boss had fled.

When quizzed by the Americans, Nameer said he had been a specialist police dog trainer until one day when he was abruptly summoned to Saddam's palace. The dictator told Nameer he was now his personal veterinary surgeon and instructed him to dissolve his old practice.

Defying Saddam was not something you did if you wanted to

live. It only was Nameer's professional expertise that kept him on the dictator's payroll, not Ba'athist loyalty.

Or so he claimed. Nameer did have some difficulty explaining why he had been a Ba'ath Party VIP card carrier, but one has to be careful of being too judgmental of what happened in those days of terror.

However, it's impossible not to be judgmental about Nameer's skills—or perhaps lack thereof—as a veterinarian. When Brendan and Farah went to inspect the bear at Nameer's practice they were shocked rigid. She was only three years old, about five and a half feet tall, and squashed so tightly into a transport cage she could barely move. The cage was roughly six feet by six feet and placed on bricks so bodily wastes could slide though the gaps between the bars, which meant the bear was in effect continuously standing on a suspended iron grid. This had rubbed her paws meat raw and, coupled with foul hygiene, caused the pads to turn septic. It was agony for her just to stand. The floor under the cage was slick with gore and excrement.

A large suppurating abscess on her buttock—her "wounded ass"—was weeping with rancid puss, and sections of her back, flanks, and abdomen were scraped to bare skin from the tight fit in the cage.

The only treatment she was getting appeared to be a pink-colored antiseptic mist that Nameer periodically sprayed on the sores. That a doctor of medicine with supposed compassion toward fellow creatures had allowed this to happen was, in Brendan's eyes, beyond repugnant.

With the vet was a sinister-looking man with a scimitar nose and bushy beard. His entire being prickled with hostility toward Brendan, no doubt intensified by the fact that he had an attractive Arab woman with him. Brendan decided this was tactically not the time or place to start a debate about ethical care of animals. He and Farah shook hands with the men and smiled, making it obvious they were not there to inspect the place.

However, they couldn't miss the two emaciated pelicans, crippled badgers, and skeletal dogs in tiny cages piled up against the office walls. Their revulsion toward the vet in front of them tilted over the abyss. But Brendan and Farah kept their cool. They could not let personal animosity pervert their judgment; they had to keep options open.

Nameer was initially hesitant to talk to Brendan as he believed he either was American or had contacts with the military. Brendan explained he was South African—"you know, Nelson Mandela country"—and was not involved with the army in any capacity.

The vet loosened up a little and grudgingly acknowledged that the bear was not in the best of health but said he didn't have the money to treat her properly. Brendan suggested they move the animal to the zoo, where she could get more intensive treatment, not just for her injuries but also for possible internal ailments such as screwworm.

This sparked some aggression from Dr. Nameer. He curtly refused, saying she was not his property. She belonged to a man called Abu Sakah, who reputedly was a prominent wild animal black-market dealer. The vet went further, intimating he would be in serious danger from black-market racketeers if the bear was harmed—which was a bit rich considering the atrocious conditions she was being kept in.

Nameer then changed the subject, saying he knew a lot of "secret places" in Saddam's palaces and perhaps he could assist the Americans. This was a covert way of intimating he might be of more use than just as a vet.

Brendan and Farah said they would pass that information on and left with a vague promise of meeting him again sometime.

About a week later they returned to Nameer's surgery and, as luck would have it, the black-market hustler Abu Sakah was there as well. A swarthy man with hooded eyes, he had brought in a sick lion cub to be treated. Like Nameer, Abu Sakah was wary of speaking to foreigners, but Brendan again explained that he was South African and had nothing to do with the occupying powers.

Farah used her extensive charm as well to ease the tension.

They started talking about the black market and Abu Sakah pointed to a photo of a tiger on the wall, saying he could get Brendan a prime specimen from Iran. Brendan then switched the topic to the bear and said she was in really bad condition—was there any way they could get her to the zoo for treatment?

Abu Sakah mulled over that for a few moments and asked if the zookeepers knew how much money they would have to pay him in compensation.

That was the core of the issue. No one, except us, was interested in the actual welfare of the animal. It was purely a question of money. Brendan suggested Abu Sakah come to see us at the zoo and we could discuss it further.

A couple of days later Nameer arrived at the zoo asking for Brendan. Sumner was there and, as Brendan had already told him of the vet's claims of knowing Saddam's palaces inside out, took Nameer into the office for a chat.

Nameer then asked Sumner if he could pave the way for him to be employed as a police dog trainer, something he claimed to be particularly good at. In return, he would give the military all the information he had on Saddam's palaces. However, although Nameer knew a lot, it was nothing Military Intelligence didn't already know.

The topic then moved back to the bear, with Nameer saying that it would be expensive to buy the animal from the black marketers. Sumner said no problem, but first Nameer must give the bear to the zoo as a sign of good faith. They could talk about prices afterward.

Nameer said he would relay that to Abu Sakah, but if he relinquished the animal unilaterally, his life could be in danger. Sumner repeated that he would discuss prices with the black marketer directly and stressed the military would not arrest anyone—but first the bear must be handed over.

Indeed, getting Wounded Ass proper medication had now become the top priority for the rescue team. Like everything we tackled, it was a race against time, as we knew she wouldn't survive for long in those horrific conditions. Nameer's staff was also serially abusing her. Whenever they wanted her to move they just banged on her cage or poked her with iron rods, forcing her to stand on her rotten paws. There was no doubt her life depended on us getting her to the zoo as quickly as possible.

Brendan in particular fretted about that constantly. He wanted to storm Nameer's surgery and just take the animal, but we couldn't do that without serious military backup. This was the black market, after all, and we were worried there could be retaliation against our staff. They lived in the community and could be easily traced by thugs seeking revenge.

Eventually Nameer agreed that since he couldn't afford to treat the bear, he would anesthetize her and the zoo team could come and fetch her.

However, as he was walking out he said in Arabic to Dr. Adel: "You inject that damn bear yourself. I'm not doing it."

In one breath Nameer had told Sumner one thing; in the next he was saying exactly the opposite. However, Sumner and Brendan didn't quibble. If the vet didn't have the professional integrity to anesthetize an animal under his care himself, zoo staff would do it for him.

Like most of our seat-of-the-pants rescue operations, this one also didn't start off on the right foot. I was not present, but I got a graphic description afterward.

On the way to the vet's clinic Adel's beat-up vehicle was rammed by another car in the middle of Baghdad's gridlocked anarchy euphemistically called traffic. Adel looked in his rearview mirror and shrugged. So did the driver behind him, who was actually at fault. In strife-torn Iraq, you just drive away from a crash and count your losses, particularly if you have a bear cage in the back. If you stopped for too long, looters would steal it. If you want, you can have a street fight, but it won't make any difference. There were no traffic police or accident claims in those chaotic times.

Once they arrived at the surgery Adel rapidly prepared the sedative and jabbed the syringe into the bear's butt. They wanted this rescue to be short and sweet.

But after a while it was obvious that wasn't going to happen.

Even with a full dose of tranquilizer, the bear resolutely refused to go down. And as with Last Man Standing, anyone within earshot was lectured by Adel on the legendary toughness of the Iraqi brown bear—"because they come from the mountains." It seemed to be almost a source of national pride.

Brendan merely shook his head, resigned to the bizarre fact that every bear that came our way seemed more difficult to sedate than the last.

After half an hour Adel decided to dart the animal again. To facilitate this—and before Brendan could intervene—Nameer's staff forced her into a corner of the cage via their usual method of viciously poking her with metal rods.

Not surprisingly, this infuriated the terrified bear. She screamed and grabbed the rods, twisting them as if they were pieces of spaghetti. For the first time Brendan realized her strength, that this was a really powerful bear they were dealing with. All the other times he had seen her she had just been lying down in her cage, too traumatized to do much.

Adel got the dart in, and again everyone waited. By now about ten people had gathered in the clinic and were making a hell of a noise and banging the cage, stressing the already-panicked creature no end. Brendan managed to quieten them down, and the bear started dropping her head and getting drowsy.

Then some youth who had arrived out of the blue to buy a dog from the vet walked up to the cage and kicked right where the bear's head was. She jumped up in alarm, now wide awake. Brendan stormed over and threatened to thump the guy, but it was too late. The bear was too agitated for the tranquilizer to take effect.

Adel prepared another injection and again inserted it near the wound. That, too, didn't work.

There was nothing further they could do, except write the day off as another bad mission. There was a sense of dread at the zoo. Everyone knew the bear would be dead before the weekend.

Two days later Sumner organized a convoy with a group of military engineers to attempt another rescue. This time the plan was not to sedate the animal (you know, tough Iraqi bears from the mountains, etc.) but to coax her from her current cramped quarters into the zoo's transport cage—similar to what we had done with Luna Park's Last Man Standing.

As always, nothing went smoothly and they faced immediate problems, not least because of the inconvenient discovery that the bear cage's door opened outward, making it impossible to place our mobile cage flush against it. After some head scratching it was decided to saw the door off at the hinges and then move the transport cage—which had a drop door—into position. Once the two cages were square against each other, the sawed-off main door could then be yanked up and discarded.

They cut through the metal as rapidly as possible to avoid spooking the animal more than necessary.

But they needn't have bothered about stress. For the clinic workers again went ballistic with their metal rods, violently prodding the animal to get her to move into the other cage. This further vexed the already-distressed animal and she scurried wildly around her tiny confines, howling in anguish as she tried to snatch the rods from her tormentors.

The poor creature's frenzied scrambling resulted in ripping the savage wounds on her paws even deeper. She also started defecating all over the cage, due to both terror and rage. That this proud and beautiful animal had been degraded and reduced to such pitiful circumstances was absolutely criminal.

Thankfully, through the red haze of fear and fury the semi-starved creature finally noticed the food placed as bait in the new cage and scampered in. The drop door was slammed down, the padlock bolted home, and at last we had her.

The cage was then winched onto the back of the hemmit and driven back to the zoo without further incident.

With proper diet, care, antibiotics, and a flat surface to walk on, the bear's suppurating wounds and ripped paws healed rapidly. Zoo staff spray her daily with water to keep her cool, and like Last

Man Standing she has an outside section to her enclosure with a shade cloth on the roof.

All things in life are relative, but Wounded Ass considers her new quarters to be luxurious. She is thriving. The potentially gangrenous abscess on her butt is now covered with glossy thatch, but the name Wounded Ass still sticks.

The zoo team was ecstatic with the success. We now had two new bears—although the drama in getting them to the zoo perhaps should not be considered classic textbook rescue missions.

But given the extreme circumstances the rescue team had no choice except to wing it as best they could. There was no other option. This was no First World Disney situation. They could only use what they had at their disposal and, crucially, no one—either human or animal—got hurt.

That's the nub of it. The true story behind the two bear rescues was the gritty determination of everyone at the zoo to save them at all costs. In extremely hazardous armed-conflict situations, using makeshift equipment and homemade, rudimentary cages with barely functioning wheels, the rescue team managed to move starving, dangerous, wild animals from conditions of appalling squalor to as decent a home as possible.

Few can dispute that's what care for our fellow creatures is all about.

HOWEVER, IT WAS NOT ALL WORK and no play, and a couple of days after the Wounded Ass bear rescue, Jeremy arrived at the zoo in a black SUV with darkened windows and yelled, "Do you want to see the test match? We're playing Kiwis and a couple of my mates have jury-rigged up a satellite feed."

Rugby is the national sport in South Africa and an international between the Springboks and our archrivals the New Zealand All Blacks is the highlight of the year.

"Excellent!" Brendan shouted back. "Where?"

There was one "minor" problem. The TV was in a hotel on the other side of the city, somewhere Jeremy and his crack team would go, but not civilians like me and Brendan.

I started asking questions. I knew these guys, and for them a shoot-out on the way was just another day at the office. On their last trip into the city they had ended up in a spontaneous gunfight and killed an insurgent on the street.

Seeing my concern, Brendan pulled me aside. "What the hell," he said. "They have got enough weapons to stage a coup, and it's a test match for God's sake. Let's do it." We were joined by two other SUVs and sped out from Al Zawra in a convoy through the checkpoints and into the Red Zone. As we drove, the windows went down, the weapons came out, and the men at the doors turned in their seats and took up positions so they could observe and return fire. Whenever the vehicle was slowed by traffic, the guns went out the windows and they screamed at pedestrians in Arabic to stay away from the car. If the traffic got too slow, we drove along the sidewalks, speeding like maniacs with the horn permanently on, swerving past pedestrians, donkeys, and pavement stalls.

"The insurgents target SUVs, so we do anything to avoid stopping," said Jeremy. "But if we have to stop, we all get out and take positions, one at each corner of the vehicle, facing outward, rifles at the ready, until we are on the move again."

We made it, shaken but still in one piece, and leaving a guard with the vehicles hidden around the back, we rushed into the room where the satellite feed had been rigged just as the game was about to start.

Unfortunately, South Africa lost, and we left repeating the crazy high-speed drive through the city back to the zoo. The ride gave us an insight into the daily lives of VIP protection in Baghdad in those wild days. It was not a job I would do for any money—but at least we did get to see the rugby.

E L E V E N

THE CLATTER OF HOOVES hammering up Damascus Street on the east bank of the Tigris rattled like rapid rifle fire.

All guards at the checkpoint on the Al Jamhooriah Bridge jerked instantly alert. The 120mm cannons on the two Abramses swung into position.

Then they saw the horse, a magnificently muscled gray stallion, galloping at full tilt. The animal was obviously panicked out of his mind and stampeding blindly.

The soldiers watched in awe as he charged straight at them. Reinforced concrete barriers and coiled razor-wire fences protected them, but it was a still a daunting sight.

With a sickening thud of flesh the steed crashed into the concrete, then bounced off, tangling and shredding himself in the wire barbs. The horse was killed instantly.

What had spooked the animal so terribly? What had sparked such crazed terror for him to stampede headlong into a concrete wall?

The checkpoint guards extracted the ripped carcass from the wire, winched it up onto a troop carrier, and took it to the zoo. Every combat soldier in the city knew about my perpetual quest for protein to sustain our starving animals. This would be a treat for the lions.

It was. Indeed, it was probably the most expensive feast the cats would ever enjoy. The horse was one of Saddam's prized Arabian stallions, one of a herd worth millions of dollars that had mysteriously disappeared before the Americans took the city.

The lions and tigers didn't make distinctions, of course. Within thirty minutes the horse was just a scatter of splintered bones.

Despite his sad demise, the dead horse was the breakthrough I had been searching for. I now suspected that at least some of Saddam's magnificent Arabians had survived the aerial carpet bombing of the palaces and were still in Baghdad. And if I could help it, I would try to save them.

HUSSEIN'S BLUEBLOODS could trace their gene pool in a direct line back to the Crusades, and their fate in the aftermath of the invasion had intrigued me from the moment I set foot in Iraq. I had been told beforehand of this magnificent equestrian collection that the dictator kept corralled in the grounds of his Baghdad palace, and it was something I wanted to see for myself. Saddam's herd has a genealogy that is unique in the equestrian world. Indeed, it is not too much a flight of fancy to believe some of his horses' forebears were sired ten centuries earlier to steeds saddled by the legendary caliph Saladin himself.

For history enjoys such quirks of fate, which is what makes it so fascinating. Saladin, like Saddam, was born in Tikrit. But unlike Saddam, Saladin was a Kurd. And considering the genocide Saddam waged against the Kurds, if alive today Saladin—Islam's greatest warrior—would have been a blood enemy of the Hussein tribe.

As far as I was concerned, to be in Iraq and not visit something as unique as a collection of exquisite thoroughbreds of a bloodline untainted since the days of Saladin was like going to Paris and neglecting to pay homage to the Mona Lisa. But the horses had seemingly vanished into thin air. I quizzed Adel and Husham, who shrugged and said they believed the herd disappeared at about the same time as Saddam and his family fled the city. Husham was convinced the horses had gone for good. Animals as valuable as that would have been instantly seized by black marketers.

I had to agree that was the most likely scenario. But the thought of an irreplaceable breed of horses apparently evaporating off the face of the earth kept buzzing about my head like a mosquito I couldn't swat. They had to be somewhere, and if there was a chance they were still alive and corralled somewhere in the city, I would find them.

Thus what started off as mild curiosity grew into an almost obsessive quest. It was my duty, I believed, to trace this national treasure—particularly as everyone else seemed so indifferent.

After the arrival of the dead horse, at the next staff meeting I told everyone a full search was now on for Saddam's horses. And any news of the herd—whether it be rumors, hearsay, gossip, or grapevine—was to be reported back directly to me.

The zoo staff was less than enthusiastic. They were, like Husham, convinced it would be a wild-goose chase. There was no way, they told me, that animals collectively worth millions of dollars would still be on the loose amid the urban anarchy. And even if they were alive, how on earth were we going to find them in a chaotic city like Baghdad?

I assured them that "no" was not an option, so they reluctantly started asking around. Brendan and I also requested soldiers at checkpoints to be on the lookout, as well as anyone we bumped into at the Al-Rashid Hotel or the palace. Checkpoints radioed other checkpoints and soon the word was out all over the city: the zoo people wanted Saddam's horses.

All I had to go on was what the Iraqis told me: that the horses had disappeared from the palaces during the early bombing raids and, if they were alive, they were possibly being hidden in heavily disguised stables somewhere in the teeming city. I couldn't have asked for a sketchier scenario.

Staff members also regularly warned me that looking for the horses was not a road I should go down. If I did, I probably would butt heads with black-market thugs. And a bigger bunch of cutthroats was hard to imagine, as we had seen with Abu Sakah and the Wounded Ass bear. The characters involved in illicit animal trading were not squeamish about butchering anyone who crossed them, particularly when you considered what was at stake. We were not talking about the odd sick bear here. Saddam had the finest Arabian stock in the Middle East, indeed, arguably in the world. When Saddam wanted a particular horse, he got it.

According to local lore, his core breeding herd numbered about seventy and was kept in special paddocks at the equestrian Chival club near the Baghdad airport. Where they were now was anyone's guess.

Looking at the arcane crisscross of streets on a Baghdad map only made me more confused. Where does one even begin? There was no logical kickoff point, so I reverted to the only option open to me: word of mouth. Surely someone somewhere would have noticed a herd of prime horses being moved around the city? Surely the regal steeds must have stood out among the donkeys and goats?

Apparently not. After weeks of intensive questioning at every roadblock I encountered, all we had seen was one shaking head after another. This, of course, confirmed the zoo staff's belief that the horses were now either dead from falling bombs or so deeply enmeshed in the underworld's murky web that they were irretrievable.

However, the death of this splendid stallion, tragic as it was, gave me new hope. There must be others around. According to eyewitnesses, it appeared as though the incredibly valuable horse was being used to draw a cart like a donkey but had broken loose and, in an unhinged stampede for freedom, had bolted blindly up the road until he thudded into the concrete blocks at the checkpoint.

This meant our initial theory was probably correct; that the other animals were still somewhere in or around Baghdad. So we resumed our quest with vigor, again pestering patrols to be on the lookout for horses being covertly moved and to get word to the zoo instantly if any were found while soldiers were searching transport trucks. These horses were stolen property, we stressed, and as the last direct descendants of the "Crusade" herds, they were worth a fortune.

Eventually our persistence paid off. One day out of nowhere a man called Dr. Abu Bakker appeared at the zoo and whispered to a staff member that he knew where the horses were. This news was relayed to Farah faster than one could kick a ball, but frustratingly, when she rushed over to meet him, he had disappeared and hadn't left an address.

We thought we were back to square one. But fortunately not, and one morning Adel arrived at the zoo to find the elusive man waiting for him.

Yes, said Abu Bakker, he knew exactly where the horses were hidden. He had been Saddam's chief equestrian vet and was intimately acquainted with the animals.

Adel summoned me and we moved into the zoo office, as Abu Bakker was reluctant to be seen discussing the matter in public. He told us that a few days before the Hussein family fled their palaces the horses had been taken to a secret complex of stables were they would be kept until Saddam's "return." To my dismay, the stables were right in the middle of one of most dangerous places in Iraq at the time—Abu Ghraib.

Abu Ghraib is a district about twenty miles west of Baghdad on the edge of the city's shanty suburbs that sprawl uncontrolled into the desert, a seething, densely populated ghetto, home to thieves, black marketers, smugglers, and hash dealers. And now fedayeen and al-Qaeda-linked operatives, who lurked in the lawless, dark alleys, were filtering in as well.

The town is also synonymous with the Abu Ghraib jail—the most brutal in Arabia—where unspeakable torture was inflicted by Saddam's henchmen on the regime's opponents, and which ironically would later become a massive embarrassment for the American military, resulting in court-martials and a deluge of anti-American outrage.

All in all, Abu Ghraib was a town one did not want to visit unless absolutely necessary. We would need serious military backup to pull this rescue mission off, and so I took Farah along to discuss the matter with Coalition Provisional Authority Director L. Paul Bremer's popular chief of staff, Pat Kennedy.

To my relief Kennedy instantly grasped the significance of the issue and asked for the coordinates of the stables' location, which he could pass on to a general who would follow it up. Kennedy pledged a tank and troops to do the job.

Indeed, he said, this would not be the first time U.S. soldiers had rescued priceless horses during conflict. During the Second World War men from Gen. George Patton's Third Cavalry saved the Lipizzans, a herd of top-pedigreed high-stepping classical riding horses that had been seized by the Nazis. Patton was a horse lover, and when he heard the unique steeds were being held at a German depot in Czechoslovakia he vowed to rescue them. But as the Russians were advancing from the east, with the United States further back in the west and south, it seemed certain the Russians would get there first. So Patton cut a deal with the Germans to turn these horses over to the United States and prevent the Red Army from capturing them. It was said at the time that had Soviet soldiers—who were basically living off the land and close to starving—found the herd, the animals would have been butchered and eaten. Thanks to Patton's prompt action, the horses were shipped to America, where their unique genealogy has been retained.

Kennedy said as far as they were concerned, Saddam's Arabians would be as important as the Lipizzans to future generations of Arab equestrians.

Unlike Lipizzans, which are a "niche" pedigree, Arabian bloodlines are found in all today's top racing breeds. The Bedouins first tamed them around 1500 B.C. and there's no question these noble horses were absolutely intrinsic to the desert economy. Without a good speedy horse, a Bedouin could not successfully plunder his neighbors and grow rich.

Consequently these tough desert tribes believed the steeds were a gift direct from Allah. Even Muhammad commanded "every man should love his horse."

In those days the most prized Arab horses were bred deep in the desert, as only the hardiest survived. They were—and still are—rugged, brave, wild, fast, and beautiful. Not surprisingly the ancient Greeks fashioned the mythical Pegasus in the image of an Arabian stallion.

The effect of the Arabian on the global equestrian industry is inestimable. Virtually every quality light horse in Europe and America today has Arabian blood in its veins, and the belief among breeders is the higher the percentage of that blood, the better the horse. The conquistadors used Arabian offshoots to conquer South America, the forebears of the famed mustang.

A purebred Arabian has a distinctive "dished profile," with prominent eyes, large nostrils, and a small muzzle. The Bedouins attached mystical significance to these features; the large forehead was said to hold the blessings of Allah, and the arched neck and aggressive stance were a sign of the horse's courage. But the true power lay in its muscle-ridged chest, short, powerful back, and strong, sloping shoulders. No European horse could touch it for speed and hardiness, and when the Crusaders first clashed with the Muslims in 1094 captured Arabian horses were prized booty. They were shipped back to Europe as breeding stock to "lighten" the ponderous workhorses used by the Europeans. Today, from Ascot to Churchill Downs you will not find a racehorse that is not a carefully mixed cocktail of bloodlines, with the dominant strain being Arabian.

The horse still is a powerful symbol in the Arab mythology. One of Osama bin Laden's favorite quotes is that people will always follow the man on a strong horse, which explains his penchant for being photographed on a muscular white stallion.

Saddam also liked to be considered an expert horseman. Hence his desire to own the finest collection of Arabians in the world.

ALTHOUGH ABU BAKKER'S INFORMATION provided a potentially vital breakthrough, further proof was needed. We also wanted some form of documentation to establish his credentials as Saddam's horse doctor, so the next night Farah drove Brendan in her battered little Passat to the vet's house in the Al Saydeiah suburb. He furtively let them in, hurriedly closing the door behind Brendan, fearful that some spy would snitch to the terror networks that a foreigner had come to his home.

In his small study he brought out piles of Iraqi Arabian Horse Association documents and CDs that recorded the details of each of Saddam's horses to back up the authenticity of the herd's bloodlines. This certainly confirmed Abu Bakker's credentials, and he confidently told us he would be able to provide proof of pedigree of any of Saddam's steeds we found.

Brendan then asked the key question: how we would recover the Arabians? As they were mixed with other horses, it would be virtually impossible to identify them on the spot. We would just be guessing, taking the finest-looking ones on the off chance.

Abu Bakker nodded. He had given this some thought. The stable hands, he said, knew which horses were which. They could probably be persuaded to assist if their security was guaranteed. In fact, he knew of one who would definitely help us.

The following Friday morning, Farah, Ali, Abu Bakker, and Brendan went to the Abu Ghraib stables to meet the stable hand who had agreed to turn informer. They left at sunrise, long before the racecourse down the road opened, and were surreptitiously ushered into a secluded stable block. Red-haired Brendan stuck out like a sore thumb and the meeting was conducted hastily; it was just too dangerous to have a white person in the area without hefty military muscle.

According to the fidgety informer, Saddam had indeed moved his horses to Abu Ghraib when the Americans started bombing the palaces. But now that the dictator had fled, black marketers had taken the steeds from the stable hands at gunpoint. Once everything quieted down, no doubt the objective was to put these majestic animals up for sale where they could fetch more than one hundred thousand dollars from aficionados. That's being conservative, as the tag "Saddam's horses" would probably add an impressive collector's premium.

The informer claimed forty-one Arabians were still in the area and being rudimentarily cared for. He said they were poorly groomed and some even had been shoed, absolute sacrilege for prime Arabian breeding stock. In their unkempt, debilitated state, they could not easily be picked out among the scores of mixed-breeds stabled with them.

The stolen horses, their true origins disguised, were also surreptitiously being raced, a massively popular pastime in Baghdad, and with the racecourse in an area pretty much away from military scrutiny, there were meetings three times a week.

Then came the key question: would the informer help to identify the horses? The man who, judging by his diminutive stature, probably also was a jockey, swallowed hard. Yes, he said. Neither he nor the other grooms had any love for the grim bandits who had stolen the horses. But the Americans must assure his safety.

No problem, said Brendan. They would handcuff all the stable hands at the onset of the raid to deflect suspicion that any could be involved.

The groom nodded, satisfied.

The group then ghosted away from the stable block as stealthily as they had arrived.

Brendan reported back to me that the horses were "Porsches being treated like Passats" and suggested we get a rescue mission going as soon as possible.

I WAS AGAIN SCHEDULED to meet potential donors in America and reluctantly left Baghdad International on a military C-130 to catch a connecting flight from Kuwait. This meant I would miss out on the climax of the horse adventure, just as I had the bear rescues, and it galled in the extreme, as I had started this hunt as a personal quest. But it was critically important that I met with relevant organizations to garner international aid for the beleaguered zoo, and postponing the trip or the horse rescue was simply not an option.

Thus it was left to Sumner, Brendan, and Farah to reconnoiter the racecourse and stables the next Saturday morning and see first-hand what they would be up against.

It wasn't encouraging. In fact, it was downright terrifying. There were hordes of people swarming everywhere, and a large expedition would soon attract attention and lose the initiative. The mere whisper of a posse of military vehicles about to thunder into Abu Ghraib would see the horses being whisked away in an instant. All that would remain would be a line of empty stables.

The zoo team watched the busy area silently from the closed windows of their car. Eventually Sumner motioned to the driver to move on.

"It's gotta be a quick in-and-out," he said. The others agreed. A lightning raid was their only chance of success. And even that would be hazardous in the extreme, as terrorists could mingle with the seething crowds at will.

They decided to request that the military authorities provide a smallish but heavily armed convoy to storm the stables, load the horses into the cattle trucks as quickly as possible, and speed off.

However, despite Pat Kennedy's assurances that the army would provide backup at the highest level, this did not happen, much to the disappointment of the rescue team. Kennedy was away at the time, which was extremely unfortunate, for I knew if he had been there things would have happened exactly as planned. Thus the initial two proposed raids were spectacular flops.

The rescue team's first escort, led by "some big Texan guys," pulled out at the last minute, as they were "worried about security arrangements." The effect that had on the team was—to put it mildly—profound. If the soldiers were scared, what about us civilians? To make matters worse, the escort withdrew at the last minute, which meant the rescue team could not cancel the hired cattle trucks in time. The zoo ended up having to pay the drivers for the aborted mission.

The next group to step forward was an engineering unit based at Al Zawra Park that volunteered to provide men and equipment. But once they heard the strike would be deep in Abu Ghraib, they also apparently got cold feet. However, at least they gave several hours' notice and the rescue team was able to postpone the trucks.

Brendan and Sumner realized that if the operation was to go ahead, they would have to plan it themselves. This meant the manpower would be a lot sparser than perhaps was healthy, but Sumner knew they had no option.

The date was set for the next Tuesday, a nonrace day to ensure minimum crowds, and the rescue team set off with a squad of marines under Capt. Gavino Rivas. The convoy consisted of a Bradley fighting vehicle, four Humvees ferrying the marines, and two cattle transportation trucks for the horses.

It wasn't exactly a big-league assault team, but that's all Sumner could muster. However, he reckoned that with some nifty planning and nerves of steel they could pull it off.

Brendan, Farah, and Abu Bakker were waiting in Farah's car for the convoy at a gas station about five hundred meters from the stables with three jockeys from the Arabian Chival Club who had worked with Saddam's horses before. They kept in touch with handheld radios, and when the convoy arrived on schedule they followed as it rumbled into the stable courtyard, taking the grooms completely by surprise.

However, to their dismay they found the hand-drawn maps of the area provided by Abu Bakker and the jockeys were grossly inaccurate. For instead of the stables leading onto a single courtyard, there were two yards, the second one leading off into a suburb rather than open space. This made it extremely difficult to seal off, and the horse thieves could simply vanish into the residential area with the animals.

Improvisation was now all they had, and everyone just "hung around" while Sumner and Rivas urgently discussed what to do.

Watching all this commotion were two ancient white-bearded Iraqi men sitting at a fold-up table about fifty yards away drinking chai. Nothing was going to stop their morning ritual, not even a tank brimming with soldiers. So they carried on sipping chai, studiously pretending the Humvees, shouting Americans, and frantic stable hands were not there. After some minutes the men finished their tea, slowly picked up their plastic furniture, walked back inside a building, and shut the doors. It was like an old Western movie, with civilians clearing the sidewalk as the gunslingers hit town—but at their own pace, thank you.

The two commanders quickly summed up their options. With only the tank, four Humvees, and six cattle trucks, there were not nearly enough vehicles to circle the courtyard area as they had planned. And to compound problems, one of the Humvees had broken down en route to the stables and was now being towed. This could pose serious security problems; the golden rule all American soldiers religiously observed in the Red Zones was never to spread themselves too thin.

Sensing they were losing momentum, Sumner and Rivas started barking orders. They instructed the Bradley driver to park at the gate where its brooding hulk radiated menacing gravitas while a group of marines closed off the area as best they could. The rest of the soldiers rapidly rounded up the grooms and jockeys, demanding to know where the stolen horses were kept. The cooperation of the grooms was vital as there were so many horses it would have taken far too long for the team to identify each individual animal. The success of the mission depended on quick action.

In the confusion the soldiers also forgot to handcuff the informer to show he was there "under duress," which understandably alarmed him considerably. Fortunately, the other frightened grooms soon acquiesced as well, agreeing to point out which horses were from Saddam's prized herd and also to help load them. But to Sumner's and Brendan's acute disappointment, the grooms claimed there were only sixteen horses, not the forty-one the informer had promised.

Sumner ordered the animals to be rounded up. This was easier said than done, as it involved raiding each stable individually, a potentially hazardous exercise, as the black marketers were reputed to be armed with AK-47s and could be lurking anywhere in the sprawling labyrinth of cubicles. There was only one way to find out—by kicking open every door and storming in.

By now Sumner was a worried man. All around him was bedlam; stable doors being smashed, agitated horses bolting and kicking, and no one was quite sure who in the rapidly gathering crowd of Iraqis was friend of foe. The confusion was aggravated by billowing clouds of dust that hung in the air like surreal sepia mist. In the blazing heat, everything appeared as though it were happening in dreamlike slow motion, as if even chaos were lethargic.

Sumner and Rivas had to think on their feet. There was no standard procedure handling this incident. And problems were exacerbated by the fact that the grooms didn't understand a word the Americans were saying.

This is where Farah really came into her own. Amid all the mad stampeding and shouting, she was the only one able to communicate with both sides. And she did so with an icy control that only those under fire could really appreciate. Such was her authority that the grooms never questioned taking orders from a woman—not something taken lightly in Arab society. Her coolness and grace in such chaos were truly heroic.

According to the plan (if one could call it that), once all the Arabians had been accounted for and tethered to the Humvees, the grooms would then load them into the cattle trucks.

But in the wild melee several horses snapped their rotten halters and went galloping down the track with the grooms in frantic pursuit. Fortunately, the grooms managed to keep the animals under control and the horses finally calmed enough so that they could be loaded into the transport trucks.

As the horses were being loaded, one animal's hoof shot straight through the rusted metal floor of the dilapidated cattle truck, gashing its leg to the bone. The animal panicked and started kicking wildly. Sumner shouted at the groom to cut the rope around its neck before it could strangle itself.

Showing tremendous initiative and courage, another groom darted under the truck and grabbed the flailing hoof. A shard of rusty metal had snapped off, embedding itself in the animal's leg. The Iraqi yanked the shard out and then shoved the wild-kicking leg back through the hole in the floor.

Both Iraqis and Americans crowded around the injured horse, everyone now quiet. Would the horse go lame? To have to shoot an animal now, after such a valiant rescue attempt, was unthinkable. All they could do was swab the open wound with disinfectant and hope for the best.

The roundup had now lasted for almost five hours, and the soldiers decided they would be tempting fate by sticking around much longer in such a high-risk area. So much for the quick in-and-out raid they had planned! There was no doubt that word was already spreading through Abu Ghraib like a brush fire; Americans are here—and they're only a small group.

The zoo team loaded the sixteen Arabian horses as well as one other whose pedigree they weren't sure of, and Sumner said that was enough for the day. It was anyone's guess where the remainder of the informer's tally of forty-one were—and when quizzed, the grooms told Sumner and Brendan that two of the better Arabians had been snuck out while all the drama was going on and were tethered down the road at a gas station. The two men debated whether to grab these as well, but with their position becoming more and more tenuous as minutes ticked by, they decided to head back to base instead.

Glancing at his watch, Sumner shouted to the truck drivers to step on the gas. With one injured horse, two crowded cattle trucks, exhausted men, darkness setting in, and a busted Humvee, they would be tempting fate if they lingered.

A FEW DAYS PRIOR to the raid, Sumner, eager to do things by the book, had contacted the World Arabian Horse Association and asked for specifics for transporting thoroughbred Arabian horses. They e-mailed him back an eight-page instruction booklet strictly outlining all the absolute essentials.

The booklet was an eye-opener. For amid the mayhem, dust, and anarchy, Brendan, Farah, and Sumner had barely managed to comply with even the simplest of the stipulated rules.

One rule, for instance, stated each horse should have a special breakaway rope so if it fell, it would not snap its neck. Brendan said that did cross his mind as he watched the first Arabian dangling from a rope with its leg through the rotten truck floor. There also was no mention in the rulebook on how to speed things up in case terrorists lobbed a grenade or two.

Like everything else, they had been forced to fly by the seat of their pants and . . . well, just do it. The most important factor was that all the horses rescued in the mission survived; even the one with the injured leg recovered completely.

However, saving the horses wasn't the end of the saga. We sud denly had a serious fight on our hands to make sure they would be properly cared for in the future.

Although everyone agreed that the herd was a genetic gold mine and national asset, enthusiasm tended to diminish rapidly whenever the cost of their upkeep was mentioned.

Through Brendan's bullheaded persistence, the City Council eventually came to its senses, grasping these horses were not only an exquisite historical treasure but potential money spinners for the city as well. They now plan to set up a fully subsidized equestrian program in Al Zawra Park using these magnificent animals as the prime attraction. Thankfully, the future of those seventeen horses whose lineage dates back to the Holy Land wars and who were rescued in a chaotic modern-day mission in the heart of the Abu Ghraib badlands now seems secured.

But where is the rest of the herd that is still unaccounted for? Perhaps they have been sold on the black market; perhaps they are doing menial work such as dragging carts in rural areas; perhaps they are being raced at the Abu Ghraib racecourse. We don't know.

However, at least some of the gene pool of this priceless Mesopotamian bloodline has been saved.

When I returned from America I spent some time with these magnificent creatures. It was an absolute privilege and I was completely entranced. They were so regal I had the urge to stand at attention in their presence; I imagined how many times Saddam, too, had stood admiringly in front of them.

While to the casual observer a thoroughbred Arab may look like any other horse, to those in the know these animals are kings of the equestrian world; muscular, tough, and as unyielding as the desert in which they were born. There is also a particular gleam in their eyes—the windows to their wild spirit. You cannot help revering them as they effortlessly command respect.

To me the greatest thrill was knowing that against incredible odds we had found these noble creatures secreted away in an anarchic city. What began as an impossible dream had become a reality.

I also derived immense satisfaction in the fact that saving these horses was a huge victory for us, not only over vicious black-market thugs but also in doing something really worthwhile for the Iraqi people. This, after all, was their national herd a priceless asset steeped in the rich history of the region. If it had not been for us, the horses would have ended up scattered in various collectors' herds or being raced to death. Or even worse, being cruelly used as beasts of burden

Brendan, Sumner, and Farah later debriefed me on the raid and the pernicious problems they had overcome. I looked at them and said one word: "*Unesibindi.*"

Only Brendan understood, as it was a Zulu saying. Directly translated it means "you have liver."

In other words, great courage.

TWELVE

D R. ADEL pulled me aside. His voice was urgent.
"Must speak with you."
"What's the problem?"
"The people say Saddam's secret police are here. Mukhabarat."
"What?"

I scanned the throng swarming at the zoo's gates, still dangling precariously on torn hinges. There was always a large, noisy crowd in the morning clamoring for work. Sometimes a few would be hired to do odd jobs for the day, cleaning cages or helping staff find donkeys for sale. One man in particular caught my eye: an Arab with pale skin and green-blue eyes, a genetic throwback to the Crusades, when soldiers from both sides raped and ransacked at will. But he certainly didn't look like a security cop on the run.

"People say Saddam's spies are going to places where Iraqis are working with Americans and threatening them with death."

"Any of our people been threatened?"

Adel shook his head. "Not yet. We tell them we are working

with South Africans, not Americans. We say we are just interested in getting the zoo right."

"Tell the staff to let me know if anyone is threatened."

As I spoke, a volley of gunfire crackled at the far end of the street, scattering the civilians, who flattened themselves among the dusty mounds of bomb-blasted rubble still strewn carelessly around the park. This volley was followed by the deeper *thud-thud* of American M-16s returning fire.

We were standing beneath a towering bullet-chipped eucalyptus and glanced briefly over our shoulders to see if we should be worried.

Nah . . . it was just the usual Baghdad boogie. There was always the sound of gunfire and explosions, every day, and it became part of our lives, most of it in the distance outside of the Green Zone but on occasions in the streets around the side of the park that were open to the Red Zone.

However, threats to Iraqis working within the system were an escalating problem, and Brendan, Sumner, and I were getting some idea of just how gutsy the zoo team was. One of the reasons we were able to travel relatively safely around Baghdad's Red Zones without the phalanxes of bodyguards that surrounded the growing number of Western civilians was because there was always someone from the zoo to vouch for us.

It was also thanks to Adel and Husham that the staff obeyed us unquestioningly. The two directors' unswerving support of the work Brendan and I were doing to keep the zoo functioning during those dire days was made plain to the Iraqis. They knew we were on their side.

For our part, we went out of our way to make friends and ally ourselves with the staff in particular and Iraqis in general. We thus managed to remain marginally separated from the conflict, emotionally if not physically. Well, as far as one could in a simmering war zone.

However, the threat of assassination or kidnapping by militants aimed at anyone even vaguely perceived to be assisting the coalition government hung like a pall. In one case assassins broke into the home of a particularly courageous Iraqi logistics contractor who was working in the park just outside the zoo and shot her dead in front of her children.

Also, a few days before we heard these rumors about spies, a well-armed group of insurgents had sneaked past American troops in broad daylight and mounted a machine-gun attack on an amateur radio station in the park just a couple of hundred yards from the zoo, killing several people. The gunmen were apparently unhappy about the broadcast content, and this vicious shoot-out right next door scared the hell out of us. The radio staff knew Adel and regularly came over to the zoo for a chat, so we could be forgiven for getting a little paranoid when we heard that the attention had now turned to us.

Closer to home, on one occasion zoo staff were cooking lunch outside on open fires when a man walked up and without a word spit into the pot of stewing chicken. He sauntered off, leaving the animal caregivers too stunned to do or say anything.

An attack on our people was bound to happen; that we all knew. It came just days after Adel voiced fears about the Mukhabarat when a trainee animal supervisor, who for his own safety shall remain nameless, was savagely beaten and stabbed three times in the head one night at his home.

What was worse was that the knife wielders were his uncles, his mother's brothers, and we learned that it wasn't the first time he or his mom had been beaten up. Apparently the militants were trying to extract information about U.S. troop movements at the zoo and Al Zawra Park. But despite repeated assaults, the young Iraqi showed immense courage and refused to be cowed, saying he was working with South Africans. Fortunately, none of the knife wounds penetrated his skull, but it still took him three days to recover from the savage thrashing. Undeterred, he reported back for duty as soon as he could.

At times like this even the hardiest must have nursed unspoken doubts. It could seem at times as if we were fighting against quicksand, but the example of those Iraqis who remained unbowed in the face of such savagery was an inspiration.

I relayed the staff's growing trepidation about security to Sumner, who said he would do what he could to bolster a military presence at the zoo. But he didn't hold out much hope, as similar problems were mushrooming everywhere in what was now being called the Sunni Triangle—Saddam's key support zone. The triangle roughly comprised a line drawn west from Baghdad to Ramadi and north to Tikrit, Saddam's birthplace. In this concentrated area of Sunni Muslims a heavily armed fanatical few were able to terrify the many, which is terrorism's prime motivation.

But the mounting security headaches could not be allowed to cripple our work and all I could do was urge our people to be careful out there. And somehow we kept the wheel of survival grinding. If we weren't scrounging the city for donkey meat, we were plugging leaking pipes or treating a host of animal infections with our rapidly depleting supply of medicines. There were no hard-and-fast rules on how to stay alive. You just had to remain constantly alert and observe the obvious. If a situation looked dangerous, don't question why—just get the hell out of the place.

Maybe it's stating the obvious, but it still needs to be said: The heroism and commitment of the Iraqis at the time, led by Adel and Husham, was one of the most outstanding fundamental aspects of the fight for Baghdad's Zoo. They put their lives on the line daily just venturing out to work.

When I mentioned the threats to the South African bodyguards, their response was instant. They would keep coming to the zoo whenever they could, and they repeated their offer to bump off a few troublemakers as "a lesson." I again refused, and they shrugged.

"Your funeral, *boet*," said Jeremy.

TO COMPOUND THE VOLATILE SCENARIO, another ominous trend was gathering momentum. Suicide bombers, who had always been on the periphery, now seemed to be radically on the increase, and I was worried this terrible publicity would scare other conservation agencies off from coming forward with aid.

At least, that was my suspicion. For the past two months the only two foreigners continuously at the coal face had been Brendan and myself. We had received some welcome aid from Stephan Bognar and Barbara Maas. Stephan had stayed for about a month, Barbara for a week, although she was scheduled to return. But for the most part, it was just Brendan and I working directly with the Iraqis and the military.

It was obvious we would have to get some serious financial and material backing soon; we couldn't go on living hand-to-mouth forever. But I had little idea who to approach.

The first chunk of financial aid we received fairly soon after I arrived was largely thanks to a group of South Africans guarding Gen. Jay Garner, the initial interim administrator for Iraq before the Coalition Provisional Authority (CPA) was formed. By all accounts General Garner enjoyed the company of his tough South African minders immensely, and when they told him about a group of mavericks keeping animals alive with little more than spit and sweat, he asked his men to arrange a visit.

He arrived one morning surrounded by the South Africans carrying enough weaponry to quell a major insurgency. Although the zoo was in the still-to-be-designated Green Zone, its northeastern boundary was wide open to the chaotic Red Zone and easy to infiltrate. The bodyguards protecting the highest-profile member of the U.S. force in Iraq at the time were taking no chances.

Garner was friendly and approachable and I could see why he was such a popular general. We walked him around the zoo explaining what we were doing, and as we went from enclosure to enclosure it was obvious that he had empathy with animals. At that stage Stephan and Barbara were still there and we had only just started sourcing regular food for the animals. Garner was visibly shocked at the debilitated state most of them were in. He also went out of his way to talk to Adel, Husham, and as many of the Iraqi staff as possible.

But most important, he was genuinely interested in the project and how we were doing it on less than a shoestring, grasping instinctively that this was a vital community asset. Finally, we did a quick video shoot where he thanked us all, and out of the blue he told me twenty thousand dollars for the zoo was on its way.

Just before they drove off, one of the guards whispered that Garner had remarked the zoo was "the only goddamn place that worked" in Baghdad. Huge praise indeed, coming from the man in charge. I passed this on to Adel and the staff and there were smiles all round. It was a welcome boost to morale.

The cash, though helpful, was instantly swallowed up in a quicksand of expenses such as animal food, staff wages, and repairing basic infrastructure. The speed at which the money vanished hammered home just how much money we needed to get the zoo beyond its current critical level. If twenty thousand dollars evaporated so quickly, we would need hundreds of thousands to keep the momentum going. Where would it come from?

Without an answer, I decided not to dwell on that. The seeming hopelessness of the big picture could drive you crazy.

So the struggle for survival continued, hour by hour, day by day. From keeping water flowing with spluttering pumps to lugging buckets of detergent and scrounging for food, the daily routine was relentless.

However, fate plays quirky tricks and the major breakthrough for us didn't come from some high-powered CNN report or tub-thumping politician but from a story published thousands of miles away in a regional South African newspaper, the *Zululand Observer*. The twice-weekly community paper was much respected in its circulation area and had run a feature on me as a local boy in a foreign war zone. The fact that the managing director and editor in chief was my mother, Regina Anthony, just might have helped as well.

Sarah Scarth, the International Fund for Animal Welfare (IFAW) director of emergency relief in Cape Town, picked up the story on the *Zululand Observer*'s Web site and phoned Regina—or Reg, as she is known by her friends. IFAW does not turn a blind eye to emergencies, and Sarah wanted confirmation of what she intuitively knew: that this was something they should be doing something about.

My mom was in regular contact with me via satellite telephone and told Sarah that Brendan and I were the only foreigners at the beleaguered zoo. We seriously needed help, the type of help the IFAW specialized in.

That was all the info Sarah required before she swung an international Emergency Relief (ER) team into action. A few weeks later the first convoy of trucks rolled into Baghdad carrying three tons of food; essential medical supplies such as drip feed kits, suture kits, drugs, and antibiotics; building equipment such as angle grinders, welding machines, and electrical and plumbing parts; and gallons of detergent and pesticides.

It was the wish list I had long been asking for. The cavalry had arrived.

Indeed, the mountain of equipment and food being off-loaded in front of us was something we had scarcely believed possible. From laboring with buckets and banged-up hotel carts and killing donkeys with axes to suddenly having tools and medicines and huge food supplies all hygienically packed was beyond comprehension.

IFAW's advance guard was made up of logistics experts Mariette Hopley and Amed Khan. They were joined later by Jason Thrupp, a veterinarian from New Zealand; Jackson Zee, a zoologist who manages IFAW's moon bear sanctuary near Hong Kong; and Ashraf Kunhunnu, a wildlife veterinarian from India.

With the exception of Jackson Zee, all were specifically contracted for this particular ER mission. Jackson works full-time for IFAW and has the whole of Asia as his stomping ground. His usual work focuses on saving moon bears, which in China are captured and caged in abominable conditions, as their gallbladder bile is milked for medicinal purposes.

Our main aim now was to get away from a hand-to-mouth survival situation and function as normally as possible under the abnormal circumstances. Once that was achieved, I wanted to "plug" the Baghdad Zoo into the American Zoo and Aquarium Association, who would work closely with the Iraqi administration. AZA, one of the most respected zoo organizations in the world, would be there for the long haul in an advisory capacity, guiding the Iraqi administration in developing the Baghdad Zoo according to internationally accepted standards and assisting with transforming it into a habitat rather than caged environment. Animals would eventually be kept in open enclosures with surroundings imitating their natural habitat as closely as possible. The bears, for example, would have large outside enclosures with trees and other foliage similar to that of the mountains of northern Iraq. The stress for the animals would be lowered immensely in comparison to being caged in cold concrete.

The effect of the new team in Baghdad was instant. We could dare to start believing in the future—and at long last we had antibiotics to treat our sick and injured animals holistically. It was no longer a case of ministering to life-threatening wounds and illnesses with basic antiseptics or whatever else we could scrounge.

Our newly stocked dispensary had wider-reaching implications as well. Adel and Husham had lived under stringent economic and academic sanctions for many years, and although both were highly competent vets, they had little idea of the massive strides made in international veterinary and zoological science over the past decade. Through no fault of their own, they had never visited modern zoos. Much of their reference works concerned diseases that had long been eradicated in the Western world or had no relevance to current zoo husbandry.

For the Baghdad Zoo, those dark ages were now about to end.

HOWEVER, OUR JUBILATION at IFAW's arrival was dealt a massive blow from another quarter.

It happened a few days later when soldiers arrived one morning and demanded to see Dr. Husham. I asked why, but they merely repeated that they wanted the Iraqi vet.

When Husham appeared he was immediately arrested—right in front of the dismayed staff, who could only watch in angry silence.

Before marching him off, the soldiers told me he was a member of the Ba'athist party and would be investigated accordingly. Demanding more information, I was told an edict had been issued by the coalition stating all Ba'ath Party members above a certain rank were to be interrogated and would no longer be able to hold any position in government departments. As the zoo was a civic institution, they were under orders to arrest Husham.

I retorted that if they really wanted to destroy the city and any goodwill the Americans still had, they were going about it the right way. Who did they think was going to run things? The irrefutable reality was that the majority of Iraqis with administrative experience were Ba'athists. They had to be—you didn't get a senior-level job in any state or civic department under Saddam's regime unless you were a card-carrying party member. In most instances this membership was a matter of simple expediency rather than idealism. Saddam's government was no democracy in which you had a political choice. That, I said, was almost certainly the case with Husham.

I was wasting my breath. The soldiers bundled Husham into a Humvee, and as they drove off I called out that we would soon have him released.

But inwardly I was stunned. Husham's contribution in those hellish initial weeks cannot be overstated. He was the first civilian to come to the zoo's rescue, and the lifesaving water "feed" into the cages was solely due to his creative improvisations.

Indeed, if he was a Ba'athist he showed no material gain whatsoever from being one. In fact, he used to wear the same faded shirt to work, day in and day out. It was always impeccably ironed, and no doubt his wife washed it for him when he went home, drying it overnight in the desert air.

My mission now was to get him reinstated. We at the zoo owed it to him, and the next day I started banging on the Coalition Administration's doors, pleading Husham's case.

However, things didn't look promising, particularly when Ted Morse, the interim mayor of Baghdad, bluntly told me their policy was to purge the administration of every single Ba'athist and there was zero chance of Husham ever being on any state payroll ever again.

I took the matter up with Tim Carney, the interim minister for industrial and mineral affairs. He had been the first to take an interest and support my rescue mission when I hatched my plan back at Thula Thula, and had helped get me first into Kuwait and then into Iraq. I stressed to him that Husham was one of our key people. Indeed, the man deserved a medal—not being fired.

Carney, always the diplomat, said he would see what he could do behind the scenes. I must just be patient.

While I was working my way through the bureaucracy, Brendan was like a jumpy kid on Christmas as he sorted through all our new supplies. He and Ashraf, IFAW's Indian vet, drew up scientific feeding programs for the animals. The biggest change for us was that the carnivores would now be fed vacuum-packed buffalo chunks imported from India in order to halt the number of donkey deaths. No longer did we endlessly have to scour the streets for protein, and Kazim, our axman, overnight became virtually redundant, his job outsourced, although we obviously still kept him on our payroll as a charity case.

While welcoming the fact that my men no longer had to wander around an exceedingly dangerous city trying to find donkeys, we never really understood why some of the IFAW guys insisted on hugely expensive imported frozen meat being the preferred diet. Okay, they believed donkeys shouldn't be killed—but didn't that mean Indian buffaloes were being slaughtered instead? Brendan and I also knew from bush experience that fresh meat, bone, and organs were far healthier fare for the cats than slabs of prepackaged flesh. But despite our questions about the value of buffalo rather than donkey meat, we were extremely grateful for the much-needed help and the amount of time saved by having a regular source of protein. The plain fact is that animal welfare can often seem paradoxical when the animal you're attempting to save is a voracious carnivore.

The plans for renovating cages to make the zoo more habitat orientated also generated much discussion among the team. Indeed, at times it became a touchy issue. Just fixing up the bear quarters to top international specifics would cost a fortune, and we would need a huge amount of money to uplift the entire zoo to state-of-the-art standards.

IFAW's vet Jason Thrupp openly wondered whether it was worth it. He believed no wild animal should be kept in captivity and argued passionately that it was pointless raising money for a single bear cage if we couldn't upgrade the whole complex as well. As it was unlikely we would ever obtain the necessary funds to do that, he said perhaps it would be better to destroy the zoo.

Brendan, Sumner, and I argued differently. The zoo was a reality and would continue to be so no matter what we foreigners did or said. And while a spacious, habitat-focused bear cage might not mean much to the naysayers, it mattered a whole lot to the bear.

Generally speaking, I do not support the concept of zoos. It's difficult to get away from the fact that they are animal prisons. The great majority of zoos, particularly in the Third World, are absolutely horrific. The only facilities I would support are those that are scientific institutions with habitat-oriented environments and focus on education, such as the San Diego Zoo. I was in Baghdad for the animals, not the zoo, but while I was there I would do everything I could to help improve the facilities, bring Baghdad Zoo out of isolation, and connect Dr. Adel and his staff to the international fraternity of zoos.

Fortunately, it never became a problem between Jason and us. We agreed to disagree. A true professional emergency aid worker, Jason focused on the project at hand and did a great deal of good.

IFAW's logistics controller Mariette Hopley was an absolute

gem. She tackled her job with Herculean energy, and things were always happening around her. I introduced her to the CPA's chief of staff, Pat Kennedy, and a couple of weeks later, presto!—we had a spanking-new black SUV for the zoo.

"How did you do it?" I asked.

"It's my job," she said, smiling.

For the first time since the Kuwaitis left with my car, we had reliable transport. No longer did we have to take our chances in our old street-salvaged jalopy or rely on lifts to get anywhere.

On another occasion we heard we were about to be evicted from the now-renovated Al-Rashid Hotel, where we stayed for free in the relatively safe Green Zone, to make way for the scores of contractors pouring into the country. This intrigued me, as Brendan and I were by far the longest residents at the Al-Rashid and despite all the work at the zoo we were still not even on the administrations' radar.

As unflappable as ever, Mariette went to see Kennedy. She returned a few hours later giving a triumphant thumbs-up.

"He says we can stay. We've been put on the official list."

That was a close call. Brendan and I nearly ended up camping in the zoo grounds, which was my original plan.

As interim administrator of the Baghdad Zoo, I was at this stage moderately pleased with our progress. Despite the bleak financial situation, something always seemed to crop up at the last minute. Such as when an army officer called Brian Hoyback arrived out of the blue one afternoon for a look around.

His department was responsible for financing restoration projects, and Brendan escorted him around the premises. Brian told us he had always enjoyed taking his kids to zoos back in the States, and after inspecting the lions' cages he asked Brendan if we were happy with the current situation. Brendan said, "No," and outlined what we were trying to achieve and what already had been achieved under crippling circumstances.

Hoyback was impressed. "Tell me how much you need right now to make a difference to these animals."

Brendan was caught off guard and said he couldn't quote a figure off the top of his head. We hadn't done any formal bookkeeping at the time, as everything had been so chaotic. We had been living hand-to-mouth and just spent whatever we had available and tried to scrounge more. All we did know was that it had cost us many thousands of dollars.

Brian and Brendan agreed to meet the next morning to discuss it, and Hoyback promised to get us funds.

He was as good as his word. Within a day he had cleared fifty thousand dollars with the CPA's Baghdad Central office and handed it over to us. The only condition was we gave ten thousand dollars to the Ministry of Irrigation to help fix the water systems . . . well, we could have thought of worse demands.

The money was an absolute godsend, but like General Garner's donation, it soon disappeared in the swamp of daily survival demands.

What we really needed was a shove from somewhere high up, some frictionless momentum to glide the project through the mountain of obstacles confronting us. In other words, out of the "emergency" situation where we could guarantee food on a daily basis, materials to finish building the enclosures to acceptable standards, and a budget for the staff salaries and running costs. After that, the zoo could be handed back to the Iraqis with full international sponsorship.

The bottom line was simple: money. But how could I persuade the coalition to prioritize the zoo among the barrage of other urgent demands? It was an elusive problem but one that had to be solved soon if the zoo was to prevail in a meaningful way.

One morning while chatting to Adel I asked out of simple curiosity how many people used to visit Al Zawra before the war.

"Zoo get half million people each year," said the Iraqi. "Park— one million."

I was astonished. So many! This battle-trashed tract of real estate we were sitting on had previously attracted 1.5 million people a year. That was more than a quarter of Baghdad's total population.

In a flash I had the answer. The coalition was desperately trying to get the city back to normal, and it didn't take a sage to deduce that the Al Zawra complex was one of the biggest social institutions in the city by far.

But somehow nobody had yet realized that!

We needed to do a complete about-face. To "sell" the rescue project it was crucial we focus on recreation and a return to normality—not animal welfare. The only way the zoo could get the cash injection it desperately required was for us to convince the Coalition Administration it was sitting on a golden "human" public relations opportunity. Even though to me this project was in its widest sense about the plant and animal kingdom, to get the hard sell across I had to plan things another way. Our new proposals had to fixate on what direct benefits restoring Al Zawra and the zoo would have on the people of Baghdad, not the animals of the Baghdad Zoo. In order to help the animals, we had to focus on the zoo's value for humans.

Mariette and I immediately set off for the coalition headquarters at the Al Salaam—now known as the Four-Headed—Palace to speak to Pat Kennedy. Kennedy was not in, and while waiting we bumped into the interim minister of irrigation, Eugene Stakhiv. I outlined my new proposal that we restore the park for the people, emphasizing how many Iraqis visited Al Zawra each year.

He was immediately interested: "Give me that in writing and I personally will get it to Ambassador Bremer."

So I sat down and wrote the proposal right there in the waiting room. The words flowed and I stressed that the zoo and park had been a vital cog of Baghdad's leisure life in the past. It was more than just a zoo; it was the city's only green belt, and as most Baghdad residents lived in cramped concrete quarters, it was the one place they could get out and breathe some fresh air under date palms and eucalyptus trees. They could have a picnic. Indeed, 3.5 million people each year had done just that.

I was presenting to the administration a blue-chip option for showing some signs of a return to normality and strengthening of community relations with the people of the city—if they could only see it. Rescuing the animals, the most important thing for me, was barely mentioned. But as they would be the prime beneficiaries, it didn't matter.

However, even in my most optimistic moments, I had set my sights low on this one. At best, I was expecting a replay of General Garner's visit, a minor check of perhaps twenty thousand dollars, accompanied by the usual put-down that the coalition was resurrecting a shattered infrastructure. The zoo, as we were endlessly told, was way down the priority list.

I was wrong. The powers-that-be grasped exactly what I was getting at—that Al Zawra Park and the zoo offered a gilt-edged chance to show the people of Baghdad that the Americans meant business in fixing their city. If their smashed park was rebuilt, it would be both a tangible and symbolic signal that life was gradually returning to normal. That Baghdad was starting to function again.

We found this out several days later when Sumner sped over to the zoo in his Humvee to tell us the coalition was acting on my proposal "big-time." A tentative budget of $250,000 was set for restoration work, and the military was instructed to send in its crack engineering unit, the Second Brigade's Fortieth Engineer Battalion.

We received the news in dumb shock that soon turned into "it's too good to be true" disbelief.

Then "where's the catch?"

Then exultation.

That night we celebrated hard. Well, as best we could—for celebrating in Baghdad, where party treats were nonexistent, meant sitting up late in Mariette's room, sharing a few warm beers, joking and excitedly discussing what we were going to do to improve enclosures and life for the animals at the zoo.

The highlight of the evening was when Brendan found a hookah and some awful rose-scented tobacco that rasped your throat like sandpaper. We all tried it.

WITHIN A WEEK, the gears started to shift. Wherever you went in the park you could hear welders hissing blue-hot heat, angle grinders carving through concrete ruins, and generators kicking long-dead electrical installations into life.

It was a formidable assignment. Al Zawra Park had been a key battleground in the fight for Baghdad and covered two square miles, with the zoo taking up three-quarters of a square mile in the center. The area was in ruins, littered with wrecked buildings, bombed bridges, stagnant lakes, and unexploded ordnance. Just clearing that would be a mammoth exercise.

But American ingenuity is a wonderful thing. Soon pumps were spurting water from the river Tigris into the park lakes, electricity was reconnected to the city's stuttering power grid, and the mangled buildings were rebuilt. Burnt-out military trucks and other pulverized relics of war were towed away. The hundreds of lamp posts, all of which had been unbolted and heaved over so looters could yank out the copper wire, were set straight once again.

To our intense relief, all remaining unexploded ordnance was finally cleared and detonated. It was now safe to walk in the park without sticking to the paved pathways.

However, the most impressive renovation was the sprinkler system that kept this green haven in the sweltering sands alive. Piping shredded by tank treads had been replaced, and the whole area was backlit by a rainbow as zillions of droplets scattered across the earth. Al Zawra was becoming an oasis once more.

I watched all this activity with amazement. The zoo would soon be reopened to the public, although no firm date was set. Who would have thought that possible in those early desperate days?

Normality was fast approaching and yet another crisis loomed. This time from a completely unexpected source, threatening to put an end to the zoo itself.

THIRTEEN

S ADDAM'S SON'S LIONS to be Freed in African Wilds," trumpeted the headline.

I stared at the newspaper story again to make sure I was reading it correctly. There it was in black-and-white. Uday Hussein's cats were apparently about to be moved out of Iraq and none of us at the zoo knew a thing about it.

The article continued in the same triumphant vein as the headline, stating Uday Hussein's "war-traumatized" lions were currently in a "bullet-ridded cage," but the three adults and their six cubs were now about to be freed from an "Iraqi hellhole" to a lush private reserve in South Africa.

Furthermore, in a separate operation Saedia, the blind brown bear, was to be moved to a mountain sanctuary in Greece.

Surely not Saedia! Dr Adel would never let her go, and in any event, she was far too old to move. Someone had to be putting me on.

I quickly scanned the page to find the source of the story. I recognized the name: SanWild Wildlife Sanctuary, a small animal rehabilitation facility in South Africa's Limpopo Province, and they seemed pretty confident the cats were coming to them.

Further down, backing up everything SanWild said, was our colleague Barbara Maas of Care for the Wild International—and also a former ad hoc member of the Baghdad Zoo Committee.

During the next few days the international media pounced on the story with gusto. It was good copy: Lion cubs born among ricocheting bullets and belonging to a brutal despot's psychotic son were getting their freedom. A blind bear, traumatized by war, would live out her final days in an idyllic mountain retreat. Emotive headlines such as "Free at Last," "Return to the Wild," and "War Zone Cubs" took root and flourished in newsprint.

The Arabic media initially did not run with these stories, but when a copy of one of the foreign papers finally reached the zoo the shock to the staff was massive. Although the Zoo Committee had in the past spoken of relocating some of the lions and even given tacit support, at no stage had it progressed beyond casual discussions.

I was in South Africa on a brief fund-raising trip and phoned Brendan in Baghdad to get an update. He told me Adel was incensed, particularly with the news that the bear was "included" in the relocation package, as Saedia was zoo property. He wasn't happy about the lions going, but said that was out of his hands. The big cats came from Uday's palace and technically did not belong to the zoo.

However, Adel's view was that as Uday had plundered the country's national wealth, his assets, which included the lions, should be bequeathed to the state. It was a powerful argument.

But then again, equally powerful was Barbara Maas's case: was it not better for the lions to roam free in the wild?

A bitter dispute with the Iraqis over relocating animals was the last thing we needed, coming just as the rebuilt zoo was on the cusp of being reopened.

IFAW in particular was recoiling at what they believed was going to be a huge public relations fiasco and a raging row over whether animals should be caged or released. They frantically got hold of me and called me back to Iraq.

I canceled all meetings and caught the next available flight out.

But by the time I was able to say "whoa" and ask everyone to take a deep breath, it was too late. The situation was flaring out of control. The Iraqis were adamant that Uday's lions and the bear must stay. Care for the Wild International was equally determined to relocate them.

The project was on the verge of collapse. Everything I had done, all that we had achieved under incredibly difficult circumstances, the risk and danger, the effort and discomfort of life in Baghdad, all for the sake of the animals, could now go down the drain. The whole rescue initiative was always precarious and never needed much to knock it off the rails. Now it looked like we had another mountain to climb. The difference was this time it was about relationships and the trust of Adel and the Iraqi staff.

THE IDEA TO RELOCATE Uday's pride of three adults and six cubs was, in fact, first put forward by me as soon as I realized that Xena was pregnant—just days after the Green Berets had taken us to them.

I was uncomfortably aware that the zoo had too many lions—even more than the massive San Diego Zoo—and soon there would not be enough room to accommodate them. An adult lion eats about twenty-two pounds of meat a day, and having too large a pride would severely tax our lean resources. Lions also breed like cats, because . . . well, because they are cats.

My initial idea was we find a suitable reserve in South Africa and run the relocation program as a joint Iraqi–South African venture. Dr. Adel and the Baghdad Zoo staff would be closely involved and it would be an educational as well as humanitarian project.

Adel was originally open to the idea as long as it didn't involve the zoo's animals. But the Iraqi vet was adamant that nothing should be rushed, as the issue was extremely sensitive. The zoo had already lost almost all of its inhabitants and on no account did we wish to appear to be imperialist foreigners decreeing that more must go. We were thus content to let the idea proceed at its natural pace.

All of this had been discussed at a zoo committee meeting attended by Barbara during her first visit to Baghdad. Adel had stressed to the ad hoc committee, which at the time consisted of himself, Brendan, Captain Sumner, Stephan, Farah, Barbara, and me, that it was essential there should be no publicity whatsoever; otherwise the lions would never taste freedom.

The SanWild press release was a serious miscalculation of the political dynamics involved. By being associated with it, Barbara unfortunately alienated Adel and the Iraqi authorities—and, as we later discovered, unwittingly placed Adel's life in grave danger.

Barbara arrived in the Middle East on the same day as I did and we bumped into each other at the American air force base in Kuwait, where she was persuading a marine helicopter crew to ferry her to Baghdad. She told me she had specifically flown out from London to oversee the animals' relocation and was literally bouncing with excitement.

I said little, dread mounting in my gut at what I knew was going to be an explosive confrontation with the Iraqis.

Slim and dark-haired, German-born Barbara is absolutely dedicated to her cause of relocating animals into the wild. While I normally find such dedication admirable, in this case it was blurring the current situation. Once we arrived in Baghdad she would tell anyone within earshot of her "Uday's war cubs back to Africa" project, and such was her infectious enthusiasm, she would blow complete strangers away with her passion. She also had apparently clinched a deal with a London-based newspaper to do a feature on the relocation. She said they were prepared to pay for an exclusive, which would help cover the costs of the project. Once the newspaper story appeared, she said, TV stations were scheduled to do follow-ups.

"This will be the best news story of the war," she told me, eyes glowing.

That was not quite Adel's viewpoint, and on the afternoon of my hasty return he cornered me outside his office, his normally placid face hard with anger.

"The animals belong to the Iraqi people," he kept repeating in his lyrically accented English. "What is happening?"

To test the waters, I gently put the counterargument to him. The zoo would have nineteen lions once Uday's pride was brought over. It was obvious some of the animals would eventually have to be relocated, either inside Iraq or elsewhere. Sending the extra lions back to Africa would be good for the cats and good for the zoo. He could send some of his staff with the animals to settle in, as part of the relocation program. What did he think of that?

He mused for some moments. Okay, he said. Perhaps he didn't have an intractable problem with Uday's lions going, although he believed the Baghdad Municipality would need much persuading. But the bear—he shook his head.

"She is too old; she will die in the move," he said, which was likely the truth. And what would his staff think if they saw one of the zoo's stalwarts being carted off?

Adel's body language told me that if the bear was taken away, he would have nothing more to do with us. To him it would be the ultimate betrayal. We foreigners could come and go, but Adel and his team were there for the long haul. Baghdad was their home; the zoo was their livelihood.

A rancorous internecine dispute had to be avoided at all costs, and I assured Adel he had my support. The bottom line was that the zoo was going to be handed back to the Iraqis soon and we—the international groups—were simply helping out. Whether the lions were relocated now or later wouldn't alter the big picture. But it was obvious that if they were moved out now in the current hostile climate, causing irreconcilable resentment, the entire project would collapse in acrimony.

The zoo had lost almost 90 percent of its animals in the looting spree, and the Iraqis were adamant that none of the survivors should be relocated. We had to treat this with extreme sensitivity.

An emergency meeting was scheduled for the next day so Barbara could put her case before the Zoo Committee and hopefully we could thrash the issue out amicably.

In the interim, Brendan, Sumner, Farah, and I gathered at the Al-Rashid to discuss the issue. They updated me on the news from their side, warning we could not underestimate the Iraqis' anger. What did I think?

My heart, I said, wanted the lions to go free. But my head said they must stay until the Iraqis gave the go-ahead. At that stage I believed Adel could still be persuaded if the matter was treated delicately. But my greatest fear was that Barbara would try to force the issue, particularly with the bear. The bear belonged to the zoo, and that had to be respected.

Brendan interrupted me. "Guys," he said. "Are we talking about Uday's three lions—the Special Forces lions? Brutus, Heather, and Xena?"

"Yes," I replied.

"That's crazy. Heather and Xena have been declawed. How are they going to hunt? They'll never survive in the wild. No way!"

"What! Are you sure?"

"Absolutely. Xena and Heather actually have to take their food in cupped paws," replied Brendan.

Farah also nodded. Apparently Uday Hussein had enjoyed parading his cats on a leash when they were cubs and to prevent himself being scratched he had had their claws surgically removed.

There was a stunned silence. This was a whole new ball game. In fact, as far as we were concerned, all arguments concerning Uday's three lions and their cubs being returned to the wild were now moot.

"And don't forget they're also heavily rumored to be maneaters," Brendan reminded us. "How are we going to explain that away?"

Of course!

Unfortunately, we had to break early, as Sumner, Brendan, and Farah were going to a symphony concert in the fortified conference center, the first to be held in Iraq since the invasion. Brendan is not your average classical music aficionado, but he said he was so starved for entertainment that anything would suffice. He dressed up for the highbrow cultural event in his typical fashion: khaki trousers, bush boots, and jungle green shirt with the Thula Thula elephant logo embroidered on the pocket.

The group was back in an hour, thanks to a power failure. Brendan claimed he had enjoyed the music. However, what he did not know was that Iraqi TV had filmed the show and, according to Adel, there had been a fine shot of Brendan snoring his head off.

WHATEVER THE ARGUMENTS, there was no escaping the fact that some lions did need to be relocated and it was a problem we eventually would have to face. But at the moment the situation was clear: to protect our excellent relationship with Dr. Adel and his staff in the current hostile climate we had to convince the Iraqis that no relocations whatsoever would go ahead without their approval.

All this I hoped could be cleared up at the meeting. But we were off to a bad start even before talks started when Adel cornered me to say the headline story on local TV news directly accused foreigners of wanting to remove Iraqi lions to South Africa.

I went cold. The fact that South Africa was regularly being mentioned was serious cause for concern. As Brendan and I were South Africans, the Iraqis would now almost certainly believe the two of us were involved in the deal as well.

On that disconcerting note, the meeting began. I asked each present if they supported the proposed relocation of some lions in principle. I was first to go on record as saying I did, provided Adel and the Iraqi authorities concurred, and the others around the table nodded their assent as well—except Adel, who sat tight-lipped.

Barbara was then asked to explain her position and immediately stood up, arguing her cause with fervor. Yes, she said, everything in the papers was true. Uday's lions, Brutus, Xena, and Heather and their six cubs were going to SanWild. The crates were already in Kuwait and a vet was on standby to accompany them to Africa, courtesy of the Emirates airline. There, she said, they would be kept in an enclosure where they would be fed mechanically and have no human contact. They would later be released into the wild on a game reserve, where they would fend for themselves.

Brendan interjected, asking if Barbara knew Xena and Heather had been declawed. How were they going to survive in the bush if they could not hunt? A lioness was a pride's key provider and needed razor claws to grab and pull down her prey; otherwise she and her dependents would starve.

Barbara replied that the cubs would grow up and hunt for their parents.

The meeting went silent. Anyone with any understanding of the African bush knows there is no such thing as a free lunch. If you can't feed yourself or chase others off a kill, you die. To release lionesses with no claws into the wilderness meant a cruel death sentence. Death by starvation: simple as that.

The South African authorities were also unlikely to grant permits for imported, declawed lionesses to be kept in domesticated enclosures, particularly after recent "canned lion" hunting scandals, in which retired circus animals were shot by despicable trophy hunters, had caused a huge outcry.

Then there was the question of Uday's lions having tasted human flesh. The rumors that Saddam's son had fed his opponents to the animals were simply too prevalent to ignore. Even if there was no tangible proof, could we still take the risk? If someone was killed and eaten, how could we as a committee ever justify our decision to relocate a pride of suspected man-eaters?

Although Barbara said the lions would have no human contact, in Africa rural people do not necessarily respect fences. Declawed lions would probably have no alternative but to go for easy prey—like humans.

While the desire to give Uday's lions their freedom was undeniably noble, the reality was somewhat different. It was plainly impossible, not to mention inhumane, to successfully release the pride as a unit. The animals would instead have to be kept in an enclosure and fed for the rest of their lives, no different from what we were currently doing.

Barbara went on the offensive, saying it was too late to backtrack. Everything was now arranged and SanWild was ready to take the animals. She added that she had gone to a lot of trouble to find them decent homes, far better than they would have in Iraq.

Finally, she pointed out what we already knew: that there were too many lions in the zoo and if some were not relocated, how would the others survive?

We then moved on to the bear. Barbara "confirmed" the old blind bear, Saedia, was going to a bear sanctuary in Greece where she would have her cataracts surgically removed and her sight restored. She would live out her remaining days in freedom.

Even Jason Thrupp, the IFAW vet who usually had little love for zoos, was particularly reluctant to relocate Saedia into the wild. For a start, she was thirty years old and had lived in captivity for almost her entire life. An average brown bear's life span is thirty-five years, which meant she was nearing her end days. There were other younger bears in cages, such as Wounded Ass, who was only three. Shouldn't the thousands of dollars be spent on something a little more . . . well, long-term?

Those with little knowledge of the natural world think of a bear retiring as a human would: in well-deserved comfort after a lifetime of toil. In reality, Saedia was so old and so traumatized from the war she probably wouldn't survive the sedation or journey. She also would possibly be frightened out of her wits if she was set free at her advanced age. Her security blanket, heartbreaking as it was to admit, was the zoo and her handlers. Freedom was just a word.

I held up both hands. "We're forgetting something very important here. Dr. Adel opposes the relocation, and if the Iraqi authorities don't buy into this, it is not going ahead. These are, after all, their animals."

I turned to Adel. "Please explain your position."

Using Farah as his interpreter, Adel said he was vehemently

against any of the animals being removed. They belonged to the Iraqi people and could not leave without Iraqi permission.

Barbara interrupted, pointing out that Adel had initially agreed to the relocation and on the strength of that she had incurred costs and invested a lot of her own and other people's time and money in the project. And now, at the last minute, he was changing his mind.

Adel conceded Barbara had raised the matter some while back, but as far as he was concerned that had simply been talk and nothing had been finalized. Then suddenly through the press he discovered the animals were being taken from his country.

Barbara shook her head, exasperation creeping into her voice. She repeated that in her view the committee had agreed to the idea. She had gone forward on that basis.

Adel turned in his chair and faced Barbara directly. He spoke quickly and angrily in Arabic, and Farah had to translate at speed.

"Do you remember when you were last here and I said these are very bad times for us Iraqis? I said we had to be careful and any talk of moving animals was too soon, as people would start asking me questions I did not want to answer. Everybody then promised to keep all of this private, to protect us Iraqis while we talked. But you continued on your own and also went to the newspapers. Because of that you have put all of us Iraqis who work with foreigners at the zoo in a very dangerous position. Now gunmen know we work with foreigners. Now we are not safe. Our families are not safe."

I tensed. We were getting to the crux of the issue.

"I did not do any press release," Barbara replied. "It was done by SanWild. I knew nothing about it."

"Nevertheless, the damage has been done," said Adel.

Barbara turned to me. The Americans, she said, were the controlling authority and they certainly had no objection to relocating the animals, no matter what the Zoo Committee said or did.

I looked at Sumner. "We need to get hold of Ted Morse immediately and find out the coalition's standpoint."

Within a few minutes, Morse, the acting mayor of Baghdad, was on the line.

"I thought the animals had already gone," he said. "What's the delay?"

That was news to everyone.

Adel's face went black as a thundercloud. He muttered, "This is not an American decision," and stormed out of the room, beckoning me to follow.

"You understand some of our people are already saying I have sold the lions for my own pocket," he said once we were outside, his brow creased with worry. "They say the animals are going to South Africa—your home and Brendan's home. They say I am taking money to let the lions go. This is very bad for me."

IT WAS NOW BECOMING CLEARER. This dispute wasn't solely about animals, and to grasp the underlying currents one had to delve into the mind of an Iraqi. Not just any Iraqi, but an Iraqi living in Baghdad, a war-torn, rumor-filled city that had long been traumatized by paranoia and fear beyond comprehension by the Western mind.

One has to remember that for three decades Baghdad had been under the tyrannical heel of Saddam's Gestapo-style secret police, the Mukhabarat. Their influence spread everywhere. Informers lived on every street, and their word could be a death sentence.

Nobody escaped this iron fist of terror; they experienced it either directly or through the treatment of their family and friends. No one was unaffected. It was that sinister, that pervasive. Although ousting Saddam Hussein was a powerful relief, the corrosive psychological aftermath of his brutality was too entrenched to be lifted instantly.

As Iraqis regularly pointed out, during the 1991 Desert Storm invasion Saddam had been resoundingly defeated but somehow still held on to power. Thus the people of Baghdad understandably were taking no chances this time around. They were living in a dreadful limbo, not sure whether the Americans had removed Saddam for good or the murderous Mukhabarat was still flourishing underground, watching and waiting.

The rules of survival were simple: keep your head down, your mouth shut, and don't openly cooperate with the coalition forces. Above all, don't attract unwanted attention, especially press attention. You never know what deadly menace will come for you out of the shadows.

Adel was in an extremely tenuous position, as he was openly working with foreigners, even though it was generally known we were neutral South Africans. He also was a Shia Muslim, whereas the Ba'athist underground insurgents were predominantly Sunni, two groups that have often been at odds with each other.

He was genuinely terrified when hordes of Iraqi press and TV reporters arrived banging on the zoo's doors and demanding to know if it was true Uday's lions were going. And if so, under whose authority was this happening: American or Iraqi?

These were loaded questions. They put not only Adel but his entire family at risk. If he conceded that relocating Uday's lions was under consideration, it unequivocally meant he was working with the coalition. To admit collaboration in those hostile times was life threatening.

But if he said no, they would ask why one of his own committee members, Barbara Maas, was contradicting him.

So he grasped the only lifeline he could. He flatly denied knowing anything. As far as he was concerned, no lions were going anywhere.

The fact that the lions had once belonged to the Hussein family had massive iconic implications as well. The issue had gone far beyond moving a handful of animals; it was now about human lives.

THAT NIGHT we gathered at IFAW logistics controller Mariette Hopley's room in the hotel and sent someone down for ice-cold (we never lost our optimism) drinks and a pile of chicken and French fries.

Mariette's room was a magnet for any gathering, as it was the tidiest and she was a fine hostess. But even she was downcast that evening. The Barbara Maas–Dr. Adel feud put a pall on everything.

Until now, the team had worked together under often-difficult circumstances with one final goal; to get the zoo operational. There had been no time for sideshows.

On the one hand, what worried Mariette was that rescuing zoos was not something IFAW usually did, and she was concerned about potential adverse publicity. IFAW focused on freeing or caring for animals in their natural habitat, and this was one of the few times they had been involved in zoo rehabilitation. Mariette feared that a messy public spat over freeing animals, which IFAW stood for, would jeopardize their standing in the conservation world.

Sumner, on the other hand, succinctly summed up the dilemma from our perspective: If we estranged the Iraqis we might as well shut down the entire project. The zoo was soon to come under the authority of a new Iraqi-controlled Baghdad City Council. If we did backdoor deals before that, the damage would be irreversible. The real losers would be the animals.

I then gave the others the background on Adel's situation. He and his staff had been at pains to make it known on the street that the foreigners they were working with were neutral South Africans.

And where were the lions going?

South Africa.

This had potentially devastating consequences and unless handled carefully would raise intractable suspicions about our involvement. It could destroy our credibility with the Iraqi staff or, worse, the staff's credibility with the community at large.

There was no doubt Adel was in potentially serious danger. As he had mentioned at the meeting, not only had he been exposed through the press as someone working closely with foreigners, but he also had been erroneously fingered as being behind the removal of the Hussein family's lions. And perhaps even profiting from it.

If Saddam's underground supporters wanted a symbolic public execution, Adel was a prime candidate. We urgently had to promote

Adel's side of the story. Somehow we had to get the word out that he was implacably opposed to the relocation and not some foreigners' stooge.

There was no time to waste. Sumner and I composed a statement from the Baghdad Zoo Committee declaring we were totally against any animals being moved without Iraqi consent. This was released to the press.

We also instructed the media that in the future all press inquiries must be referred exclusively to Dr. Adel, which would clearly prove that the Iraqis, not foreigners, were in control.

Or so we hoped.

In the middle of this internecine strife Stephan Bognar arrived back. I had spoken to him earlier in San Francisco and suggested that as he and Barbara were in touch about the lions, his presence at the zoo might help smooth things over.

"Get me an official letter, signed by you as administrator of the zoo, requesting my return, and I will do what I can," he said.

Brendan and I brought him up to speed and I told him about my recent visit to Baghdad's soon-to-be-installed deputy mayor, Dr. Faris Abdul Razaq al-Assam, with Dr. Adel to discuss the relocation issue.

Faris was adamant; the lions must stay. "We have a suitable location and when the city settles down we want to build a drive-in lion park like they have in other countries. It will be a great attraction."

"Dr. al-Assam," I said in a last attempt to change his mind, "lions are not indigenous to Iraq; it's much too hot for them here. Let's rather stock the zoo with indigenous Iraqi animals and at least let the lions with claws go. We can do a joint program with you."

"Ah, but that's where you are wrong," he replied confidently. "My grandfather was named after a magnificent lion seen on the outskirts of Baghdad the day he was born. There have been lions in Iraq for thousands of years."

His statement took the wind out of my sails. That was that; the conversation was closed.

But Stephan gamely believed he might have more success. "Let me go back to him and at least try," he said.

The next day Stephan came back dejected. "They will not release them; they're not interested. I'll have to go and tell Barbara," he said.

As far as the Baghdad Municipality was concerned, the issue was no longer negotiable.

FOURTEEN

I F WE THOUGHT the zoo's uncompromising announcement that
the lions would not be relocated was the end of the matter, we
were seriously mistaken.

The release had barely gone live before reporters from a TV network in Lebanon arrived and started questioning our staff members. The first to have a microphone stuck in front of him was
ex–Republican Guard Jafaar Deheb, who worked with the lions.
What did he think of the animals being removed?

They weren't going, he said.

That wasn't their information, said the TV interviewer. They
had spoken to a German woman at the zoo who said not only were
Uday's lions and Saedia going, but they would soon be followed by
a cheetah, a wolf, and a jungle cat.

What?

Jafaar called over his colleague Ahmed, who was in charge of
feeding the zoo's animals.

"It's true," said the TV interviewer.

The two men told other zoo workers and within minutes a posse stormed into Adel's office.

"Why is Lebanon TV saying all our animals are going to be taken away?"

Adel explained that certainly was not the case, but he could see they didn't believe him. "It's on TV," they said.

He hurriedly summoned me and Sumner and we listened to the story with increasing consternation. Sumner said we had to clear this whole mess up once and for all. He was going to call a meeting where Barbara herself could explain what was going on and why she thought the animals should go and the staff could question her directly.

After that Adel would tell the staff categorically that no animals were going and they never would without the consent of the Iraqis. The animals belonged to them, not the foreigners.

We got a message to Barbara at the hotel, and to her credit she agreed to attend what could be a lively meeting. Unfortunately, earlier that morning she had claimed Jafaar had made "a throat-slitting gesture" while sitting next to her in Ali's taxi. Brendan, who was also in the car, said that Jafaar was actually in a good mood, even wearing his new CWIT-shirt, which Barbara had given him, and was laughing and playing the fool.

But Barbara had no doubts. Back at the hotel she told a group of soldiers an Iraqi zoo worker had threatened to cut her throat, and that's not something an American GI takes lightly. In no time an armed guard had been formed to escort her to the zoo.

When Brendan and I arrived at the hotel to collect her, she said she wasn't going with us; she was going with the soldiers. They were her bodyguards, her life had been threatened, and they were going to "sort things out" at the zoo.

We stared at her, stunned, but sure enough, standing behind Barbara was a contingent of fully armed soldiers, ready to leave.

This had disaster flashing in neon lights all over it.

"Barbara," I said, "this is all completely unnecessary. There is no threat to anyone. William Sumner is a U.S. Army captain. He is there and he is in charge of security."

I knew full well that in the volatile Baghdad climate American combat troops arriving at the zoo with Barbara could spark an extremely inflammable situation. The soldiers were angry, believing that a woman had been threatened, and there was no doubt they were keen to teach Jafaar a lesson. Zoo staff would possibly now also believe we foreigners were plotting against them, even calling in soldiers. This could destroy everything.

Brendan and I decided our best bet was to get to the zoo first and cancel the meeting. Ali was outside and we sprinted toward his taxi, shouting at him to step on the gas.

To my dismay I saw the entire zoo workforce had assembled by the office, ready for the meeting. They wanted some straight answers. We rushed out of the taxi and ran over to Sumner, shouting that armed soldiers escorting Barbara were on their way.

"You must be joking," he said. "When will they be here?"

As he spoke, two SUVs loaded with troops arrived at the gate.

"Shit!" cursed Sumner. "Break up the meeting, quick. Get the staff out of here! Now, now!"

Brendan and I turned to the staff. "Get back! Get back!" we yelled, trying to disperse the workers. They looked at us bemused, not understanding what was happening or what we were saying.

"Go back to work," I yelled. "We'll call you later."

The SUVs skidded to a halt and the soldiers leaped out, rifles at the ready. Barbara jumped out after them and stayed in the background. The staff started milling around, confused. As the soldiers came toward them, they fled.

Adel ran up. "Why have you got your guns out? Have you come to kill my people?" he shouted.

At that moment Sumner reached the soldiers. "What's going on here?"

Seeing an officer, the soldiers stopped. Sumner informed them he was in charge of security and there was no need for their presence at the zoo. He ordered them to leave immediately.

The tension eased and the soldiers decided to go, happy to know everything was under control. Barbara went back to the hotel with them.

No further meaningful dialogue between Dr. Adel and Barbara was possible. The next morning the agitated Iraqi vet met with Baghdad's soon-to-be-installed deputy mayor, Faris al-Assam, who drafted a letter from the town council banning Barbara from the zoo and had it delivered to her at the Al-Rashid Hotel.

THE NEXT DAY Ted Morse unexpectedly pitched up at the zoo. Barbara had been in his office with a final plea for the animals' release, and although he initially had sanctioned the move, he now wanted more clarification.

He first met privately with Adel before asking Sumner and me to join them. After listening to all sides of the story, Morse finally made his decision. Uday's lions and Saedia, the bear, belonged to the Iraqi people and would not be moved without the formal approval of the Baghdad Municipality. In the future no zoo animal would be relocated anywhere without the municipality's expressed consent.

The matter was closed.

Seeing that Morse was in a reasonably good mood, I again brought up the issue of Husham getting his job back. Morse's smile dropped like a guillotine and he abruptly shook his head. That matter was closed as well, he said.

But I wasn't going to give up on a man I considered a conservation hero and once more phoned Tim Carney, arguing the case for the brave Iraqi vet.

It was a tough call, but Carney suggested I refer the matter to the Baghdad's deputy-mayor-in-waiting, Faris al-Assam. Carney figured the Iraqis themselves would know Husham wasn't some sinister Saddam supporter; he had been required to be a Ba'ath

Party member in order to keep his position, like hundreds of thousands of other Iraqis.

The end result was a compromise. A few days later Husham was reinstated as a vet but lost his position as deputy director, which kept both the Americans and us at the zoo happy.

He arrived at work the next morning and we embraced. It was good to have him back.

Unfortunately, it did not end there. Six months later, in January 2004, he was dismissed again in a new round of "de-Ba'athification," and it now seems permanent. Most regrettably, he has not been seen or heard of since. But whatever happened, no one can take away from him the fact that he risked his life to help the starving, thirst-crazed animals of Baghdad Zoo. The zoo will always be indebted to him.

Husham, I'm afraid, was a victim of the times. De-Ba'thification may have got rid of some bad eggs, but it also barred a lot of talented professionals from working for the new Iraq. The fact that many had to join Saddam's Ba'ath Party to survive is well documented, and sadly, many innocent people may have had to pay a price for that.

I COULD NOT HELP SMILING. There, at the entrance to the zoo, the staff was walking in a circle, solemn faced and holding hand-scrawled placards: "Iraqi lions for the Iraqi people."

Some of the banners were in English; others, in Arabic. The protesters, about thirty in all, waved as we drove in while soldiers at the gates monitored the gathering with vague interest, just in case it got out of hand. This was nothing unusual for them; they came from a democracy. But in Iraq, a protest that wasn't cynically stage-managed by the former regime for the benefit of international cameras was a heady new experience. In fact, this was probably the first authentic citizens' protest in the new Iraq, and Uday's lions had unwittingly heralded a new era of freedom. The thought filled me with pride.

The saga was now over; the animals were staying and Barbara had left Iraq. It was unfortunate she and the Iraqis parted on a sour note. She had the guts to come in alone during the highly volatile initial stages, and she provided the dart gun that had been vital to our rescue missions. For that alone she has our enduring gratitude.

There is no doubt Barbara is a committed, courageous conservationist and her heart is in the right place. One of the only regrets of my time in Iraq is that she and the Iraqis clashed so bitterly at the end. When one distills it to its essence, the sole cause of the dispute between her and the Iraqis was the timing of the proposed relocation, not the theme. Like everyone else, Barbara genuinely wanted a better life for the animals she had chosen for relocation. It was her overriding concern.

To her, the politics and dynamics of the situation were secondary.

FIFTEEN

J ULY 4, America's Independence Day, was fast approaching and the rumor on the streets was that Saddam's loyalists were going to stage some spectacular retaliatory hits against the Americans. Civilians affiliated with the Coalition Administration were warned against venturing out of the heavily guarded Green Zone on America's most celebrated day, and military patrols throughout the country were massively stepped up.

At the zoo we were usually blasé about such rumors, as they whizzed around all the time, but I thought if the insurgency was planning something big, Independence Day would be when it happened. Even Ali, who had planned to take Mariette Hopley and Jackson Zee to the meat market that day, decided we should all stay in.

However, the Americans weren't letting anything get in their way. This was the biggest holiday of the year. Even if they were in a war zone, they were going to have one hell of a party.

On the day itself, anyone not on duty in the Green Zone was invited to Saddam's Four-Headed Palace. Free beer was on tap around the swimming pool, and the luxury of quaffing a cool(ish) brew on a hot desert night and cavorting in the ex-dictator's swimming pool on Independence Day was not lost on the crowd.

The pool was almost Olympic size, with a twenty-foot-high diving board and a fountain in the middle. As beer stock sank, more and more revelers found the courage to plunge from the high board with wildly varying levels of acrobatic competence. The number of soldiers nursing red bellies and backs from ill-advised somersaults or other fancy aerial maneuvers, not to mention sore heads from the beer, must have been astronomical the next morning.

The Four-Headed Palace itself was typical of Saddam's gargantuan ego culture. It was officially called the Al Salam Palace, but due to the fact that it had forty-foot bronze busts of Saddam's profile on each of the rectangular corners everyone called it the Four-Headed Palace.

The building had been specifically earmarked as a future administration complex before the war and thus was spared most of the bombing. Sections of the right wing, however, had been damaged. When the Americans found a miniature architectural model of it, they put it in the entrance hall and broke off pieces corresponding to the real-life bombed sections to make it easier for newcomers to navigate their way around the labyrinth.

Saddam's palaces are bigger and grander than any castle you will find in Europe, and all have enough kitsch and decadent opulence to overwhelm the senses, particularly when you see the squalor millions of Iraqis live in.

But perhaps the most telling feature was the huge palace mosque. Pride of place among the devotional paintings lining the walls of this place of prayer was a gaudy twenty-foot mural showing Scud missiles pointing toward heaven, giving serious thrust to the phrase "praise the Lord and pass the ammunition."

The scene of utter humiliation for the Führer of the Arab world couldn't have been be more complete on that Fourth of July 2003, with enemy soldiers whooping it up, downing beers in his private swimming pool and running irreverently around his gardens.

Despite the talk of threats, there were no serious incidents on Independence Day. The same thing had happened on April 29, Saddam's sixty-sixth birthday. It was whispered on the streets that the day would be "celebrated" by fierce attacks on coalition troops and poison gas releases to "thank" the people of Baghdad for supporting the Americans. Saddam's birthday was usually one of forced gaiety and compulsory street adulation for most people, but on this occasion it was marked by an eerie tranquillity. Some later said the "calm" had been Saddam's gift to the people of Iraq.

The more prosaic view was that he was scared out of his wits.

WITH ONLY DAYS TO GO to the official handover of the zoo to the Iraqi nation, we held our breath as we watched military engineers toiling flat out to get everything shipshape. I looked out over the refurbished buildings, and I couldn't recognise the place as the same hellhole I had walked into all those months ago. Everything was green, lawns were neatly trimmed, the paths were clean, and the lakes that meandered through enclosures were fresh and I could see fish swimming in the clear water. Enclosures were repaired and repainted. Little vending outlets were sprouting up and selling sweets and sodas. A restaurant had opened on the island in the lake where I had entertained mercenaries with barbecues in the anarchic early days, begging them for protection. I remembered how firefights had raged in the city and flares exploded overhead as we spoke.

I walked over to the tigers; both were robust with health, and I recalled how we had battled to keep them alive. The lions had a huge outside area and spent most of the day lazing in the sun or lying under the cool netting we had provided. Lumpy the camel's once-mangy coat was growing back, now thick as a carpet. The "suicide" ostriches had an expansive area to run in. The bears were glowing with well-being. The cheetahs, their dapples making them almost invisible in the shade, were sleeping contentedly.

I marveled at our growing animal population. When I first arrived there were only thirty or so survivors—those with sharp claws or wicked teeth to defend themselves. Now apart from the lions and tigers we had desert foxes, jackals, badgers, a camel, a wolf, a lynx, rhesus monkeys, wild pigs, boars, gazelles, a pelican, a swan, ducks, an Egyptian vulture, porcupines, hyenas, ostriches, eagles, cheetahs, the original zoo bears, Saedi and Saedia, and our Luna Park dogs—which I still found strange to see in a zoo. Also there, of course, were Uday's lions and the Last Man Standing and Wounded Ass bears.

As head of the new SPCA—now named Iraqi Society for Animal Welfare—Farah had already started getting dogs out of Iraq. She eventually got over a hundred street dogs out to homes in America. An absolutely astonishing achievement given the logistics and difficult circumstances she was working under. Farah had helped simply for the love of the animals and had made a vital contribution to the rescue.

All the cages were clean and most of them now had extended outside enclosures with shade cloth roofs to cut the harsh desert sun. The animals had settled nicely into their new surroundings; they were all well fed and healthy, and hygiene standards were high.

Morale among staff was also high. They were now on the city payroll and earning much-increased salaries thanks to new minimum wages laid down by the Americans. Dr. Adel had books on modern zookeeping and animal husbandry courtesy of Barbara Maas, as well as a new computer, and we were trying to get him an Internet connection. Plans were afoot with David Jones of the American Zoo and Aquarium Association to take Dr. Adel and his key staff to the London Zoo for an educational tour, and they were leaving shortly to visit a more modern zoo in Jordan to see how other countries built and ran zoos.

But even so, the refurbished Baghdad Zoo was still far from perfect. The improvements, while a great leap forward, were in essence only better relative to when I arrived, and a lot of work still needed to be done to lift it to acceptable international standards. I had found out earlier that it was modeled on the Cairo Zoo, which was in turn based on the London Zoo of the nineteenth century. The evolution to spacious habitat-oriented wildlife enclosures that had taken place all over the First World had not reached Baghdad. This was to be a long-term project, something that would have to be addressed by the Baghdad Municipality, and I briefed them extensively on the subject. Whether anything would happen I didn't know, especially with the ongoing war, but we intended to keep in touch.

Brendan came up and snapped me out of my reverie: "It's strange to say, but the war was the best thing that could have happened to this zoo."

I looked at him, puzzled.

"Think about it," he continued. "It's better now than it was before the war, Adel and his staff are going to be connected to other zoos, they are better paid, and for the first time ever they have access to modern animal husbandry and veterinary techniques and outside universities. Things can only get better from here."

He was right.

BAGHDAD'S COLORFUL CITY MARKET, situated across the Tigris River in the Shwaka district, was back in full swing. Farmers were once again bringing in meat, vegetables, and other necessities to feed a hungry city, and the exotic bazaars bustled with thousands of buyers haggling noisily with merchants over prices and quality.

For some time now we had been making regular buying trips, traveling to the market with fistfuls of dinars to obtain necessities for the zoo. From a security point of view the market was a gray area for Westerners, so Ali would always be there, acting as a bodyguard, guide, and chaperone, explaining away the presence of his Anglo-Saxon friends to anyone who became too interested. On more than one occasion he would warn us off the trip saying, "Today market bad, no good for you." And we would always heed his advice, thankful for his inside knowledge.

IFAW's Mariette Hopley and Jackson Zee were on just such a

shopping excursion with Ali one morning when, standing in the entrance of a crowded meat stall, Mariette heard what sounded strangely like huge hailstones striking a tin roof. She turned around and was surprised to see holes suddenly appearing along the side of a refrigerated truck parked in front of them. She froze and then her military experience kicked in, and realizing what was happening, she grabbed Jackson and turned, and the two of them frantically dived into the meat freezer in front of them for shelter.

They lay there horrified as the shooting went on, interspersed with the screaming of terrified shoppers prostrating themselves on the walkways. Suddenly Mariette and Jackson's butcher walked to the entrance of the stall with an AK-47 in his hands and, firing on full automatic, emptied his magazine in the direction of the shooters. Other stall owners rushed out also carrying AKs, shooting randomly. Then silence. It was over.

"Ali Baba," said the butcher, turning to Mariette and spitting on the floor.

Ali, who had taken refuge in the next stall, came rushing in as soon as the shooting stopped, greatly relieved to see everyone was okay. "Ali Baba steal money, better we go," he said anxiously. As they left, Mariette grabbed a fistful of AK-47 shells as souvenirs.

Back at the zoo, Mariette and Jackson energetically recounted the story with Ali standing by nodding. "I must phone Sarah Scarth at the head office and tell her all about it," said Mariette, her adrenalin still pumping. "She won't believe it."

"Mariette," I said, "do you still want to stay in Baghdad after this?"

"Are you joking? Of course I do," she replied. "I am definitely not going anywhere."

I told her to think carefully about what she was going to say in that call. Though she has military experience and views things like this differently, I knew it would seem much worse to a civilian on the other side of the world. I was sure that when Sarah heard what happened she would want to bring the IFAW team home.

Unfortunately, that is exactly what happened. Mariette phoned and, despite her tact, Sarah, already worried silly about all the bad news coming out of Baghdad, saw the shooting incident as the last straw. Despite my pleas on Mariette's behalf, the IFAW team was immediately pulled out for good. Mariette, who was crestfallen at the decision, made arrangements with Farah to handle the funds they were leaving behind for the zoo, and they solemnly packed up and left. Their commitment and courage had been exemplary, and I will always be grateful for their help.

EVENTUALLY THE MOMENT ARRIVED and on July 19, 2003, the repaired and renovated Al Zawra Park and Baghdad Zoo were officially reopened by Ted Morse, accompanied by a U.S. Army general, Dr. al-Assam, and a retinue of senior American and Iraqi officials surrounded by soldiers and bodyguards.

Only a few dozen Baghdad residents were there, but we expected that. In a city that was still lawless, a stroll in the park was difficult to contemplate. But that was the significance of it all. If they wished, the people of Baghdad were now able to take a stroll in the park. All of those who came said they liked what they saw.

For the authorities, both the coalition and the Iraqis running the City Hall, it was the symbolism that counted, not the lack of crowds. This was the first tentative step toward normality. As Ted Morse said in his official speech, "The park's reopening is symbolic of the new freedom in Iraq. The zoo is a place for the community to go and reflect on the meaning of life."

In battle-scarred Baghdad, that was no small request. That was what we at the zoo had been fighting for.

Dr. Adel spoke for the zoo, thanking everyone responsible for winning the battle for the animals' lives. The biggest miracle of all, he said, was that there was anything to hand over after the carnage of war.

But perhaps the most poignant observation came from Emad

Abbas and his young son Ali, who were among the first visitors. Abbas, a former Iraqi soldier, said his son had specifically wanted to see wild animals.

"We haven't been able to enter this park for many months, but now it looks good. Saddam deprived us of so much," he told a Reuters News Agency reporter.

The Reuters reporter then asked young Ali whether he was more scared of the lions or Saddam Hussein.

"The lions," the little boy said. "Saddam's gone now."

SIXTEEN

BOUT SIX WEEKS LATER, it was time for me to leave Iraq. It was time to go home—back to Africa.

The zoo was now under the control of the Iraqis and I was confident they would do a good job. Brendan would stay on for as long as necessary to help with the day-to-day running and provide practical know-how where needed. He would also accompany Dr. Adel and key staff on trips to other zoos, to show the Iraqis how modern menageries were run.

The good-byes were both emotional and dignified. Every zoo worker came to shake my hand; we had been through a lot together. Sumner was also there. We clasped each other's hands hard and promised to keep in contact.

I looked around to see if Husham had magically appeared. I really wanted to say good-bye to the brave Iraqi who had been with me from the start, but no one had seen or heard of him for weeks.

Brendan drove me to the Four-Headed Palace, where I would catch a convoy-escorted bus to run the gauntlet to Baghdad Airport.

"It's been fun . . . well, most of the time," he said, punching me lightly on the shoulder.

I laughed. "Sure has."

IT WAS LATE AFTERNOON when I arrived back at Thula Thula. The lush African wilderness was like a balm after the harsh desert landscapes that had been my home for the past six months.

That evening my elephants came up to the house to visit, as they always do when I return from a trip. I went out to greet them. They were in beautiful condition, their gray coats pulsing with health.

The babies were growing fast and Nana and Frankie pushed them forward to show them off.

"I've missed you, my girls."

Françoise called me. She said Brendan was on the phone from Baghdad.

I rushed back inside.

"They've killed the tiger. Malooh is dead," Brendan said, his voice echoing in the receiver.

"What?"

"Yeah. Some American soldiers got drunk at the zoo and a couple wandered around the cages. Then one brain-dead moron struck his hand in the tiger's cage, obviously freaking it out. So Malooh bit the guy's finger off and mauled his arm. His friend pulled out a nine-millimeter and shot the tiger. Malooh slowly bled to death overnight without us even knowing. We only found out in the morning."

Then Brendan, who seldom raises his voice, suddenly shouted over the phone. "That beautiful cat was in a cage! It couldn't have gone anywhere! It couldn't have run off! And those fucking drunk bastards killed it!"

A picture of the majestic Bengal tiger flashed through my mind. He was my favorite animal. When I mused alone on the futility of everything, I often found him looking at me and I took comfort from his presence. He was our most stressed animal, just fur and rib cage when we arrived, and we fought long and hard for his life. We nurtured him daily. We searched the streets of Baghdad to find donkeys to feed him, and we lugged water from the canals to slake his thirst. We did all we could to ease his torment. Toward the end we succeeded.

Now he was dead. Shot by drunken cretins who put their hands in the cage of a wild animal.

I put the phone down.

This fight for the planet is not over. Not by a long way.

I DIDN'T SLEEP MUCH that night, and when I did I woke with the image of that beautiful tiger engraved on my mind. Just as Marjan, the Kabul Zoo lion, had been a spur to my trip to the Baghdad Zoo, Malooh, the Bengal tiger, would become iconic for me in a far wider sense.

Had it all been in vain? Had a drunken imbecile who put his arm in a wild animal's cage undone all our successes achieved in the direst conditions imaginable—in a war zone? Was the symbolism just too stark, that no matter what you do, someone will just come along and undo it? Was it always other creatures that had to pay for man's follies with their lives?

The next morning I went for a long walk in the wilds and reflected on the amazing adventures of the past half year. One thing stood out: The beautiful tiger's pointless death was our only casualty. Since I had arrived in Baghdad and found those pitiful, starving, thirst-crazed survivors in their filthy cages, not one other animal had died. Against the odds, we saved them all. The tiger had been the first fatality, but not through any fault of the Babylon's Ark team.

Slowly I started to put it all in perspective. By saving the Baghdad Zoo at least we had set an example that no one could take away from us.

Although the bitter gall still burned my gut, I began to feel a little better, and I remembered all those who had helped us in this once seemingly hopeless quest: soldiers, civilians, life-threatened zoo staff, and volunteers who cared enough to do something about a handful of criminally neglected, dying creatures.

I thought of the elite Special Forces, the frontline soldiers who in the thick of war risked their lives to find food for Uday's lions. It was certainly no easy task searching among flying bullets for meat every day.

I remembered Lieutenant Szydlik and his soldiers who would toss their own rations into the starving animals' cages; and Capt. Larry Burris and his men from the Third ID who gave me protection, a place to sleep, water and food, and transport to Al Zawra Park.

I recalled how ordinary soldiers would arrive at the zoo on their own accord to ask if we were okay and how they could help . . . the unknown soldier who out of the blue gave me a generator, the sergeant who "loaned" me batteries for the water pumps, the "mercenaries" who regularly came around to check that we were safe.

There were many others, such as the CPA chief of staff, Pat Kennedy, a man with huge responsibilities who always made time for me when I needed to discuss something, squeezing me in somewhere in his tight schedule.

And, of course, my Iraqi friends, Adel, Husham, and the zoo staff, who are the true heroes of this story, men who risked their lives daily to come to work in an incredibly hostile environment where to be seen cooperating with Westerners was often a death sentence. It is difficult to record in mere words their absolute courage.

I then thought back on my first walk around the Baghdad Zoo. At first, I had been so dismayed by what I saw that I genuinely considered whether shooting each animal would be the most humane thing to do.

Today I can still scarcely believe it. I had never seen animals in such dreadful condition. Even worse, that harrowing initial scenario was soon surpassed by the brutality and squalor of Luna Park and other private menageries we found. Nothing but nothing could have prepared me for those hellholes. It is a terrible indictment against the human race that it's possible for such places of brutality to exist. The Baghdad Zoo experience certainly altered my perception of my own species and inexorably pushed me to explore in more depth mankind's near-suicidal relationship with the plant and animal kingdoms. The most crucial lesson I learned in Baghdad was this: If "civilized" man is capable of routinely justifying such blatant abuse of trapped wildlife, what of the other unseen atrocities being inflicted on our planet?

We already know that an extraordinary extinction of species is taking place all over the world, breaking vital links in the chain of life.

We are aware that most large-fish species, including cod, marlin, swordfish, and tuna, are critically endangered, and huge dead zones are appearing in our oceans, silent places devoid of life.

It is no secret that massive tracts of wild places and habitat are vanishing forever, taking countless animals, birds, and insects with them. Most of the planet's rivers and streams no longer function naturally, and many coral reefs and mangrove swamps, the priceless breeding grounds for aquatic life, have started dying off.

It's a cold fact of life that factory farming, where untold numbers of stressed animals are squashed into tiny pens, is the "new agriculture," and our insatiable demand for space is denuding nature of its support systems, the same life systems we depend upon for our own survival.

We know, too, that Earth's life-giving environment is under direct threat. The very air we breathe is being altered by billions upon billions of tons of poisonous gases that are pumped into the atmosphere each year. Many of our best scientists say these gases, which are also capable of trapping the sun's heat, are causing global warming, changing weather and climate patterns, melting glaciers, and perhaps even thawing the polar ice caps.

It is, quite frankly, a litany of disasters, and if that's all common knowledge, I shudder to think of what must be happening without our knowing.

It took billions of years for nature to develop dynamic, viable relationships between Earth and its countless life-forms. Now, in just over a hundred years, these natural balances are threatening to fall irrevocably out of kilter. We are witnessing firsthand a massive disruption of Earth's life systems, and all fingers point to one culprit: *man*.

For the first time, Mother Nature has real competition. Our ability to transform the environment is second only to Nature herself, and we have been brutally imposing our newfound technological dominance on a long since conquered and now overwhelmed natural world.

In our ruthless quest for technology, material wealth, and scientific progress, the humanities have been sorely neglected. And, as most of us are almost completely ignorant of the character and function of other forms of life, we abuse the natural world and diminish once-robust survival systems without any real understanding of the consequences—especially for our own continued existence.

Why do we so willingly inflict harm on the only home we have? Most people intrinsically have empathy with nature. Everybody I speak to is against cruelty to animals; everybody wants fresh air, open spaces, unpolluted rivers, and a healthy livable planet. So why do we so dreadfully abuse our sole life-support system?

The answer to that is fundamental to our survival as a species.

The basic common denominator of all life is the urge to survive, and the survival of life on Planet Earth is achieved only as a shared initiative with and through all life-forms. Life is a joint effort; none survives alone. There is no other way. We are all in this game of life together. There is no divide, no "us" and "them"; no "man" separate from "nature." Homo sapiens as individuals and as a species are as much a part of life's overall thrust for survival as any other species. As living organisms, we are all part of the greater whole, and as such, we are embodied with exactly the same fundamental purpose: to survive. And to do so—as individuals, families, groups, and as a species—we have to live in dynamic collaboration with the plant and animal kingdoms in a healthy, life-sustaining environment.

There is no greater imperative. Mankind's superior intellect and deep spiritual heritage will count for naught if we fail in this quest. Life will simply pass us by as we succumb to our own devices, and more successful life-forms will evolve to replace us. The fate of uncountable species that have already disappeared into oblivion after inhabiting, sometimes dominating, the Earth for millions of years bears stark testimony to this. And we are not immune.

On the contrary, all the evidence is that we are extremely vulnerable. A report published in London's *Guardian* newspaper in March 2005 backed by 1,350 scientists stated that "Two-thirds of the world's resources are now used up," and "recent studies show that human activity is putting such a strain on the natural functions of Earth that the ability of the planet's ecosystems to sustain future generations can no longer be taken for granted."

This report is complemented by the insightful words of respected environmentalist and Catholic monk Thomas Berry, who said, "Mankind has a sense of homicide and genocide, but no apparent sense of homicide or geocide, the killing of life, or the killing of the Earth itself."

These and many other similar observations by environmental experts reveal a fundamental overestimation of the capability of the Earth to continue to sustain life as we know it. The systematic degradation of the plant and animal kingdoms and the environment absolutely staggers me. And if you still have any doubt about what is going on, fly over the African rain forests as I have just done and see for yourself the deforestation, slash and burn, and uncontrolled human intrusion into these precious areas; or follow my paths through the Asian subcontinent, where untold millions living in miserable poverty suffocate the land with human waste; or into Eastern Europe, where children cough persistently from pollution; or the Middle East, where animal rights are all but nonexistent. If you can't travel, use the Internet. I must warn you: Prepare yourself for a shock for all is decidedly not well.

It seems incomprehensible that in the face of this planet-wide tragedy the authorities continue to apply ridiculous industrial terms such as "resource takeup" or "demand utilization" to living, breathing wildlife or wild lands, of which we are an integral part, and upon which we are so utterly dependent for our own survival.

I, for one, have never felt a need to accept the status quo, or pay homage to the authorities. We are laying waste to the natural world and, in the main, the authorities, secular and nonsecular, are conspicuous by their absence of imperative, rational initiative to correct this.

Our inability to think beyond ourselves or to be able to cohabit with other life-forms in what is patently a massive collaborative quest for survival is surely a malady that pervades the human soul.

And speaking of the soul, will the unthinkable happen if we continue down this road to nowhere? We are activating so many survival suppressors against life that if we carry on in this way our future as a species may no longer be taken for granted. And then, what next? What other order could possibly host the human spirit? The religious implications alone are profound. Ensuring that our home planet is healthy and life-sustaining is an overwhelming priority that undercuts all other human activities. The ship must first float.

Our failure to grasp these fundamental tenets of existence will be our undoing. And one thing is for certain: No cavalry is going to come charging to our rescue; we are going to have to rescue ourselves or die trying.

Workable solutions are urgently needed. Saving seals and tigers or fighting yet another oil pipeline through a wilderness area, while laudable, is merely shuffling the deck chairs on the *Titanic*. The real issue is that our elementary accord with Earth and the plant and animal kingdoms has to be revitalized and re-understood.

The burning question is, How?

The prophets of doom are already saying it is too late, that the crude and uninformed impact of man on the planet's life systems is just too great and that we don't have enough time to turn it all around.

I don't happen to agree, but I do know that we are entering the endgame. Unless there is a swift and marked change in our attitudes and actions, we could well be on our way to becoming an endangered species.

I recall my initial reaction to all this as one of overwhelming helplessness, and I found myself slipping into comfortable apathy about it all. Perhaps this was just the way life worked; species do, in fact, come and go as part of life's grand design and *Homo sapiens* is not meant to endure forever. Massive global extinctions have already taken place—several times, in fact. There have been plenty of ice ages before. The Sahara Desert was once tropical.

In fact, it appears that dynamic, sometimes devastating, change is part of nature's weft and warp; death nurtures life and that life must continually morph its survival mediums and evolve new species as part of its overall strategy to endure. But this time around it may not be a natural phenomenon; it may well be ignorance and neglect of the natural world that will prove to be our undoing.

This is no fun subject to brood over, and closing my mind to it all and simply focusing on Thula Thula and some very special wild elephants was to me a very attractive alternative indeed.

But something niggled at me. The popular cry that overpopulation was the cause of our environmental woes didn't ring entirely true. It appeared too simplistic, too primary, and I felt that it somehow disguised the truth.

I started researching the subject extensively, and I now believe that overpopulation is just an excuse that the prophets of doom are using to embrace the hopelessness of it all. Fast-developing advances in science and technology have the potential to ensure we stay fed, housed, and clothed, and in any event the birthrate in First World countries has already dropped substantially. In some cases it has gone into negative numbers.

I believe the merchants of fear are wrong, that the planet can be turned around. If people are responsibly informed and allowed to grasp for themselves what is actually going on, a great many will act. A friend of mine put it in a way that has stuck with me: "When one registers the fact that our very own survival depends upon the wellbeing of *all* life on our planet, one starts to understand that we are the ones responsible for the state we find Earth in today."

Individuals. It's all about individuals. Huge corporations and governments may appear to be impenetrable juggernauts, but individuals run all organizations. Individuals make the rules, set the pace, and individuals can change their minds.

The time is right for new conservationists to come together and dispel the tarnished "greenie" image, awaken people to the reality of what we are up against, and build ethical bridges linking commerce and industry responsibly to the environment. I have no doubt a lot of people will embrace such an initiative.

Using what my experiences in Baghdad and South Africa had taught me, I decided to do something. The symbolism of saving a handful of war-traumatized, starving animals in a square-mile tract of land was to me far beyond the actual significance of the zoo itself.

I felt I should take it further. When I returned from that walk in the wilds in honor of a slain tiger in faraway Iraq, I sat down and drew up the outline for a new conservation society that I would call The Earth Organization. I would get together an international group of like-minded people with the ability to get things done, and we would strive to foster ethical treatment of our planet.

Ethics is the key theme. Ethics are essential to establishing a granite moral code as an environmental touchstone. That the animals of the Baghdad Zoo had been left starving and critically dehydrated was grossly unethical; that much was obvious. But what I wanted to get across now was the equally obvious fact that unless we treat our entire planet ethically, the consequences could be apocalyptic.

The Earth Organization, founded on hard lessons learned in a war zone, will focus on the most vital and mystifying question of our age: Why do we so mindlessly abuse our planet, our only home?

The answer to that lies in each of us. Therefore, we will strive to bring about understanding that we are—each one of us—responsible for more than just ourselves, our family, our football team, our country, or our own kind; that there is more to life than just these things. That each one of us must also bring the natural world back into its proper place in our lives, and realize that doing so is not some lofty ideal but a vital part of our personal survival.

People may feel angrily powerless in trying to stop rain-forest logging in faraway countries, but they have huge power to assist in life's survival on their doorstep. As I discovered in Baghdad, a few people on the spot can make a huge difference. There is only one way we are going to hold together this little island we call home, and that is the hard way, making as many individuals aware, one by one, of what is at stake.

Trustworthy news and reliable information about what is actually going on around us is a major priority. Man's traditional links to nature, which once formed part of all cultures and used to be passed down generation to generation, have now become lost in a sea of "civilization" and technology.

The Earth Organization will rigorously help and defend our life-giving environment, and there is a crucial need for this. We will set up carefully selected projects that will make a real difference and we will see them through to a successful conclusion.

There will be additional objectives, which will include raising awareness of how life-forms need each other to persevere. Individuation from our association with nature is one of the root causes of our planet's problems and needs urgent attention.

It is also vital that our relationship with nature and the environment be included in our education systems. This is no longer something cute or nice to do; it is now a singular imperative. I would start with my nearest school board and encourage others to do the same.

Religious leaders who hold sway over billions of people now have a moral obligation to join in and play their part. I have researched the writings and teachings of many religions, and without exception there is reference one way or another to the importance of nature. If we are to attain spiritual emancipation, we have to have a healthy, life-sustaining place to attain it from. Interaction with spiritual leaders will be a particular focus of The Earth Organization

The Earth Organization will also create a definitive guide of what can be done in our personal lives to make a difference.

There is, unfortunately, no magic wand, no easy way out. We are going to have to face up to this and do it ourselves, each of us playing our part, each setting an example for others to follow and demanding of our leaders that they do the same. The future has its price and pay it we must. We have a lot of catching up to do.

And what is the alternative? Well, isn't that what we have right now? For in the absence of a workable understanding of how life survives and our part in it, placing a consumer or financial value on other life-forms and the environment has become man's only real motivation for condoning their existence. If it's worth money or has a use it survives—otherwise, why care? Just how wrong can you get? Dead wrong.

Thankfully, progress is already being made, and I have found that there are more than a few people around who share these ideals and want to do something about the situation. But we need many more of us to get on board to make a real difference. The focus may be on what individuals can achieve for themselves, but there also has to be a collective will in treating our planet ethically. We stand, or fall, together in the most crucial battle of the twenty-first century.

Consequently, The Earth Organization will now take this fight directly to the United Nations. We will strive for the creation of an international environmental agency with cross-border teeth to police and enhance biodiversity in each land and ocean and to ensure the balanced existence of every facet of the natural world. Such a global agency will be charged with ensuring the optimum survival of all life forms in all lands.

We truly do live in a global village. The oxygen we breathe today or the pollution darkening our sky can come in overnight on winds from a country thousands of miles away. The wholesale destruction of nature on huge tracts of the planet's surface impacts on everyone, everywhere, and must now be impeded by sensible international laws. There is no higher imperative.

And as we all know that sadly the human race will never stop waging wars, we will also campaign for zoos, menageries, game reserves, animal sanctuaries, and veterinarian facilities to be classified alongside hospitals and schools as illegitimate targets of war in terms of the Geneva Convention.

There must under no circumstance be a repeat of what happened to the Baghdad Zoo.

Of course, I am aware that I am being optimistic. I know that we have an enormous uphill battle, even in overcoming skepticism. For there are many who have not yet grasped what is actually going on, and others, who even in the face of overwhelming evidence to the contrary, still believe mankind has an inalienable right to abuse the environment and suppress other life-forms. We ignore such people at our peril.

But succeed we must, and we have to start somewhere. So much of our world has been brutally wrested from us; we now have to say enough. No more. Perhaps if enough individuals find out what is actually going on for themselves and start doing something about it, then maybe we can stave off the fast-advancing crisis and create a beautiful, healthy, livable planet where all life flourishes and man is free to rise to greater heights.

And I hope against hope that the battle for the Baghdad Zoo, no matter how humble, was a line in the sand.

Acknowledgments

MY GRATITUDE GOES TO THE FOLLOWING: Rod Macleod, who made
the expedition possible. Martin Slabber, without whom I would
never even have got into Kuwait. Tim Carney, the consummate
diplomat whose guidance was crucial. Dr. Fahad Salem Al-Ali Al-
Sabah and Dr. Mohammed Al Muhanna in Kuwait, who gave their
official support. Col. Jim Fikes and Maj. Adrian Oldfield, whom I
badgered mercilessly to give me military access into Iraq. Capt.
Larry Burris, Lt. Eric Nye, Ed Panetta, and the brave men of the
Third ID. Sarge for the Baghdad Café. Dr. Al-Assam Faris, Baghdad's deputy mayor and a friend, who lost his life for working with
foreigners. Dr. Abu Bakker, for finding the Arabian horses. Liz, for
her friendship and help with an impenetrable military administration. Sarah Scarth, who sent in the cavalry. The "bodyguards" for
their protection; Dave and Sandy Hodgkinson for their great company and advice. David Jones of North Carolina Zoo for his financial support and advice. OB Mthethwa, a true friend. Minister

Ihsam in Kurdistan; Terry Jastrow and Anne Archer for their interest and friendship; Kelly Preston for the use of her quote; Susan Watson and the staff of CC for their care; Bruce, Barbara, Dennis, and Bunny for believing in the story. Barbara Wiseman for throwing her weight behind me; my editor, Peter Joseph, for his guidance; Gavin, Mandy, Laurie San, Boom Boom, Terrie, Paul, Cameron, and of course, Graham Spence for the use of his talent; Lisa Hagan for her confidence; my sons, Jason and Dylan, for their precious support, care, and assistance; and humanitarian and environmentalist L. Ron Hubbard, whose works offer practical solutions for the problems facing the plant and animal kingdoms and the planet we live on.

A Note on the Photographs

We would like to thank Gracia Bennish for permission to include her photographs of the Baghdad Zoo and its inhabitants. She has been a photographer and painter of wildlife for twenty-five years. Her art has been featured in a U.S. billboard campaign, "Some Things Can't Be Duplicated," and in publications such as *Audubon* magazine and *Africa Geographic*, plus an international limited-edition publication, *A Monograph of Endangered Parrots*, which showcases twenty-eight of her paintings. To see more of her photographs and other artwork, please visit www.graciasart.com.